HIDDEN®
Wine Country

HIDDEN ®

Wine Country

Including Napa, Sonoma and Mendocino

Marty Olmstead and Ray Riegert

FOURTH EDITION

Ulysses Press ®
BERKELEY, CALIFORNIA

Published by: ULYSSES PRESS
          P.O. Box 3440
          Berkeley, CA 94703
          www.ulyssespress.com

ISSN 1527-747X
ISBN10: 1-56975-598-1
ISBN13: 978-1-56975-598-3

Printed in Canada by Transcontinental Printing

10 9 8 7 6 5 4

MANAGING EDITOR: Claire Chun
COPYEDITORS: Lee Micheaux, Lily Chou
EDITORIAL ASSOCIATES: Elyce Petker, Kat Brooks, Ruth Marcus
TYPESETTERS: Lisa Kester, Matt Orendorff
CARTOGRAPHY: Pease Press
INDEXER: Sayre Van Young
COVER PHOTOGRAPHY: Robert Holmes Photography (winery),
    photos.com (grapes)
ILLUSTRATOR: Doug McCarthy

Distributed by Publishers Group West

To Beckett

Write to us!

If in your travels you discover a spot that captures the spirit of the Wine Country, or if you live in the region and have a favorite place to share, or if you just feel like expressing your views, write to us and we'll pass your note along to the author.

We can't guarantee that the author will add your personal find to the next edition, but if the writer does use the suggestion, we'll acknowledge you in the credits and send you a free copy of the new edition.

ULYSSES PRESS
P.O. Box 3440
Berkeley, CA 94703
E-mail: readermail@ulyssespress.com

What's Hidden?

At different points throughout this book, you'll find special listings marked with this symbol:

◀ HIDDEN

This means that you have come upon a place off the beaten tourist track, a spot that will carry you a step closer to the local people and natural environment of the Wine Country.

The goal of this guide is to lead you beyond the realm of everyday tourist facilities. While we include traditional sightseeing listings and popular attractions, we also offer alternative sights and adventure activities. Instead of filling this guide with reviews of standard hotels and chain restaurants, we concentrate on one-of-a-kind places and locally owned establishments.

Our authors seek out locales that are popular with residents but usually overlooked by visitors. Some are more hidden than others (and are marked accordingly), but all the listings in this book are intended to help you discover the true nature of the Wine Country and put you on the path of adventure.

Contents

Maps

OUTDOOR ADVENTURE SYMBOLS

The following symbols accompany national, state and regional park listings, as well as beach descriptions throughout the text.

▲	Camping		Waterskiing
	Hiking		Windsurfing
	Biking		Boating
	Horseback Riding		Boat Ramps
	Swimming		Fishing

ONE

Wine Country Wanderings

Wine is produced in every state in the union now, but nonetheless, when Americans use the term "Wine Country," they most likely are talking about northern California. The triple threat of Napa, Sonoma and Mendocino counties are home to hundreds of wineries famous for producing world-class wines. The region—bounded by San Francisco Bay, the Pacific Ocean, the northern Mendocino county line and the mountains that define the eastern edge of the Napa Valley—is not only the country's most prestigious grape-growing region, it is also the most easily accessible from major cities. It is only an hour's drive from San Francisco, Oakland and Sacramento.

In 2006, California winemakers toasted the 30th anniversary of the legendary Paris tasting. Also known as the Judgment of Paris (now the title of a book on the subject), the competition was a closely watched event in which nine experts (eight of them French) conducted a blind comparison of red and white wines from both France and the New World. The white wines were tasted first; the winner was a chardonnay from Chateau Montelena in the Napa Valley. When the reds were assessed, a cabernet from Napa's Stag's Leap Wine Cellars took top honors.

The Paris Wine Tasting of 1976 had a revolutionary impact on the reputation of American wines in general and continues to create repercussions and enhance the status of California winemaking in particular. Without it, California wine sales would doubtless have never reached a record high of 441 million gallons in the U.S. alone—and 532 million gallons worldwide—in 2005. And, for better or worse, there would most assuredly not be so many consumers fighting for a chance to buy one of Napa's $200-a-bottle cult cabernet sauvignons.

Despite the exalted status of winemaking and all its attendant hype, this region is, at heart, farm country. The major crop may be grapes—hundreds of millions of dollars' worth by the time they are turned into wine—but for the most part, Sonoma, Napa and Mendocino counties are rural or at least semi-rural. Some world travelers are fond of saying that the heart of the California Wine Country reminds them of Provence or Tuscany; they share a Mediterranean climate, grapevines and olive trees, rolling hills and a certain hedonism, for sure. But those who come here first and truly sample the bounty of these counties, from the landscape to the lifestyle, may one day visit those European provinces and say, "Hmmm, reminds me of Sonoma."

Parts of the Wine Country can be toured in a day's drive, although that would be a pity, as there is so much to do and see. The preponderance of visitors are in fact not from out of state but from around the nine-county Bay Area. As a result, perhaps, the population of Sonoma County has soared dramatically in the past five years; Napa has also grown substantially (though Mendocino is still in no danger of overpopulation). So to the rural sensibility so prevalent in Wine Country, you can add a growing populace with a certain sophistication and a penchant for fine food, art, music and theater as well as the fervent hope that they can keep things the way they are. To wit, heavenly.

Hundreds of miles of two-lane country roads curve and climb through the gently sloping countryside. Travelers are almost always in view of one mountain or another, or close to a river or a farm or a winery. In winter, especially, it's possible to drive some of these roads without seeing more than a couple of other cars. Only a few cities—Napa, Sonoma, Santa Rosa, Sebastopol, Healdsburg and Ukiah—are really worthy of the term. The Wine Country is truly characterized by towns such as Calistoga, Guerneville and Yountville. Or by tiny settlements such as Rutherford, Geyserville and Boonville.

In short, you won't see any highrises. What you will see are scenic vistas: a mountain topped with forests, deer grazing by the roadside, jackrabbits hopping down vineyard rows, grape leaves changing colors in the sun, historic wineries, gently flowing rivers, Western falsefront buildings, soaring redwood trees, apple orchards, and at least one town plaza that is home to a free-ranging band of chickens.

There is so much to do and see in this part of the world that you could stay busy and quite content without ever visiting a sin-

Text continued on page 6.

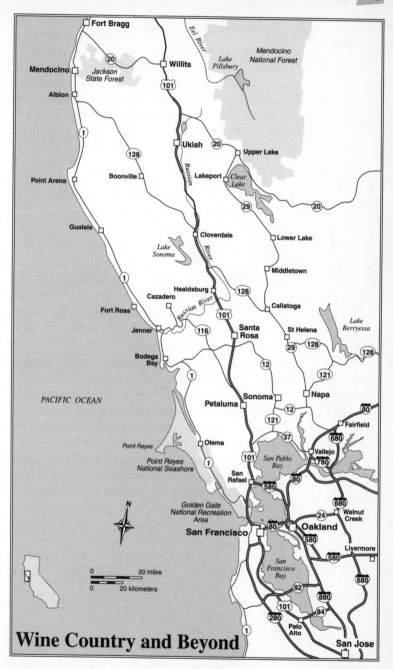

Fort Bragg

20

Mendocino

Jackson
State Forest

Willits

101

Albion

1

128

Point Arena

Boonville

Gualala

1

Eel River

Lake
Pillsbury

Mendocino
National Forest

Ukiah

20

Upper Lake

Russian River

Lakeport

Clear
Lake

29

20

Lake
Sonoma

Cloverdale

River

Lower Lake

Middletown

Healdsburg

128

Cazadero

Russian River

Calistoga

Lake
Berryessa

Fort Ross

101

St Helena

128

128

Jenner

116

Santa
Rosa

29

128

Bodega
Bay

12

121

1

Sonoma

Napa

80

PACIFIC OCEAN

Petaluma

12

Fairfield

121

680

37

Point Reyes

Olema

Vallejo

780

Point Reyes
National Seashore

101

San Pablo
Bay

San
Rafael

80

580

1

N

Golden Gate
National Recreation
Area

680

24

Walnut
Creek

San Francisco

80

Oakland

580

Livermore

580

580

San
Francisco
Bay

680

0   20 miles

92

880

0   20 kilometers

101

84

280

Palo
Alto

1

San Jose

Wine Country and Beyond

Three-day Weekend

While it would take many visits to check out every winery and attraction in this part of the world, you can certainly experience the flavor of the Wine Country in a matter of days. All it takes is a little planning. This sample itinerary encompasses parts of Napa, Sonoma and Mendocino counties, and includes specific suggestions for winery visits, outdoor activities, shopping, restaurants and lodging.

Day 1
- Begin in Napa's Carneros district with a tour (reservation only) of the **Di Rosa Preserve** (page 38), a world-class collection of art from around the Bay Area. (Allow 2 hours)

- Head north on Route 29 and enjoy a Cal-Italian lunch at **Bistro Don Giovanni** (page 49).

- Turn into Yountville and browse the shops at **Vintage 1870** (page 66) before crossing Route 29 and taking the tour at **Domaine Chandon** (page 54).

- Visit the nearby **Napa Valley Museum** (page 54) for an introduction to the regional wine industry. (1 hour)

- Continue north on Route 29, stopping at the **Robert Mondavi Winery** (page 56) in Oakville or take a detour up the Oakville Grade to visit **Chateau Potelle** (page 41).

- Drive north to **Calistoga** (page 85) and book a spa session, a mud bath and/or a massage at Dr. Wilkinson's Hot Springs or another of the town's many facilities dedicated to relaxation.

- Enjoy a hearty steak or some seafood pasta at the **Flatiron Grill** (page 94). Spend the night at a spa hotel or one of the town's inns, such as the **Cottage Grove Inn** (page 91).

Day 2
- Start the day with a **balloon ride** at dawn, weather permitting. (2 hours)

- Head north along Route 128 through the **Alexander Valley** (page 145), stopping to taste at one of several roadside wineries. (1 hour)

- Drive into Healdsburg for lunch at **Bistro Ralph** (page 150) or stop into the **Oakville Grocery** (page 151) for picnic supplies to enjoy in the town's plaza.

- Take Route 101 north from Healdsburg to the outskirts of Cloverdale and turn west onto Route 28 to drive through the **Anderson Valley** (page 191). (1.5 hours)

- Stop at **Navarro Vineyards** (page 194) and/or **Scharffenberger Cellars** (page 194) to sample local vintages. (1 hour)

- Return to Route 101 and detour a few miles north to Hopland and have dinner at **The Crushed Grape Grille** (page 185).

Day 3
- Head south on Route 101 to Healdsburg and take Westside Road south. Turn right at River Road and ride along the river to Guerneville; pick up Route 116 south. (1.5 hours)

- En route to **Sebastopol** (page 158) you can visit wineries that open in mid-morning, or save your energy for the antique stores in and around Sebastopol. (1.5 hours)

- Turn east on Route 12, a California Scenic Highway that leads to **Kenwood** (page 120). On the outskirts is **Château St. Jean Winery** (page 120). (1 hour)

- Enjoy a leisurely lunch at the **Kenwood Restaurant and Bar** (page 124).

- From Kenwood, take Warm Springs Road south to Glen Ellen to visit **Jack London State Historic Park** (page 125). (1 hour)

- Depart Glen Ellen via Route 12, bound for the town of **Sonoma** (page 106). Park at the Plaza, take a walking tour of the mission and the barracks, and browse the shops around the square. (2 hours)

- Have dinner at **Deuce** (page 112), one of Sonoma's top restaurants where a reservation is necessary.

- Spend the night at one of the inns near the plaza.

gle winery. There are many family-friendly activities, from riding a miniature train in Sonoma to horseback riding in Napa, canoeing in the Russian River, or hiking the hills of Mendocino. Bocce ball and *petanque*, the Italian and French variations of the steel-ball-hurling game of yore, are increasingly popular; several wineries have installed courts open to the public.

Community centers are incredibly ingenious at coming up with free and low-cost entertainment. The Wells Fargo Center for the Arts attracts headliners from all over the world in fields as varied as the circus arts, jazz, rock and chamber music. In the summer, there seem to be festivals or fairs practically every weekend. In addition, many wineries offer mini-festivals (often at no charge) throughout the year, especially in spring and fall.

This piece of paradise has been attracting visitors and new residents since the beginning. When California wines were finally recognized as the world-class contenders that they are, the migration became more of a stampede. Although winemaking as well as feature filmmaking continue to lead as economic juggernauts, the telecommunications industry is about to take first place. When Silicon Valley began to run out of room, dot.com entrepreneurs looked north of the Golden Gate Bridge and saw the 101 Corridor (the highway between Petaluma and Santa Rosa) as the promised land. They have joined longtimers like Hewlett-Packard into making Telecom Valley a force to be reckoned with. The presence of these successful, non-polluting businesses has pumped even more money into Sonoma's economy.

In the Napa Valley, most arable land is restricted as an agricultural preserve, resulting in scant available land for development. Most of the traffic in this valley is produced by visitors, who add to the growing number of commuter cars.

Mendocino remains resolutely rural, mostly because of the rugged landscape and its distance from San Francisco; even the county seat, Ukiah, doesn't have a major hotel, let alone a commute-traffic problem.

As you travel about the Wine Country, you'll find few major highways. Route 101 runs north from San Francisco through the area, in fact all the way to the state line. Although it is four to six lanes wide, the highway runs right beside some wineries. And Route 29 is its Napa equivalent, four lanes from the bottom of the valley to Yountville, and then two lanes north to Calistoga. Most of Napa's major wineries front this road, but there are exceptions.

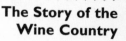

The Story of the Wine Country

GEOLOGY

The natural elements that allowed for successful wine-making were in the makings for eons; once the geography, climate and soil evolved to the critical point, sure enough, someone came along and discovered that, all together, they made ideal conditions for growing grapes. Of course, things are still evolving, as continual shudders from the Rodgers Creek, San Andreas and lesser faults shake everybody up a bit. But they're nothing compared to the dramatic tectonic movements in the last 100 million years ago that transformed the area from an underwater landscape to the beginnings of what you see today. More recently—about three to four million years ago—a mammoth number of volcanic eruptions changed the landscape almost as dramatically, creating underground fissures of piping hot water that still spew forth today in the form of little hot springs and sizable gushers.

As a result of millions of years of earth movement, the Wine Country has natural phenomena such as the Russian River (more or less in the same place it's always been) as well as Mount St. Helena (the tallest peak in the region, towering over 4000 feet). Another result of volcanic activity is that several valleys—most notably, Napa, Sonoma, Dry Creek, Anderson, Alexander, Sanel and the Russian River—are protected by mountains from the cold winds and rain along the Pacific coast.

HOME SWEET HOME

By the turn of the 20th century, Sonoma County was attracting new residents including horticulturist Luther Burbank, who settled in Santa Rosa. Novelist Jack London resided in the nearby town of Glen Ellen in 1904, living there until his death in 1916. Interested in ranching as well as writing, London exchanged farming lore with Burbank, who lived just up the road. Over in Napa, meanwhile, the state's first millionaire, Sam Brannan, established a hot springs resort with the odd name of Calistoga, and author Robert Louis Stevenson visited the valley, lodged in a cabin on Mount St. Helena, and called the local wines "bottled poetry."

HISTORY   Some 5000 to 10,000 years ago, the Pomo Indians were the first to discover the Wine Country's hot springs, heading south once they had crossed the land bridge connecting Asia with North America. They settled in present-day Mendocino and Sonoma. The Wappo also settled in Sonoma as well as Napa, where they seem to have co-existed peacefully with the Nappa tribe around the Napa River. They gathered berries and acorns, fished the waters of nearby San Pablo Bay, and stalked the mountains for bear and deer.

Winemaking in California dates back to the 18th century when Spanish padres planted vineyards at the missions. The Franciscans in particular grew black grapes for sacramental wines, crushing them by foot in hide troughs, then fermenting the harvest in leather sacks.

Spanish vineyards spread north to Sonoma, where in 1823 a Spanish priest named Father Jose Altimira came north from Mexico to establish an outpost that would be called the Mission San Francisco de Solano. The town of Sonoma sprung up around that mission.

In Napa Valley, across the mountains east of Sonoma, George Yount, the area's original settler, cultivated grapes in 1843. During the next decade numerous Europeans, drawn initially by the Gold Rush, forsook prospecting for planting. A Prussian immigrant named Charles Krug became a pioneer in commercializing Napa wines. He also taught other early vintners like Jacob Beringer and Carl Wente, whose names even today adorn wine bottles.

The American Indians who had this place to themselves for thousands of years could never have conceived of what these new arrivals would do to their civilization, their population and their sacred places. While tribes still exist in small numbers, little visible evidence remains of their one-time culture. A museum here, an exhibit there and an Indian celebration from time to time is all a visitor is likely to see.

By the 1830s, the Mexican government decided to secularize their last mission and replace it with a presidio. General Mariano Guadalupe Vallejo was commissioned for this task, establishing the town of Sonoma in 1835. Vallejo installed his soldiers in newly minted barracks and laid out the plaza, the largest of its kind in the state. In his push to settle the area, including Napa, he found a kindred soul in George Yount, the first white settler in Napa.

Yount benefited greatly from the relationship, securing prized land grants and establishing the 11,814 Rancho Caymus in the central area of the Napa Valley.

Despite Vallejo's considerable power, in June of 1846 a band of roughhewn Americans arrested Vallejo and declared California the Bear Flag Republic (symbolized by a flag sporting a grizzly bear). The reign lasted some 25 days. By July, the United States, having captured Monterey and claimed California as its own, took control. Four years later, California became a state (and in 1911, the Bear Flag was adopted as the California state flag).

Recent count revealed that the Napa Valley now boasts nearly 400 wineries; Sonoma County, over 200; and Mendocino County, over 60.

In 1857, Agoston Haraszthy, a Hungarian count, founded the Buena Vista Winery in Sonoma. Commissioned by the California governor, he traveled through France, Italy and Germany a few years later, collecting cuttings from 300 grape varieties. Soon thereafter, the University of California perfected fermentation techniques and established a national center for viticulture and enology at its Davis campus.

California's wine business boomed. Four million gallons were produced in 1869, 28 million in 1900, and by 1911 the total rose to 58 million gallons. Then came Prohibition. From 1920 until 1933, an entire industry withered on the vine. Many wineries shut down; others converted their fields to orchards.

It took nearly 30 years for the industry to recover. Not until the 1960s, as wine became an increasingly popular national drink, did California's vineyards flourish once more. This long-awaited renaissance proved extraordinary. Within a five-year period, vineyard acreage doubled. Wineries mushroomed in the Napa and Sonoma valleys, along the Russian River, and elsewhere throughout the state. Family-run wineries blossomed, national companies like Coca-Cola and Nestlé moved into the vineyards, and French and Spanish winemakers, impressed with the quality of the wines, formed partnerships with local growers.

Winemaking is now a multibillion dollar business, with millions of people touring California's vineyards each year. And as for production, more than half a century after Prohibition, the state produced a whopping 564,735,000 gallons of wine in 2000, the last year for which statistics are available.

FLORA

They don't call it the Wine Country for nothing. Grapes lead the pack, but there are plenty of other crops being raised here, though none as lucrative as grapes. In fact, different kinds of plants bloom and a variety of produce are harvested in Napa, Sonoma and/or Mendocino every month of the year; lettuces and other vegetables can be found fresh any time of year. From the mid-1800s, when the area began supplying produce to San Francisco, Sonoma and Napa have led the nation in growing gourmet produce. Starting with orchids and winter vegetables in January and February, then azaleas and rhododendrons in March through June, the year continues with strawberries, irises and daylilies, then roses, peaches, pears and figs and plums before the full summer season of blueberries, tomatoes, corn and several varieties of apples that ripen from July into December. Grapes are harvested in the fall, and the end of the year brings pumpkins, persimmons and walnuts to the tables and hearths all around the region. Some farmer's markets are open year-round, while others are summer affairs that run from May into October. Many farms welcome visitors to their properties, and some even allow visitors to pick their own berries.

> Thanks in part to the abundance of apple orchards in the Wine Country, California generates more honey than any other state.

As for what grows in the natural world, the list is almost endless. Another term for much of the Wine Country is the Redwood Empire, which is fading into disuse and never really included Napa anyway. The farther north you go, the more you will notice these giant trees. In these forests, shared with Douglas fir, wildflowers such as trillium, adder's tongue, redwood sorrel and huckleberry blossom as early as February.

Around this time, the vineyards and virtually every other disturbed field (meaning the soil has been turned over) turns bright yellow with mustard blooms that often appear as early as January and last through March. Most likely introduced to the area by immigrants planting a cover crop for fallow fields, it's here to stay, as are two other yellow-blossoming plants: Scotch broom, a shrub, and the acacia tree, which blooms as the mustard begins to fade. The native grasses that once flourished here have been overgrown by foxtail, wild oats and other grasses imported by European settlers.

Madrone, Ponderosa pine and several types of oak trees cover most hillsides in the heart of the Wine Country, sharing the landscape with occasional stands of non-native eucalyptus, a hearty hardwood whose aroma—a sort of menthol smell—often pervades wine that comes from vineyards planted nearby. Manzanita, with its distinctive reddish bark and white blossoms, is part of the chaparral ecosystem that crowns much of the wild land in this region.

The bright golden poppy, the state flower, as well as the purple lupine, can be seen on hillsides and along roadsides throughout the Wine Country. Another plant you will see constantly is the rose, in myriad shapes and colors, which is traditionally planted on the borders of vineyards.

Residents will tell you that the animals they most commonly see, aside from sheep, cattle and horses, are deer, raccoons and opossums. If you hike far from a road, however, you are likely to run across coyotes, gray foxes and bobcats, and, less often, badgers, feral pigs, bats, tule elk and small gray foxes.

FAUNA

If you're careful, you probably won't run across a poisonous Western rattlesnake, but if you go far enough into the wilderness you may see black bears and mountain lions, which become a problem during periods of drought when they approach human habitats in search of water.

In streams and river beds reside a lively riparian population of river otters, skinks and pond turtles. Fishing in rivers at certain times of year may net you Chinook, coho or steelhead salmon. Fishing in lakes is likely to turn up small- and large-mouth bass or freshwater catfish.

Our feathered friends include hawks (six species) and owls (seven) as well as their prey. Some of the smaller birds winging their way around are woodpeckers, finches, flycatchers and warblers. Keep an eye out if you are near cliffs or high bluffs, prime cruising area for kestrels, peregrine falcons and the occasional golden eagle. The most rewarding birdwatching is around water, particularly San Pablo Bay, which borders the Carneros appellation. Habitats are being restored to encourage herons, egrets, various ducks and geese, ospreys and even enormous tundra swans.

As you will discover, the real fun of exploring the Wine Country lies along the side roads and country lanes—it matters not whether you tour the region in the order of the following chapters. We have broken down the area into roughly

Where to Go

equivalent sections, either in terms of geography or in terms of how much there is to see. You can sample the Wine Country by setting up headquarters in a single town or valley and stay within a few miles of home base, or you can easily reach all the other points on this map in a couple of hours. For your convenience, we have included a three-day itinerary at the end of this chapter.

The **Southern Napa Valley** chapter covers the lower end of the Napa Valley, including the city of Napa, Napa's portion of the Carneros appellation, and the towns of Yountville, Oakville and Rutherford. Founded on the banks of the Napa River, the city has a remarkable Victorian district, where a number of old homes have been pressed into service as bed and breakfasts. The downtown area received a big boost with the 2001 opening of COPIA: The American Center for Wine, Food & the Arts. Today, downtown Napa is enjoying a renaissance with new hotels, shops and restaurants opening in recent years and more on the horizon. Major wineries such as Mondavi and Domaine Chandon, to name just two, can be found up the highway, but several intriguing wineries are tucked away in the hills.

In the **Northern Napa Valley**, shopping, restaurants and inns become a bit more chic and generally a bit more expensive. The charming town of St. Helena is chock-a-block with boutiques and home decor stores as well as the occasional café and bookstore. For a taste of the Wild West, you can head to the top of the valley to visit Calistoga, where bathing in hot water (or even mud baths) has been known to relieve an ache or two. Nearby is a state park where Robert Louis Stevenson honeymooned.

Scenic **Sonoma Valley** runs from the top of San Pablo Bay in a crescent that tops out at Santa Rosa. Here, you can not only sample fabulous wines but also learn the history of the Spanish missions and the founding of the Bear Republic. An eight-acre plaza planted with 200 types of trees and dozens of rose bushes beckons year-round with picnic tables. In summer, the Tuesday-night market is quite the after-work scene, with music as well as abundant local produce, breads and other artisanal products. Adventure author Jack London and, much later, the late, great food writer M.F.K. Fisher both chose the Sonoma Valley—in particular, the outskirts of the town of Glen Ellen—as their home. Here you can visit a museum devoted to London in a state park and find a winery that gives tours in a tractor-pulled tram. This village is the hub

Tantalizing Those Taste Buds

If you like wine, or think you might, Northern California's Wine Country is one of the best places in the world to visit. Hundreds of wineries make infinite variations of dozens of types of wines. Whether you stop at two wineries or thirty, you can enhance each visit by knowing a little bit about how to taste wine.

Why is such a fuss made about tasting wine? At a basic level, thousands of people enjoy wine without knowing the first thing about swirling, sniffing or sipping. Let alone spitting. But the more you know about what different wines taste like, the more you'll get out of the experience.

In the tasting room, available wines are usually listed on a chalkboard behind the bar. These are listed in an order that starts with lighter wines and proceeds to heavier ones. You might begin by asking for suggestions, or choose one or two and simply ask for a taste. Virtually all Napa Valley wineries charge a fee for tasting, and a growing number of Sonoma wineries are following suit. These fees are generally applicable toward the purchase of wine.

Glass in hand, start by observing the color and intensity of the wine. Since you already know what it is, memorizing the appearance of the wine will help fix the image in your mind. If possible, hold the glass up to the light for a better look.

Next, take a few short sniffs—not a long snort—and see if the smell reminds you of anything. Then, swirl the wine gently. Unless you're good at this, you may want to set the bottom of the glass on top of the bar, hold the stem and rotate the glass quickly counterclockwise (if you're right-handed, this is the easier way). "Aerating" the wine releases additional aromas.

Now, at last, you get to taste. But alas, not to swallow—at least not yet. Sip a little wine onto your tongue and hold it there for a few seconds, letting your taste buds pick up all the flavors. It may taste of butter, olives, cherries or even violets—whatever it is, try to make all the associations you can. Is the wine heavy in your mouth, or does it feel more like water? These tactile sensations, along with how smooth or bitter the wine strikes you, all play a role.

The hard part is over. Enjoy a few sips of wine. Note how long the flavor stays in your mouth: does it evaporate or does it linger? A long finish is ideal. And if you're going to really get into this winetasting business, of course, you'll want to take some notes on all the above points. If you don't need notes but can rely solely on memory, either the wine is very good or very bad—or you have a future as a professional judge.

of this region, with excellent restaurants and shopping. Kenwood is known chiefly for its many wineries.

When the valley ends at the county seat of Santa Rosa, **Northern Sonoma County** begins. By far the biggest city in the region, Santa Rosa is also the most trafficked. Some charming neighborhoods can be found near downtown, which unfortunately was divided when Route 101 was constructed, essentially chopping off Historic Railroad Square. Yet there are underpasses that access this popular enclave of shops, hotels, restaurants, cafés and nightclubs. About 15 miles north, Healdsburg has, like Sonoma, a downtown plaza flanked by oodles of stores and eateries, including a brew pub. It also has a regional museum and a boffo movie house where first-run and avant-garde films are the bill of fare. Healdsburg, with lush valleys in all directions, is the hub for winemaking, one of which, Dry Creek Valley, ends at Lake Sonoma, a busy recreational destination.

The **Russian River Area** usually refers to the areas north and west of Healdsburg, though the river itself begins in Mendocino and runs right beside Healdsburg. Several delightful roads weave through this region, where wineries are clustered to exploit the fertile riverside soil. Sebastopol is a working town with plenty of shops and a handful of good restaurants. Most of the action in these parts happens in and around Guerneville, which somehow works as both a family and a gay summertime retreat, when visitors descend on the year-round residents.

The border of **Mendocino County** lies just beyond Cloverdale, north of Healdsburg. The inland valleys of this county, already famous for its dramatic coastline, are quietly becoming acknowledged for their excellent viticultural properties. Along with wine touring, a small museum that features exhibits on Indian life and a wonderful state park out in the Alexander Valley, a popular pastime involves hanging out at Lake Mendocino on the outskirts of Ukiah, the county seat that straddles Route 101.

When to Go

SEASONS

Once you see the landscape around Santa Rosa, you'll understand why the great horticulturist and longtime Santa Rosa resident Luther Burbank called it "the chosen spot of all the earth"—it is indeed a plant-lover's dream. The Wine Country is blessed with what most here consider an ideal climate; winter chill as well as summer heat are moderated by the proximity of major bodies of water. Still, winter does get cold, with averaging lows of around 37° in December, January and February, with highs in the 50s. Almost all the rainfall in the area occurs in these months as well, although, technically, it could rain anytime. The average May rainfall, however, is far less than half an inch. Spring is fresh and breezy, with lows in the 40s and highs warming up to 80° or so. The average summer day tops out at 83°, but there are plenty of days where the temperature soars over 90°. Low humidity helps diminish the impact of all that heat and allows most nights to cool off even following hot days. Fall days can also be quite toasty, but all the truly warm weather ends by the beginning of November.

Many visitors here are surprised by the cool nights, even in summertime. That's because fog drifts up from San Pablo Bay, at the top of San Francisco Bay, making the Carneros region and, sometimes, the town of Napa especially prone to chilliness any time of year. The fog, mostly a summertime phenomenon, tends to drift in late afternoon and dissipate under the sun. Similarly, fog and ocean breezes blow in from the coast, keeping areas like the Russian River from overheating. Inland areas that receive no moderating maritime influence tend to get both hotter and colder than elsewhere.

As for the narrow valleys, the towns of Sonoma, St. Helena, Calistoga and Ukiah experience greater temperature extremes because both heat and cold are trapped between mountain ranges. Still, compared to other parts of the United States, this part of Northern California has an enviably moderate climate.

MARRIAGE LICENSES

Weddings have become big business in the Wine Country. From big resorts to intimate inns to even hot-air balloon companies, it seems everyone has a way to get you hitched. They can take care of everything (except the license), from food to flowers to drink. A good source is the local convention and visitors bureau. Another source is a book called *Here Comes the Guide* by Lynn Broadwell (Berkeley: Hopscotch Press), which details dozens of appropriate wedding places, planners and services. If you're thinking of getting married in the Wine Country, you need a California marriage license. To obtain a license in Sonoma (707-565-2645) or Mendocino (707-463-4370), call the appropriate county clerk for details.

When in doubt, just think about those all-important grapes. They lie dormant in the winter, not minding one whit how much rain falls or how cold the ground gets. As things warm up in the spring, the vines sprout leaves and by the time summer arrives, even the casual observer can see grapes emerging in clusters. By September, the leaves turn red and gold as the grapes ripen to perfection, ushering in the harvest that reaches its peak in October.

CALENDAR OF EVENTS

JANUARY   **Northern Sonoma County**   The beginning of a monthly series, **First Weekend in Alexander Valley** features special tastings and discounts at participating wineries throughout the year.

Russian River Area   Wine seminars and tastings and entertainment are the stuff of **Winter Wineland** on the second weekend.

Mendocino County   **Crab and Wine Days** showcase two of the county's major food products at restaurants, inns and wineries.

FEBRUARY   **Northern Napa Valley**   The blooming of wild mustard marks the start of the **Napa Valley Mustard Festival**, which runs through March and includes cooking demonstrations, food sampling, art exhibits, and winetasting.

Mendocino County   The **Cloverdale Citrus Fair** is a country event featuring all the citrus grown in the exceptionally warm climate around Cloverdale.

MARCH   **Mendocino County**   Mendocino and Fort Bragg celebrate a **Whale Festival** with whale-watching cruises, art shows, and chowder- and winetasting.

APRIL   **Southern Napa Valley and Sonoma Valley**   More than a dozen wineries in this southernmost region of Wine Country, band together to offer tastings, entertainment, and wine and food pairings at **April in Carneros**. The five-day Sonoma Valley film festival, **Cinema Epicuria**, presents movies, seminars and special events the first week of the month.

Northern Sonoma County   Get your **Passport to Dry Creek** the last weekend in April for two days of food, wine and easy-to-swallow education.

Russian River Area   The entire town of Sebastopol turns out for the **Apple Blossom Festival**, staging exhibits, parades and pageants.

Northern Sonoma County   Countless blossoms are grown, cut and rearranged on floats during the annual **Luther Burbank Rose Parade Festival** in Santa Rosa.

Northern Napa Valley   The **Napa Valley Wine Auction**, the largest charity event of its kind in the world, brings bidding excitement to the grounds of the Meadowood Country Club in St. Helena.

Sonoma Valley   In Sonoma's Plaza, even vegetarians will find plenty of food to enjoy at the legendary **Ox Roast**. Enjoy the Bard's dramas alfresco with various plays occurring at Gundlach Bundschu Winery throughout the summer. The **Vintage Car Festival** features classic cars as well as classic Wine Country cuisine in downtown Sonoma.

Northern Sonoma County   The splendid, expansive lavender fields at Matanzas Creek are the focal point during the **Lavender Harvest Party**.

Mendocino County   Farmers and winegrowers converge for a long weekend, celebrating the bounty of this northern county in a decidedly unstuffy atmosphere at the **Mendocino Wine Affair**.

Northern Napa Valley   The **Wine Country Film Festival** screens features and documentaries July through August at local theaters as well as outdoors at a winery location; the first two weeks of the festival are held in Napa Valley, the last two in Sonoma Valley. The old-fashioned **Napa County Fair** at the Calistoga Fairgrounds offers down-home fun with fairs and equestrian events.

Throughout Sonoma County   The **Sonoma County Showcase of Wine and Food** focuses on the region's fine foods and wines with winery dinners, barrel tastings and educational programs.

Sonoma Valley   Sonoma's **Fourth of July** parade is the town's favorite annual event, a day-long party that culminates in fireworks near the plaza. The Sonoma Plaza is ground zero for the summertime **Salute to the Arts**, a smorgasbord of artworks and fine food and wine. Foot races and world-famous pillow fights add a country vibe to the blow-out **Kenwood Fourth of July Celebration**.

Northern Sonoma County   The **Sonoma County Fair** brings ten days of food, fun, flowers, wine competitions, livestock auctions and horseracing to the fairgrounds in Santa Rosa.

AUGUST   **Throughout Napa Valley**   The **Music in the Vineyards** series of chamber concerts plays at various vineyards throughout the month.

Sonoma Valley   The second half of the **Wine Country Film Festival** (the first half is in Napa in late July) showcases shorts, features and documentaries in theaters. Formal or far-out, anything's fine as long as the colors are right at the **Red and White Ball**, a wine, food and music charity affair also in Sonoma's Plaza.

Russian River Area   Held at the height of the picking season, the **Gravenstein Apple Festival** in Sebastopol is a family-oriented weekend with an animal petting zoo, arts and crafts, and cooking demonstrations. Sebastopol's annual **Shakespeare in the Park** features the works of the Bard in a fun, summertime setting.

SEPTEMBER   **Sonoma Valley**   The **Valley of the Moon Vintage Festival** is a weekend of parades, arts and crafts, winetasting and gourmet food held throughout downtown Sonoma. The laidback **Sonoma Valley Harvest Wine Auction** takes place over Labor Day weekend with barbecues, wine auctions, winery dinners and a barrel of fun.

Northern Sonoma County   More than 100 varieties of the late-summer fruit are available for tasting at the **Kendall-Jackson Heirloom Tomato Festival**, which also features gourmet foods, food and wine seminars, and entertainment.

Russian River Area   The two-day **Jazz on the River Festival** occurs over a musical weekend at Johnson's Beach in Guerneville.

Mendocino County   The **Mendocino County Fair and Apple Show** in Boonville is a three-day event featuring rodeo, sheepdog trials, rides for kids, and country-and-western dancing.

OCTOBER   **Throughout Napa Valley**   Artists throughout the valley hold **Open Studios** during two weekends of free, self-guided tours.

Southern Napa Valley   Ghosts and goblins and an assortment of family fun are the focus each fall at **Halloween "Spooktacular"** at Vintage 1870 in Yountville.

Northern Sonoma County   The full bounty of the county is showcased at the **Sonoma County Harvest Fair**, where great weight is given to the wine competitions.

Mendocino County   The **Hopland Fall Passport Weekend** is an entrée into some of the top wineries in and around Hopland, with special tastings and discounts on purchases.

Southern Napa Valley   The big holiday tree is lit this month, **NOVEMBER** along with most of downtown Yountville, and special events and entertainment are provided as the **Festival of Lights** runs from late November through New Year's Eve.

Northern Napa Valley and Sonoma Valley   Holiday in Carneros is a full weekend of open houses, holiday festivities and food and winetastings at more than a dozen wineries in this appellation.

Southern Napa Valley   The Napa County Landmarks society **DECEMBER** arranges a **Holiday Candlelight Tour** through various historic neighborhoods.

Northern Sonoma County   Romp with the Beasts! celebrates New Year's Eve with dinner and dancing—with animals.

Several agencies provide free information to travelers. The **California Travel and Tourism** will help guide you **Before You Go** to areas throughout the Wine Country. ~ 980 9th Street, Suite 480, Sacramento, CA 95814; 916-444-4429, 800-862-2543; **VISITORS** www.visitcalifornia.com. **CENTERS**

For information on Sonoma and Mendocino counties, check out the **Redwood Empire Association,** an online resource. ~ 2 Beach Street, San Francisco, CA 94133; 415-292-5527, 800-619-2125; www.redwoodempire.com.

Also consult local chambers of commerce and information centers, which are mentioned in the various area chapters.

There are two important guidelines when deciding what to take **PACKING** on a trip to Northern California. The first is as true for Wine Country and Northern California as anywhere else in the world— pack light. Dress styles here are informal, which is a good thing because laundromats and dry cleaners are few and far between. The second rule is to dress in layers, since temperatures can vary greatly during the course of a day—a warm morning or afternoon can unpredictably become a brisk evening.

In general, you'll be safe almost anywhere in a pair of pressed jeans and a clean shirt. In Sonoma, you'll get extra points if you wear cowboy boots; in Napa, if you wear linen. The resorts are not necessarily formal, but a tie at night for gentlemen and a dress or nice pants for women will cover the bases. Wearing modest shorts at wineries is perfectly acceptable.

Other essentials to pack or buy along the way include sunscreen and sunglasses, perhaps an umbrella, and a camera with which to capture your travel experiences. And don't, for heaven's sake, forget your copy of *Hidden Wine Country*.

LODGING   The image of a country inn dominates many people's idea of Wine Country accommodations. But that's not quite half the story. For one thing, many inns are located in small towns. For another, there are a number of small hotels in the cities, although large hotels are the exception—you won't find any Hyatts or Ritz-Carltons, that's for sure. If you are careful, however, you can find inexpensive motels and even affordable B&Bs in addition to those perfect, luxurious inns.

The busiest times are summer and fall. Do not arrive for a weekend without reservations unless you like to live on the edge. The number of visitors drops sharply from late November to early March, a time when many accommodations either advertise discounts or will at least consider knocking a few dollars off the price of a room, especially mid-week.

To help you decide on a place to stay, I've described the accommodations according to price (prices listed are for the high season, double occupancy; rates may decrease in low season). *Budget* hotels are generally less than $90 per night for two people; the rooms are clean and comfortable. The *moderate*-priced hotels run $90 to $150 and provide larger rooms, plusher furniture, and more attractive surroundings. At *deluxe*-priced accommodations you can expect to spend between $150 and $300 for a bed and breakfast or a double in a hotel or resort; you'll check into a spacious, well-appointed room with all modern facilities and you'll usually see a restaurant, lounge and a cluster of shops. If you want to spend your time (and money) in the very finest accommodations, try *ultra-deluxe* facilities, which will include all the amenities at a price above $300.

Contact **California Association of Bed & Breakfast Inns** to give you a hand in finding a cozy place to stay. ~ 2715 Porter Street, Soquel; 831-462-9191, fax 831-462-0402; www.cabbi.com.

For those traveling with a large group, or those wanting to enjoy the Wine Country from a residential perspective, **Wine Country Rentals** offers elegant homes in the Napa and Sonoma valleys. ~ P.O. Box 543, Calistoga, CA 94515; 707-942-2186, fax

707-942-4681; www.winecountryrentals.com, e-mail info@wine
countryrentals.com.

DINING

Because of wonderful grapes and first-rate produce, Sonoma and
Napa restaurants excel in offering the widest array of local wines,
paired with fresh-from-the-farm vegetables and regional seafood
and poultry.

Whether it's an inexpensive taco or a four-course splurge, the
quality is highly consistent. In addition to renowned restaurants,
you'll find everyday kinds of places frequented by the locals as
well as wallet-friendly diners and ethnic places.

Within a particular chapter, the restaurant entries describe the establishment as budget, moderate,
deluxe or ultra-deluxe in price. Dinner entrées at
budget restaurants usually cost $12 or less. The ambi-
ence is informal café-style and the crowd is often a local
one. Many if not most ethnic restaurants can be found in
this category. *Moderately* priced restaurants range between
$12 and $19 at dinner and offer pleasant surroundings, a
more varied menu and a slower pace. *Deluxe* dining establishments tab their entrées above $19, featuring sophisticated cuisines,
plush decor, and more personalized service. *Ultra-deluxe* dining
rooms, where $25 will only get you started, are gourmet gather-
ing places where you should expect exceptional food and outstanding service. Restaurants that offer prix-fixe menus (where
you get a number of courses, sometimes accompanied with different wines) for a single price, tend to be extremely pricey, but are
often the best value.

> Zinfandel wines are only
> made in California, not in
> Europe. The origin of this
> grape was a mystery
> until modern DNA
> testing traced it to
> an obscure vineyard
> in northern Italy.

Lunch in the Wine Country can be a simple hamburger or
something involving salmon or foie gras. The midday meal is virtually without exception priced lower than dinner. Opting for lunch
instead of dinner is not only a money-saver, but also increases
your chances of getting a table at the restaurants most in demand.

Breakfast menus vary less in price from restaurant to restaurant.
Even deluxe-priced kitchens usually offer light breakfasts that cost
a fraction of their other meals. Dining listings in this guide serve
lunch and dinner unless otherwise noted.

**LIQUOR &
SMOKING
LAWS**

The legal age for purchase and consumption of alcoholic beverages, including wine, is 21; proof of age is required. You can buy
alcoholic beverages at liquor, grocery and many drug stores daily

from 6 a.m. to 2 a.m. Some restaurants, nightclubs and bars have licenses to sell beer and wine only, but most have licenses to sell liquor from 6 a.m. to 2 a.m. Remember when driving: the highest blood-alcohol level allowed under law is .08, which allows for about two drinks over two hours.

Smoking is illegal in California restaurants, bars, stores and office buildings, including wineries and other public gathering spaces. You won't find any special rooms set aside for smokers, either, though you might see signs outside indicating designated smoking areas.

PHONES

The area code for Sonoma, Napa and Mendocino counties is 707. It is not necessary to dial "1-7-0-7" before calling among these counties, or anywhere within the 707 area code, though longer calls qualify as toll calls. Toll-free numbers, such as those to hotels and inns, may begin with 800, 888, 877, 866 or 855; you need to dial "1" before dialing the number.

In case of emergency, call 9-1-1.

TRAVELING WITH CHILDREN

Visiting the Wine Country with kids can be a real adventure, and if properly planned, a truly enjoyable one. A number of wineries welcome children but you could also enjoy a busy and interesting vacation in this area without ever setting foot in a tasting room. After all, thousands of families live in the Wine Country and make use of its public parks and other attractions throughout the year. To ensure that your trip will feature the joy, rather than the strain, of parenthood, remember a few important guidelines.

Children under age 5 or under 40 pounds must be in approved child restraints while riding in cars/vans. The back seat is the safest.

Use a travel agent to help with arrangements; they can reserve spacious bulkhead seats. Also plan to bring everything you need on board—diapers, food, toys and extra clothes for kids and parents alike. If your visit to the Wine Country involves a long journey, plan to relax and do very little during the first few days.

Always allow extra travel time. Book reservations well in advance and make sure the lodging has the extra crib, cot or bed you require. It's smart to ask for a room at the end of the hall or away from the highway to cut down on noise. Also keep in mind that many bed-and-breakfast inns do not encourage or may not allow children as guests.

Making the Most of a Winery Visit

With hundreds of wineries, the temptation to pack too many into your itinerary is hard to resist. But it's a bad idea—those one-ounce pours can add up. The general rule is three, maybe four, in a day of tasting. One way to keep consumption to a minimum is to use the spit bucket, either for spitting or for pouring out the rest of a glass after a taste. Save those swallows for the wines you really love. Another tip is to avoid drinking anything at those wineries that offer other attractions, such as a historic building or an interesting tour.

When there are four wineries I want to see in the course of one day, I like to start early because the odds of over-consuming are less in the morning. If you make two judicious stops in the morning, break for lunch and maybe get some exercise, you can still visit one winery after lunch and another at the tail end of the day.

Winery hours are usually from 10 a.m. or 11 a.m. until 4 p.m. or 5 p.m. Expect to pay a fee anytime you taste reserve wines; as a general rule, the larger Napa wineries charge for tasting while those in Sonoma and Mendocino do not, but there are plenty of exceptions.

Large wineries schedule tours and tasting all day and permit you to drop by unannounced. Though impersonal, they're convenient to visit and provide a wider variety of wines. Small wineries, where the operation is family run and tours are personalized, create the most memorable experiences. Often the winemaker or a member of the family will show you around or at least pour you a sample, providing a glimpse into their lives as well as their livelihoods. Since the family members will be leaving their normal duties to help you, they usually insist on advance reservations.

Most towns have stores that carry diapers, food and other essentials; in cities and larger towns, 7-11 stores are often open all night (check the Yellow Pages for addresses). Chain grocery stores such as Safeway and Albertson's are open late, sometimes 24 hours a day.

Hotels often provide access to babysitters or you can check the Yellow Pages for state licensed and bonded babysitting agencies.

A first-aid kit is always a good idea when traveling. Also, check with your pediatrician for special medicines and dosages for colds and diarrhea.

Finding activities to interest children in Northern California could not be easier. Especially helpful in deciding on the day's outing are *Fun Places to Go with Children in Northern California* (Chronicle Books) and the Friday and Sunday entertainment sections of the *Santa Rosa Press Democrat*, the only major daily published in the region.

> Past movies that premiered at the Wine Country Film Festival (held in the summer) include *Eat Drink Man Woman*, *Tin Cup* and *Shall We Dance?*

WOMEN TRAVELING ALONE

Traveling solo grants an independence and freedom different from that of traveling with a partner, but single travelers are more vulnerable to crime and should take additional precautions.

While the crime rate in Napa and Sonoma is very small indeed, don't let that give you a false sense of security or override common sense. It's unwise to hitchhike and probably best to avoid inexpensive accommodations on the outskirts of town; the money saved does not outweigh the risk. Bed and breakfasts and youth hostels are generally your safest bet for lodging, and they also foster an environment ideal for bonding with fellow travelers.

Keep all valuables well-hidden and hold onto cameras and purses. Avoid late-night treks or strolls through questionable sections of town, but if you find yourself in this situation, continue walking with a confident air until you reach a safe haven. A fierce scowl never hurts.

These hints should by no means deter you from seeking out adventure. Wherever you go, stay alert, use common sense and trust your instincts.

If you are hassled or threatened in some way, never be afraid to yell for assistance. It's a good idea to carry change for a phone call and a number to call in a case of emergency. Northern California boasts nearly 900 women's organizations, including rape crisis centers, health organizations, battered women's shelters, National Organization of Women (NOW) chapters, business networking clubs, and artists' and writers' groups. You can find a complete listing of these groups at www.distel.ca/womlist/countries/usa/california.html.

Emergency services, including rape crisis and battered women's hotlines, can be found in local phone books or by calling directory assistance.

For more hints, get a copy of *Safety and Security for Women Who Travel* (Travelers' Tales).

GAY & LESBIAN TRAVELERS

In the Wine Country, the most gay-friendly area is around Guerne-ville, where many resorts cater expressly to gays and lesbians. The **Gay-Lesbian-Bi Information Referral Line** is a traveler-friendly phone line that provides information and referrals about lodging, dining and nightlife in the area, along with just about any other information you might need. ~ 707-526-0442.

The local gay and lesbian newspaper is *We the People*, which comes out once a month and is available throughout the area. The free bimonthly *Mom . . . Guess What!* serves all of Northern California with political scoops, travel tips, restaurant reviews and more. ~ 916-441-6397, fax 916-441-6422; www.mgwnews.com.

SENIOR TRAVELERS

The Wine Country is an ideal spot for older vacationers and has a growing number of retirement communities. The mild climate makes traveling in the off-season possible, helping to cut down on expenses.

The **American Association of Retired Persons,** or AARP, offers members travel discounts and provides escorted tours. ~ 601 E Street NW, Washington, DC 20049; 888-687-2277; www.aarp. org, e-mail member@aarp.org.

For those 55 or over, **Elderhostel** offers educational programs in California. ~ 11 Avenue de Lafayette, Boston, MA 02111; 800-454-5768, fax 617-426-0701; www.elderhostel.org.

Be extra careful about health matters. Bring any medications you use, along with the prescriptions. Consider carrying a med-ical record with you—including your current medical status and medical history, as well as your doctor's name, phone number and address. Also be sure to confirm that your insurance covers you away from home.

DISABLED TRAVELERS

California stands at the forefront of social reform for persons with disabilities. During the past decade, the state has responded to the needs of the blind, wheelchair-bound, and others with a series of progressive legislative measures.

There are also agencies in Northern California assisting travelers with disabilities. For tips and information about the greater San Francisco Bay Area, contact the **Center for Independent Living**, a self-help group that has led the way in reforming access laws in California. ~ 2539 Telegraph Avenue, Berkeley, CA 94704; 510-841-4776, fax 510-841-6168; www.cilberkeley.org.

There are many organizations offering general information. Among these are:

The **Society for Accessible Travel & Hospitality**. ~ 347 5th Avenue #610, New York, NY 10016; 212-447-7284, fax 212-725-8253; www.sath.org, e-mail sathtravel@aol.com.

The **MossRehab ResourceNet**. ~ MossRehab Hospital, 1200 West Tabor Road, Philadelphia, PA 19141; 215-456-9600; www.mossresourcenet.org, e-mail staff1@mossresourcenet.org.

Flying Wheels Travel. ~ 143 West Bridge Street, Owatonna, MN 55060; 507-451-5005, fax 507-451-1685; www.flyingwheels travel.com.

Travelin' Talk, a network of people and organizations, also provides assistance. ~ P.O. Box 1796, Wheat Ridge, CO 80034; 303-232-2979; www.travelintalk.net, e-mail info@travelintalk.net. Its sister organization, **Access-Able Travel Service**, also has worldwide information online. ~ www.access-able.com.

Or consult the comprehensive guidebook, *Access to the World—A Travel Guide for the Handicapped*, by Louise Weiss (Holt, Rinehart & Winston). Though out of print, it can be found through second-hand book dealers.

Be sure to check in advance when making room reservations. Many hotels and motels feature facilities for those in wheelchairs.

FOREIGN TRAVELERS

Passports and Visas   Most foreign visitors are required to obtain a passport and tourist visa to enter the United States. Contact your nearest United States Embassy or Consulate well in advance to obtain a visa and to check on any other entry requirements.

Customs Requirements   Foreign travelers are allowed to bring in the following: 200 cigarettes (1 carton), 50 cigars or 2 kilograms

(4.4 pounds) of smoking tobacco; one liter of alcohol for personal use only (you must be 21 years of age to bring in alcohol); and US$100 worth of duty-free gifts that can include an additional 100 cigars. You may bring in any amount of currency, but must fill out a form if you bring in over US$10,000. Carry any prescription drugs in clearly marked containers. You may have to produce a written prescription or doctor's statement for the customs officers. Meat or meat products, seeds, plants, fruits and narcotics are not allowed to be brought into the United States. Contact the **United States Customs and Border Protection** for further information. ~ 1300 Pennsylvania Avenue NW, Washington, DC 20229; 202-354-1000, 877-227-5511; www.cbp.gov.

Driving   If you plan to rent a car, an international driver's license should be obtained prior to arrival. Some rental car companies require both a foreign license and an international driver's license, along with a major credit card and require that the lessee be at least 25 years of age. Seat belts are mandatory for the driver and all passengers. Children under the age of 5 or 40 pounds should be in the back seat in approved child-safety restraints.

Currency   American money is based on the dollar. Bills in the United States come in seven denominations: $1, $2, $5, $10, $20, $50 and $100. Every dollar is divided into 100 cents. Coins are the penny (1 cent), nickel (5 cents), dime (10 cents), quarter (25 cents), half-dollar (50 cents) and dollar. You may not use foreign

CRUISIN' THROUGH THE COUNTRY

If you're in San Francisco and are planning to tour the Wine Country, the most unique—and likely the most luxurious—way to do so is by boat. Catch **Cruise West** at San Francisco's China Basin for three- or four-night excursions up the Sacramento River to Sonoma, Napa Valley, and Old Town Sacramento. In addition to soaking up views of the Bay and riverfront towns from the decks of these 100-passenger ships, you'll get to enjoy gourmet meals served in the dining room; and an on-board wine expert will impart knowledge about winemaking. So rest up in your comfortable stateroom before heading out to visit those wineries and historic sites. ~ 2401 4th Avenue, Suite 700, Seattle, WA 98121; 888-851-8133, fax 206-441-4757; www.cruisewest.com, e-mail experience@cruisewest.com.

currency to purchase goods and services in the United States. Consider buying traveler's checks in dollar amounts. You may also use credit cards affiliated with an American company such as Interbank, Barclay Card, VISA and American Express.

Electricity and Electronics Electric outlets use currents of 110 volts, 60 cycles. For appliances made for other electrical systems, you need a transformer or other adapter. Travelers who use laptop computers for telecommunication should be aware that modem configurations for U.S. telephone systems may be different from their European counterparts. Similarly, the U.S. format for videotapes is different from that in Europe; some souvenir videos are available in European format on request.

Weights and Measurements The United States uses the English system of weights and measures. American units and their metric equivalents are as follows: 1 inch = 2.5 centimeters; 1 foot (12 inches) = 0.3 meter; 1 yard (3 feet) = 0.9 meter; 1 mile (5280 feet) = 1.6 kilometers; 1 ounce = 28 grams; 1 pound (16 ounces) = 0.45 kilogram; 1 quart (liquid) = 0.9 liter.

Outdoor Adventures

CAMPING

The state oversees more than 260 camping facilities. Amenities at each campground vary; for a complete listing of all state-run campgrounds, send $2 for the *Guide to California State Parks* to the **California Department of Parks and Recreation**. ~ P.O. Box 942896, Sacramento, CA 94296; 916-653-6995, 800-777-0369, fax 916-654-6374; www.parks.ca.gov, e-mail info@parks.ca.gov. Reservations for campgrounds may be made by calling 800-444-7275.

In addition to state and Wine Country campgrounds, Northern California offers numerous municipal, county and pri-

WINE COUNTRY ADVENTURES

For backpackers and daytrippers, state parks in Wine Country offer a chance to escape the crowds while exploring forests, meadows and mountain ridges. **Backroads** organizes five- to six-day hiking and biking jaunts that take in Dry Creek, Alexander, Napa and Sonoma valleys; most meals and lodging are included. ~ 801 Cedar Street, Berkeley; 510-527-1555, 800-462-2848; www.backroads.com.

vate facilities. See the "Parks" sections in each chapter for the locations of these campgrounds.

Anglers in the Wine Country can drop a line in northern Sonoma County at Lake Sonoma or the Russian River north of Healdsburg. Lake Mendocino near Ukiah is also a favored spot. See "Fishing" in Chapter Seven for more information.

FISHING

For current information on the fishing season and state license fees, contact the **Department of Fish and Game.** ~ 1416 9th Street, Sacramento, CA 95814; 916-445-0411; www.dfg.ca.gov. There is also a regional office in Napa Valley. ~ 7329 Silverado Trail, Napa, CA 94558; 707-944-5500.

▼▼▼▼▼▼▼▼▼▼▼▼

Transportation

The quick, painless and impersonal way to the Napa Valley is along **Route 80.** From San Francisco, the freeway buzzes northeast to Vallejo, where it connects with **Route 37** and then **Route 29**, the main road through Napa Valley.

CAR

An alternative course leads north from San Francisco along **Route 101**, the major north–south artery in Sonoma County; parts of it are two-lane while other parts are four-lane. From this freeway you can pick up Route 37, which skirts San Pablo Bay en route to its junction with Route 29. **Route 116** runs in a southeast–northwest axis from Route 101 in Rohnert Park all the way to Guerneville and other areas of the Russian River.

For the most scenic drive, turn off Route 37 onto **Route 121**. This rural road, which also connects with Route 29, provides a preview of the Wine Country. The curving hills along the way are covered with vineyards, ranches and sheep farms. **Route 12** segues from Route 121 and leads through the town of Sonoma and all the way north to Santa Rosa.

Two airports are close enough to the Wine Country to require less than a two-hour drive.

AIR

The **San Francisco International Airport**, better known as SFO, sits 15 miles south of downtown San Francisco off Routes 101 and 280. A major destination from all points of the globe, the airport is always bustling. ~ www.flysfo.com.

Most domestic airlines fly into SFO, including Alaska Airlines, American Airlines, Continental Airlines, Delta Air Lines, Frontier

Airlines, Hawaiian Airlines, Midwest Express, Northwest Airlines, United Airlines and US Airways.

International carriers are also prominent here. Air Canada, Air France, British Airways, China Airlines, Japan Airlines, KLM Airlines, Lufthansa Airlines, Mexicana Airlines, Philippine Airlines, Singapore Airlines, TACA International Airlines and Virgin Atlantic have regular flights into San Francisco's airport.

To avoid the crowds and parking hassles at SFO, consider landing in Oakland, just across the Bay. Domestic carriers that service **Oakland International Airport** include Alaska Airlines, Aloha Airlines, America West Airlines, American Airlines, Continental Airlines, Delta Air Lines, jetBlue, Southwest Airlines, United Airlines and US Airways. International carriers here are Mexicana Airlines and ATA (Suntrips). ~ www.flyoakland.com.

Evans Airport Service provides regularly scheduled shuttle transportation to the Napa Valley from both San Francisco and Oakland airports. You can also arrange chartered limousine service to other parts of the Wine Country. ~ 707-255-1559; www.evans transportation.com, e-mail info@evanstransportation.com.

The **Sonoma Airporter** runs regular shuttles to and from SFO. Reservations are suggested and pickup can be arranged. ~ 18346 Sonoma Highway, Sonoma; 707-938-4246; www.sonomaairpor ter.com, e-mail info@sonomaairporter.com.

CAR RENTALS

Most major agencies have outlets at both the San Francisco and Oakland airports. These include **Avis Rent A Car** (800-331-1212), **Budget Rent A Car** (800-527-0700), **Dollar Rent A Car** (800-800-4000), **Hertz Rent A Car** (800-654-3131) and **National Car Rental** (800-227-7368).

Several other companies, listed in the Yellow Pages, offer free pickup at and delivery to both airports.

BUS

Greyhound Bus Lines has frequent service to the Napa Valley, Santa Rosa, Healdsburg, Guerneville, Geyserville and points farther north. ~ 800-229-9424; www.greyhound.com.

Golden Gate Transit provides bus service from San Francisco to some Sonoma County towns. Allow around two hours to reach Santa Rosa and another half-hour to reach Healdsburg. These buses serve commuters; on weekends, you must disembark in Santa Rosa and transfer onto Sonoma County Transit buses to reach other towns. ~ 415-455-2000, 415-923-2000, 707-541-2000; www.goldengate.org.

NAPA VALLEY   Napa Valley Transit operates between Calistoga and Vallejo, with links to the local valley transportation as well as the Vallejo Ferry and bus lines. Bike racks are available on all buses, which run daily except Sunday from 5:30 a.m. (6:30 on Saturday) until 7:30 p.m. Fares are based on distance traveled, with regular adult fares starting at $1. The VINE (**Valley Intracity Neighborhood Express**) provides bus service along five routes within the city of Napa. ~ 707-251-2800, 800-696-6443.

PUBLIC TRANSIT

SONOMA COUNTY   Sonoma County Transit buses connect all the cities in the county on a daily basis. Fares are usually less than $3 one-way; some stops are within walking distance of wineries. ~ 355 West Robles Avenue, Santa Rosa; 707-576-7433, 800-345-7433, TDD 707-585-9817; www.sctransit.com.

Santa Rosa CityBus serves 17 routes within the city every day, with slightly shorter hours on Saturday and Sunday. Exact change of $1 is required; children under 5 ride free. Transfers are free. ~ 707-543-3333; TTY 707-543-3926; www.srcity.org/tp.

MENDOCINO COUNTY   From Santa Rosa you can pick up coastal connections on **Mendocino Transit Authority**, which travels Route 1 from Bodega Bay to Point Arena. There's only one bus a day in either direction. ~ 707-462-1422, 800-696-4682; www.4mta.org.

Dial-A-Ride is a share-ride service that provides door-to-door transportation on a limited basis within Ukiah and its immediate surrounds. In-town fare is $4 for adults and $2 for seniors/disabled within the city limits, but the price rises drastically for trips beyond those limits. ~ 707-462-3881.

NAPA VALLEY   The **Napa Valley Cab** company ("The Red One") is available for intra-valley service around the clock and offers flat-rate service to the airports. ~ 707-257-6444.

TAXIS

SONOMA COUNTY   Vern's Taxi Service serves the Sonoma Valley. ~ 707-996-6733. The Santa Rosa–based **George's Taxi** (707-546-3322) and **Yellow Cab** (707-544-4444) serve Rohnert Park, Cotati, Sebastopol and Windsor. The **Healdsburg Taxi Cab Company** (707-433-7099) serves the city and environs and also offers personalized tours of the Wine Country. There's a 20-percent discount for service from any airport shuttle and for senior citizens.

RUSSIAN RIVER AREA   George's Taxi (707-546-3322) and **Yellow Cab** (707-544-4444) serve the Russian River area. There's a 20-percent discount for service from any airport shuttle and for senior citizens.

MENDOCINO COUNTY   **Hey Taxi Incorporated** (707-485-5560) serves Mendocino County. Limited transportation around Ukiah and on the Mendocino coast is available through the **Mendocino Transit Authority.** ~ 707-462-1422.

TWO

Southern Napa Valley

The very name "Napa" is synonymous with the best wine produced in the entire country. It is such an important distinction—and one so vital to Napa's supremacy in the hierarchy of American winemaking—that in 2006 the U.S. Supreme Court confirmed the vintners' insistence that if the word "Napa" appears on a wine bottle label, at least 85 percent of the contents must come from Napa. Corks popped at hundreds of wineries throughout the valley when the ruling became known. Napa's supremacy is often challenged by wine-growing appellations in Sonoma and elsewhere, but in fact Napa lagged behind neighboring Sonoma in its early years.

The first white explorers arrived in the lush valley in 1823 in search of a site to build Mexico's northernmost mission; they chose Sonoma instead. As a result, southern Napa Valley lacks the historical significance of its neighbor in many ways but has plenty to offer on its own merits.

One of the original 27 California counties, Napa is bounded by Lake County on the north, Sonoma on the west, Yolo and Solano on the east, and San Pablo Bay, the northwestern part of San Francisco Bay, on the south. At the top of the valley is Mount St. Helena, source of the mineral-rich soil in much of the region; through the 40-mile agricultural preserve runs the Napa River, another fount of nutrients for the picturesque vineyards that carpet the valley floor and spread up onto the slopes of the Mayacamas Mountains.

More than 160 years ago, a pioneer named George C. Yount planted grapes around present-day Yountville, using vines obtained from General Mariano Vallejo's Sonoma estate. (Yount dubbed the settlement Sebastopol, but it was later renamed in his honor. Good thing, since there is a city named Sebastopol in neighboring

Sonoma County.) From this land-grant vineyard, Yount made his first wine in 1841 out of mission grapes introduced to northern California by the Franciscan fathers in the 1820s.

While most of the first wineries opened in the environs of St. Helena as early as the 1860s, others were eventually established throughout the valley. Microclimates were observed, setting the stage for the establishment of prestigious appellations such as Stag's Leap (east of Yountville) and the Rutherford Bench (between Yountville and St. Helena) as well as the Carneros, the southernmost appellation.

In the early 1970s, vintners became increasingly aware of the potential of planting vineyards in the Carneros district that borders the bay on the south. Cool temperatures and steady maritime breezes—sometimes actual winds—are considered excellent conditions for grapes such as pinot noir and chardonnay, both of which are used in the making of California sparkling wine. Some newcomers, such as Domaine Chandon (which belongs to Taittinger, the French champagne house) and Artesa (which belongs to the Spanish winemaking family, Codorniu), established stunning facilities and make outstanding wines, both still and sparkling. Meanwhile, existing wineries in Napa began planting vineyards there and/or purchasing grapes from growers in the appellation.

On the rim of the Carneros lies the county seat, the city of Napa. Founded by Nathan Coombs (who had been a member of the Bear Flag Party that declared independence from Mexico in 1845 in the heart of Sonoma), the city lagged Sonoma in development; its first building wasn't constructed until 1848.

If you were parachuted into downtown Napa, you wouldn't recognize it as Wine Country since it looks like many Bay Area towns. You won't see a lot of wine shops or ritzy resorts but you will see a plethora of Victorian buildings, several of which have been converted into bed-and-breakfast inns.

It comes as a surprise to some visitors that Napa is a river town. The Napa River was crucial to the burgeoning wine industry as a conduit to San Francisco Bay, where wines could be distributed out of the big cities. In Napa are some unusual cultural destinations, including an opera house and an indoor-outdoor gallery devoted to regional art as well as a hillside winery with an art collection that rivals small European museums. In addition, Napa is home to the only tourist train in the entire Wine Country.

The city of Napa is the workhorse of the valley—county offices are located here along with the last batch of relatively inexpensive housing. This is where everyone goes to shop at home and garden centers, discount clothing outlets, and national chain stores. It's as if the valley residents realized they had to sacrifice some place in order to preserve the agricultural splendor elsewhere, and Napa was it.

Surrounding the town, however, are highly regarded vineyards as well as a major-league resort. Napa is a good choice to establish headquarters if you're in-

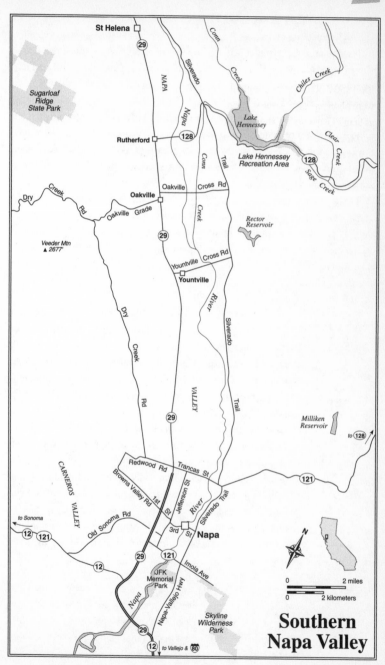

Southern Napa Valley

terested in visiting wineries in both the Napa and Sonoma valleys. Downtown is enjoying something of a renaissance, and the riverfront is finally being recognized as the fabulous resource that it is. As you will discover, there is much more to do here than sample wine. There are hot-air balloon rides, parks for hiking, the river for fishing, and walking tours through the Victorian district, now on the National Register of Historic Places.

Yountville, Rutherford and Oakville do have residents, but their raison d'être is the production of wine. Vineyards and wineries, including such world-famous names as Mondavi, dominate the landscape as well as the local consciousness. But all three have wonderful places to eat and spend the night. It's just that there is no downtown in any of these towns.

On weekends from early summer to late fall, the entire valley throngs with tourists. So try to visit during the week, and plan to explore not only the main highway, which often suffers from bumper-to-bumper traffic, but also the Silverado on the east side of the valley and the numerous east–west roads that connect the two. An ideal itinerary will carry you up the valley on Route 29, then back down along the parallel roadway.

▼▼▼▼▼▼▼▼▼▼
Napa Area

From the north shore of San Pablo Bay, the southern portion of the Napa Valley runs up to the town of Oakville. The city of Napa anchors the region, but for visitors the county seat pales in importance when compared to the world-famous vineyards that surround it on every side. Skimming the bay is the Carneros district, where pinot noir and chardonnay are the king and queen.

North of the city are the small towns of Yountville, Rutherford and Oakville, where the soils and weather patterns are considered ideal for cabernet sauvignon as well as other prized grape varietals. Yountville is a dining and shopping destination and, as of fall 2004, has a new concert hall for the Napa Valley Symphony. Otherwise, the area north of Napa, the county seat, is for the most part rural. Napa itself has the most shops, restaurants and other businesses, and continues its meteoric rise as a top tourist destination.

SIGHTS   The city of Napa, long regarded as an ugly duckling compared to the glamorous upper valley, has undergone some dramatic changes since COPIA: The American Center for Wine, Food & the Arts opened in 2001. A restored opera house, a hotel-restaurant-shopping complex on the Napa River and several new dining spots have revitalized the downtown area. Now that the riverfront has once again become vibrant, other neighborhoods, especially those with numerous Victorian homes, are breathing new life as well.

The Carneros appellation extends into both Napa and Sonoma counties along the rim of San Pablo Bay and straddles Route 29, bordered by Browns Valley Road and Imola Avenue on the north; only a small portion of the city of Napa lies within the designation.

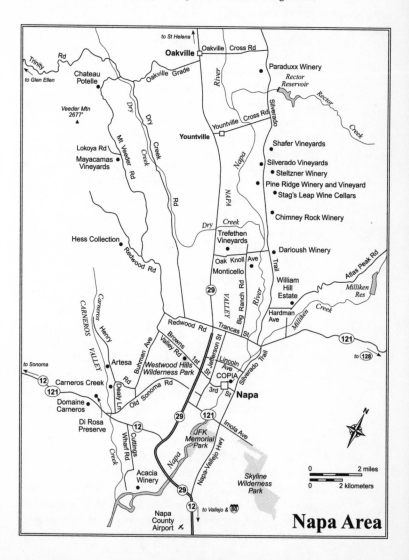

Napa Area

The varietals that flourish here are also the grapes used to make champagne, so it's not surprising that a number of wineries are known for their sparkling wines. (Unless otherwise noted, all wineries offer regular or self-guided tours and are open daily except for Thanksgiving, Christmas and New Year's Day.)

From Route 29 go north until the turnoff for Route 121. Travel a few miles towards Sonoma to find one of the most impressive assemblages of art in Northern California. Keep an eye out for cut-out sheep dotting the hillside and you'll know you've arrived at the **Di Rosa Preserve**. This unusual rural setting befits the one-man vision, perhaps the country's largest collection of Bay Area art. Rene di Rosa, a former journalist has installed thousands of drawings, sculptures, paintings and more in a series of buildings and, where appropriate, in the great outdoors on the grounds of a former winery, including on the shores of a 35-acre lake. From the whimsical to the deeply moving, the artwork is more than enough to fill the guided tours (reservations recommended). Closed Sunday and Monday. Admission. ~ 5200 Carneros Highway, Napa; 707-226-5991, fax 707-255-8934; www. dirosapreserve.org, e-mail info@dirosapreserve.org.

Almost across the road from the art preserve, **Domaine Carneros** is housed in a building that could pass as a French château. That's because it's the New World offshoot of Taittinger, the famous champagne house. In this imposing setting, you can sample sparklers in the tasting room or on the terrace. Tasting fee. ~ 1240 Duhig Road, Napa; 707-257-0101, fax 707-257-3020; www.domainecarneros.com, e-mail info@domainecarneros.com.

HIDDEN ▶ A few scenic miles from Route 121 via Duhig Road, **Acacia Vineyard**, founded in 1979, quickly built a reputation for vineyard-designated pinot noir. Named for the trees that blossom with yellow flowers each spring, Acacia is also known for chardonnay and viognier. The tasting room is small, but there's plenty of room outside to enjoy views of the vineyards and the bay marshlands to the south. Tours weekdays by appointment. Tasting by appointment; fee. ~ 2750 Las Amigas Road, Napa; 707-226-9991; www.acaciavineyard.com, e-mail acacia.info@acaciavineyard.com.

Some of Napa's prettiest and least-traveled roads can be found in this section of the Carneros district, where several wineries are tucked away. One is **Mahoney Vineyards**, which is known for its pinot noir, though it also produces chardonnay, syrah, vermentino and Montepulciano. Samples are available in the hospitality center, picnic tables sit in the shade of an arbor, and there is a large deck in back. Tours by appointment. Tasting fee. ~ 1285 Dealy Lane, Napa; 707-253-9463, fax 707-253-9465; www.mahoney vineyards.com, e-mail wineinfo@mahoneyvineyards.com.

Up the road, **Artesa** (pronounced ar-TESS-uh) opened on a hilltop in 1991. A stunning 127,000-square-foot winery that is dug into the top of the hill, Artesa boasts one of the most dramatic approaches in the Wine Country, with a sweeping staircase rimmed by waterfalls, fountains, reflecting pools and sculptures. The nearly wraparound view from the top includes hillside vineyards and north San Pablo Bay. Originally known as Codorniu Napa, the winery switched its focus to still wines in 1997. Today the winemaker makes chardonnay and pinot noir as well as other varietals. Tasting fee. ~ 1345 Henry Road, Napa; 707-224-1668, fax 707-224-1672; www.artesawinery.com.

To reach the city of Napa, return to Route 121 and head east, then turn north on Route 29; take the 1st Street exit, which will lead you to 2nd Street, heading one-way downtown. If there is no street parking, you can easily find public lots.

The **Napa Valley Conference and Visitors Bureau** is a good place to get started on a tour of the entire valley. They will supply you with maps and brochures for the area. ~ 1310 Napa Town Center, Napa; 707-226-7459, fax 707-255-2066; www.napavalley. com, e-mail info@napavalley.org.

If someone in your traveling party wants to be a fireperson when she grows up, the whole family might like a brief stop at the **Napa Firefighters Museum**, just a couple of blocks away from the visitors bureau. Engines, ladder trucks, hose carts and other equip-

sights

AUTHOR FAVORITE

I love wandering through the **Di Rosa Preserve**, an art extravaganza on the grounds of an old winery. Former journalist Rene di Rosa has been collecting Bay Area art for decades and has amassed more than 2000 paintings, sculptures, drawings, photographs and videos. In addition to exhibiting the works indoors, he's chosen to install a number of them outside. I especially enjoy the outdoor sculptures, which inject a refreshing dose of whimsy into an area that can take itself a bit too seriously. See page 38 for more information.

ment as well as uniforms and old photos would look better in a real firehouse, but it's a nice enough display. Closed Monday and Tuesday. ~ 1201 Main Street, Napa; 707-259-0609.

For anyone who's ever aligned themselves with Copia, the goddess of abundance, there's COPIA: **The American Center for Wine, Food & the Arts.** Located on the banks of the Napa River directly across from downtown, this spacious, two-story facility is a mecca for foodies, wine lovers, gardeners, art connoisseurs and others. You'll find an array of exhibits, cooking demonstrations, and classes in wine appreciation and the visual arts, plus Julia's Kitchen, a restaurant named for celebrity chef Julia Child. The building is flanked by demonstration gardens planted with herbs and other produce used in the center. Closed Tuesday. Admission. ~ 500 1st Street, Napa; 707-259-1600, 888-512-6742; www.copia.org, e-mail info@copia.org.

The **Napa Valley Opera House,** dark for some 88 years, re-opened in 2002 after extensive renovations. The landmark's impressive Italianate facade has been restored, while interior details such as woodwork and a brick wall have been preserved for posterity. There are two performance spaces—the Margrit Biever Mondavi Theatre upstairs and the cabaret-style Café Theatre downstairs—where plays, musicals, concerts and the like are presented several nights a week. ~ 1030 Main Street, Napa; 707-226-7372; www.nvoh.org.

North of Napa, the serious Wine Country begins, with wineries seemingly every 100 yards. One worth a slight detour is **Monticello Vineyard,** where a pretty if small-scale version of Jefferson's Virginia home serves as company headquarters. Best bets for tasting are merlot, cabernet and chardonnay. Tasting fee. ~ 4242 Big Ranch Road, Napa; 707-253-2802, 800-743-6668, fax 707-253-1019; www.corleyfamilynapavalley.com, e-mail wine@monti cellovineyards.com.

HIDDEN ►

Just off Route 29 is the site of one of the valley's oldest wineries. **Trefethen Vineyards** occupies an 1886 wooden winery on the National Register of Historic Places. A lovely wine library, decked out in antiques and plush leather chairs, houses the vineyards' older and larger bottlings for taste and purchase. "Library Tastings" (fee; reservations required) are held the first Saturday of the month and include five personal picks from the winemaker. Ones to try include the estate-grown cabernet sauvignon and chardonnay as well as the less-expensive versions of these two varietals. Tours are by appointment. ~ 1160 Oak Knoll Avenue, Napa; 707-255-7700, 800-556-4847, fax 707-255-0793; www.trefethen.com, e-mail winery@trefethen.com.

Not terribly far from Route 29, on the west side of the valley, you can find one of the valley's most outstanding attractions. The **Hess Collection** is where fine wine meets fine art, and the self-guided tour is unique: It is the only winery in the valley that includes two floors displaying some 130 museum-quality artworks by contemporary international artists. The Hess Collection also refers to the cabernets and chardonnays that are just being released and are available for sampling in the ground-floor tasting room. Tasting fee. ~ 4411 Redwood Road, Napa; 707-255-1144, fax 707-253-1682; www.hesscollection.com, e-mail info@hess collection.com.

From Hess, return to Redwood and take Mount Veeder Road north to another out-of-the-way winery. **Mayacamas Vineyards** ◄ HIDDEN provides an entirely different setting from the wineries on the valley floor. Located deep in the mountains west of Napa Valley, it sits astride an extinct volcano. The blocks of vineyard appear hewn from surrounding rock walls. Indeed, the fields of chardonnay and cabernet sauvignon rest on terraces along the mountainside. Like the encircling hills, the winery is made of stone, built in 1889. Tours of this special place are by appointment; it lies about ten miles off Route 29 along winding mountain roads. Closed weekends. ~ 1155 Lokoya Road, Napa; 707-224-4030, fax 707-224-3979; www.mayacamas.com, e-mail mayacama@napanet.net.

Back on Mount Veeder Road and nestled on the slopes of Mount Veeder away from the hubbub (about ten miles west from Route 29 via the Oakville Grade), **Chateau Potelle** is the dream- ◄ HIDDEN

TOURING TIPS

Most Napa Valley wineries charge for tasting their wines, often a nominal fee or one that includes a souvenir glass. The large wineries are open every day except for major holidays, while the smaller ones usually operate on a limited schedule, especially in winter. A handful require reservations, a stipulation noted in the winery descriptions where applicable. Bear in mind that wine cellars are typically cool, around 65° year-round, so carry a wrap if you plan to take extensive tours of the properties.

come-true of a French couple. The winery and its acreage, located at an altitude ranging from 1600 to 2000 feet, produces about 20,000 cases of estate-grown zinfandel, cabernet and chardonnay, plus other varietals grown elsewhere. No tours. Seasonal closures, call ahead. ~ 3875 Mount Veeder Road, Napa; 707-255-9440, fax 707-255-9444; www.chateaupotelle.com, e-mail info@chateaupotelle.com.

HIDDEN ►

Return to Route 29 and the Silverado Trail to continue your tour. Located on a hillside near the Silverado Trail, **William Hill Estate** has a pastoral feel. A third of its 200 acres have been left undeveloped, allowing extensive views of the surrounding landscape, all the way to the Mayacamas Mountains on the western horizon. The winery makes chardonnay, merlot and cabernet sauvignon, notably Aura, a limited-production cab. The tasting room is small but there is seating beneath a trellis on the lawn. By appointment only. Tasting fee. ~ 1761 Atlas Peak Road, Napa; 707-224-4477; www.williamhillestate.com, e-mail winery@williamhillestate.com.

Head north to visit several top wineries clustered in the prized Stag's Leap district, known for its top-notch cabernet sauvignons.

One of the most dramatic winery sites in the Napa Valley, **Darioush** is distinguished by 16 monumental freestanding columns with capital bulls, an exterior of textured travertine and a palatial interior, all of it inspired by the architecture of Persepolis, capital of ancient Persia. Bordeaux-style estate wines are the specialty of the house. Several wines are paired with cheeses Friday afternoons by reservation only. Tours by appointment. Tasting fee. ~ 4240 Silverado Trail, Napa; 707-257-2345, fax 707-257-3132; www.darioush.com, e-mail info@darioush.com.

Since 1989, **Chimney Rock Winery** has been producing wines from vineyards in the southern Stag's Leap district. Nine years earlier the Wilson family began converting an 18-hole golf course into vineyard land that is especially well-known for its cabernet sauvignon. The winery also produces chardonnay and a red meritage blend. Chimney Rock's bright white Cape Dutch–style buildings, distinguished by arched gables and steep roofs, are clustered around a poplar grove. The tasting room feels like a gentlemen's club; there is additional seating on a brick patio out back. Tasting fee. ~ 5350 Silverado Trail, Napa; 707-257-2641,

The Carneros District

The grape-growing appellation that spans a swath along the north rim of San Pablo Bay is unusual for several reasons, chief among them being that it straddles two counties. The bulk of the Carneros lies in Napa but also includes a chunk of the southern Sonoma Valley. While there are no historic buildings along the lines of the town of Sonoma's mission and barracks, the area shares the history of the surrounding region. Here, the wine industry grew up, matured, struggled through the last phylloxera infestation, rebounded and finally achieved recognition in the 1980s. Its prominence in wine circles has continued to grow since it was named an American Viticultural Appellation (AVA) in 1983.

Carneros shares San Francisco's marine climate, with milder winters and summers than the valleys, giving the appellation a longer growing season suited to certain grapes. Because of the slow maturation in this climate, Carneros grapes reach maturity at lower sugar levels and higher acids, resulting in a great depth of flavor extract.

The moderate climate and fertile lands of the Sonoma Valley attracted early settlers who traveled through the area that today is served by Routes 12 and 121 (the latter known in this neighborhood as the Carneros Highway). As early as 1850, while hay was still free to those who would cut it, workers traveled by barge to Carneros (from the Spanish word for the sheep, or rams, once common here) to load hay and grain for transport to San Francisco. Farmers followed, raising sheep and cattle and cultivating grapes, pear, plums, apples and apricots.

While most of these vines were destroyed by phylloxera, the Stanly Ranch survived and helped start Napa's reputation for growing quality grapes. In 1942, Louis M. Martini, a longtime buyer of Stanly grapes, bought some 200 acres of the old ranch and replanted them with pinot noir and chardonnay. But by the close of World War II, little wine was being produced in Carneros. The current crop of wineries started up in 1972, when Francis Mahoney established Carneros Creek, the area's first new winery in nearly four decades. Today, the appellation's vineyards are harvested not only by Carneros winemakers but also by wineries from other parts of Sonoma and Napa.

Most of the roads in this part of the Wine Country (once you get off Routes 12, 121 and 29) tend to be small and less-traveled than their counterparts. It would be easy to visit most of the 16 or so wineries here in a weekend.

800-257-2641, fax 707-257-2036; www.chimneyrock.com, e-mail club@chimneyrock.com.

The wine that put California on the world map came from **Stag's Leap Wine Cellars**, which wowed oenophiles by beating out even the French Bordeaux entries in the now-famous Bicentennial tasting in Paris. Tasting fee. ~ 5766 Silverado Trail, Napa; 707-944-2020, fax 707-257-7501; www.cask23.com.

Tucked into a dell in the heart of the prestigious Stag's Leap district, **Pine Ridge Winery and Vineyards** has a storybook feel, with pine-forested hills receding in the distance and a cozy, adobe-clad tasting room. The winery, which is best known for its chardonnay and cabernet sauvignon, offers a special experience in addition to the standard pours: guided, sit-down tastings in the Cabernet Caves featuring comparative tastings accompanied by artisan cheeses. Other attractions include a demonstration vineyard and a picnic area. Tasting fee. ~ 5901 Silverado Trail, Napa; 800-575-9777; www.pineridgewinery.com, e-mail info@pineridge wine.com.

Named for the mining community that once flourished near Calistoga, **Silverado Vineyards** has capitalized on Napa Valley's resemblance to the Italian countryside with Tuscan-style architecture and colors like ochre and terra cotta. The winery, which belongs to members of the Walt Disney family, clings to a steep knoll. The 4000-square-foot tasting room opened in 2000 with large windows overlooking the vineyards. It is a handsome and remarkably uncluttered space, considering how much bric-a-brac is sold at most wineries. Tours offered by appointment. Tasting fee. ~ 6121 Silverado Trail, Napa; 707-257-1770; www.silverado vineyards.com, e-mail info@silveradovineyards.com.

The nearby **Steltzner Winery** is revered for its cabernet sauvignon; several vintages are usually available for tasting. For something different, you might sample the claret or sangiovese. Tasting fee. ~ 5998 Silverado Trail, Napa; 707-252-7272; www. steltzner.com.

Paraduxx Winery offers an unusual chance to sample and compare two or three vintages of its annual red wine blend, which always includes estate-grown cabernet sauvignon and zinfandel. Inside the mustard-yellow farm-style Vineyard House—quite a contrast from the sleek tasting room furnished with leather chairs and window seats—a staff member serves the wines in stemless Riedel "O" glasses along with a small bowl of spiced almonds and a bottle of spring water. No tours. Tasting by appointment only; fee. ~ 7257 Silverado Trail, Napa; 707-945-0890, 866-367-9943; www.paraduxx.com, e-mail tastings@para duxx.com.

LODGING

You will find a handful of small inns in downtown Napa, though accommodations in this area tend towards chain lodging and small motels on the outskirts of town.

You can't see much from the road, but hidden within the 27-acre **Carneros Inn** are 96 luxurious cottages as well as two restaurants (one of them for guests only), a spa and a smattering of private homes. Each accommodation is decorated with Corbusier and Eames furniture and cherrywood floors, and equipped with fireplaces, internet access, indoor and outdoor showers and fairly private patios with landscaping and vineyard views. Opened in 2003 and set for a major expansion in 2006, this hideaway is an ideal location for exploring not only the Carneros appellation, but the Napa and Sonoma valleys as well. ~ 4048 Route 121, Napa; 707-299-4900, 888-400-9000, fax 707-299-4950; www.thecarnerosinn. com, e-mail info@thecarnerosinn.com. ULTRA-DELUXE.

The **Blackbird Inn** is housed in a meticulously renovated 1910 Craftsman-style residence within walking distance of downtown restaurants. All eight rooms are decorated with individually crafted furnishings and subdued colors like pale mus-

AUTHOR FAVORITE

If you love the sound of water as much as I do, you'll love the fountains, waterfalls and, best of all, the river itself at the **Milliken Creek Inn**. Located on three prime acres along the banks of the Napa River, the stylish hostelry offers water views from almost every room. The decor features muted colors, crisp lines and luxurious trappings. Benches, terraces and ponds lure people to the riverfront, where waterfalls and other sound barriers muffle the traffic noise. All rooms feature mini bars, TVs, DVDs and modem access; suites have fireplaces and spa tubs. Massage services a re available. Breakfast is included. Two-night minimum on weekends. ~ 1815 Silverado Trail, Napa; 707-255-1197, 888-622-5775, fax 707-255-3112; www.millikencreekinn.com, e-mail info@millikencreek.com. ULTRA-DELUXE.

tard. The more expensive accommodations have spa tubs, fireplaces and/or private decks. Breakfast is included. ~ 1755 1st Street, Napa; 707-226-2450, 888-567-9811, fax 707-258-6391; www.blackbirdinnnapa.com, e-mail blackbirdinn@foursisters.com. DELUXE TO ULTRA-DELUXE.

Even in a town heavy on Victorians, **La Belle Epoque** is a standout. A colorful Queen Anne–style number built in 1893 by noted architect Luther M. Turton, it houses five spacious rooms named for wine varietals. Antiques such as an Eastlake queen bed, silk oriental carpets, and a Belgian armoire distinguish the accommodations, several of which have canopied beds and/or stained-glass windows. The breakfasts are so elaborate that a menu for tomorrow's meal is displayed each afternoon. Tastings are held in the wine cellar each evening. The inn, which is near downtown shops and restaurants, also has two luxury suites in a Victorian across the street. ~ 1386 Calistoga Avenue, Napa; 707-257-2161, 800-238-8070; www.labelleepoque.com, e-mail innkeeper@labelleepoque.com. ULTRA-DELUXE.

Known for its cool and windy climate, the Carneros appellation is considered ideal for growing pinot noir and chardonnay grapes.

Reasonably priced bed and breakfasts are nearly nonexistent in the Wine Country, with one exception—**Churchill Manor**. Located on an acre of landscaped, flower-filled grounds just south of downtown Napa, the manor, built in 1889, is now a ten-room inn. The rooms are furnished with European antiques, and exquisite redwood columns front the main staircase. The innkeepers serve a full breakfast in the tile-floored sunroom, and on nice mornings you can take it out on the veranda, which surrounds three sides of the home. In the evenings, complimentary wine and cheese are offered. There are also tandem bikes to ride, croquet to play and a sitting room with games and puzzles to enjoy. ~ 485 Brown Street, Napa; 707-253-7733, 800-799-7733, fax 707-253-8836; www.churchillmanor.com, e-mail be@churchillmanor.com. ULTRA-DELUXE.

The three-story, red-brick **River Terrace Inn** sits within walking distance of COPIA. All 78 rooms and 28 junior suites have ten-foot ceilings, ceiling fans, whirlpool tubs, and high-speed internet access; most have balconies. Complimentary breakfast buffet. Two-night minimum on summer weekends. ~ 1600 Soscol Avenue,

Napa; 707-320-9000, 866-627-2386, fax 707-258-1236; www.
riverterraceinn.com, e-mail sales@riverterraceinn.com. DELUXE.

The **Old World Inn** is at its most glorious in spring and summer, when wisteria and jasmine and then roses and other shrubs
are at their peak of flowering. Rooms are decorated in bright
colors such as mint green or blue and yellow; the eighth room is
in a detached cottage on the far side, with an indoor hot tub. A
full breakfast is included, as is early evening wine and cheese,
and desserts at night. Two-night minimum with a Friday or
Saturday stay. ~ 1301 Jefferson Street, Napa; 707-257-0112,
800-966-6624, fax 707-257-0118; www.oldworldinn.com, e-
mail innkeeper@oldworldinn.com. ULTRA-DELUXE.

As usual, the cheapest lodging has the least desirable address,
but in the Napa Valley, that's all relative. Look around Soscol
Avenue or near Route 29 for the best deals. An example of the
latter is the 34-room **Chablis Inn**. The rooms are larger than
usual, with a wet bar, coffeemaker and small refrigerator; some
have whirlpool tubs. In summer, you'll be glad to see the small
pool and spa. Be sure to ask for accommodations on the far side
of the highway. ~ 3360 Solano Avenue, Napa; 707-257-1944,
800-443-3490, fax 707-226-6862; www.chablisinn.com, e-mail
info@chablisinn.com. DELUXE.

In a region where few people blanch at uncorking a $100
bottle of wine, the **Chateau Hotel and Conference Center** might
be considered the equivalent of a screwtop. Accommodations
here are ordinary, quite clean and conveniently situated for exploring the entire valley. Some of the two-story motel's 115
rooms have refrigerators. Continental breakfast is included.
There's an indoor swimming pool and spa. ~ 4195 Solano Avenue, Napa; 707-253-9300, fax 707-253-0906; www.thecha
teauhotel.com. MODERATE TO DELUXE.

Your own place in Napa Valley? That's the ambience at the
Cottages of Napa, a collection of charming private structures—   ◄ HIDDEN
between 450 and 600 square feet—that have been renovated and
upgraded with sophisticated Wine Country decor. Each cottage
has a king-size bed, a living area with a queen sleeper sofa, a
kitchen, a gas fireplace, a private garden and an outdoor fireplace,
plus amenities such as TV/DVD and wireless internet access. The
inn is located off Route 29 two miles south of Yountville. Two-

night minimum on weekends May through October. Continental breakfast included. ~ 1012 Darms Lane, Napa; 707-252-7810, 866-900-7810; www.napacottages.com. ULTRA-DELUXE.

DINING   The truly chic restaurants are clustered around Yountville and St. Helena, but Napa offers some bargains and your best chance at ethnic food. There are a few coffee shops downtown that can provide you with a substantial snack.

HIDDEN ►   A roadhouse-style restaurant, **The Boon Fly Café** at the Carneros Inn is a rustic gathering place for neighbors and visitors as well as guests. Breakfast brings home-baked goods, and light lunches are available for eating on the premises or taking out. The wine list highlights vintages from neighboring wineries. ~ 4048 Route 121, Napa; 707-299-4900; www.thecarnerosinn.com, e-mail info@thecarnerosinn.com. MODERATE.

HIDDEN ►   If you wonder where the locals are, you can find a lot of them at the **Foothill Café**, a modest establishment off the tourist path on the unfashionable side of town. In 2006, new owners updated the menu with lighter, more seasonal fare. They kept favorites such as smoked baby back and prime ribs and incorporated new dishes such as pan-roasted chicken with preserved lemon and a number of pasta and vegetable dishes—a delightful alternative to the fancier, pricier up-valley restaurants. Closed Monday and Tuesday. ~ 2766 Old Sonoma Road, Napa; 707-252-6178. MODERATE.

Downtown Napa isn't the easiest place in the valley to reach, but there's a restaurant that makes the trip well worth the effort:
HIDDEN ►   **Celadon**, located in the historic Hatt Market. Seafood is tops on Greg Cole's menu of "global comfort food," as are many Thai- and Indonesian-influenced dishes, a number available in small servings ideal for mixing and matching. A great selection of wines by the glass rounds out the attractions in this high-ceilinged spot. Reservations are recommended. No lunch on weekends. ~ 500 Main Street, Suite G, Napa; 707-254-9690; www.celadonnapa.com. MODERATE TO DELUXE.

HIDDEN ►   Part of the restored Hatt Mill complex, **Angele** is housed in a late-19th-century boathouse overlooking the Napa River. This rustic setting undercuts the seriousness of the food, and just as well. The chef uses restraint in presenting French classics such as *blanquette de veau*. ~ 540 Main Street, Napa; 707-252-8115; www.angelerestaurant.com.

Tucked into the Napa General Store, **The General Café** is an ◄ HIDDEN
ultra-casual spot for small plates of pan-Asian food. Typical offerings include champagne-mango crab roll, five-spice roasted
duck, curry halibut spring rolls plus pizzas, salads, sandwiches
and oodles of noodles. Kid's menu available. No dinner Sunday
through Tuesday. ~ 540 Main Street, Napa; 707-259-0762; www.
napageneralstore.com. BUDGET TO MODERATE.

Beautiful presentations in a cosmopolitan, high-ceilinged room
make dining at **N.V. Restaurant and Lounge** one of the most ur-
bane experiences in Napa. With little in the way of decor beyond
the sage-green curtains, nothing distracts from lovely courses like
a layered beet-and-goat-cheese Napoleon, sliced into wedges, accompanied by micro-beet greens and a swoosh of densely flavored beet "paint." Other vegetarian options include seared tofu
"scallops," while omnivores might prefer lavender-maple-glazed
pork chops or poached lobster with mandarin orange sabayon.
The sizable lounge—complete with sofas and excellent piped-in
music—instantly became a hot gathering spot when N.V. opened
in late 2005. ~ 1106 1st Street, Napa; 707-265-6400. ULTRA-
DELUXE.

Cole's Chop House, a sister to nearby Celadon, lives up to its
name with porterhouse steaks, beef Wellington and veal chops,
among other choices. It's the kind of gentleman's-club place that
calls for a martini—or at least a cosmopolitan—to start. Pretty
potted palms are dwarfed by the hangar-like space; one is hardly
surprised to find out this 1886 native stone building once housed
a bowling alley. Dinner only. ~ 1122 Main Street, Napa; 707-224-
6328. ULTRA-DELUXE.

AUTHOR FAVORITE

Blessed with one of the loveliest settings in the Wine Country,
Bistro Don Giovanni evokes Tuscany for some. The fare is decidedly
Mediterranean—delectables like focaccia, grilled meats, housemade pastas,
whole roast fish and pizza. In warm weather, linger on the shaded porch;
when it turns cool, warm yourself in front of the large, open fireplace.
~ 4110 Howard Lane, Napa; 707-224-3300, fax 707-224-3395; www.
bistrodongiovanni.com. MODERATE.

Serving *tapas* and Mediterranean dishes from lunch straight through dinner on weekdays (but only at dinner on weekends), **Zuzu** attracts a steady clientele from the wine industry, in part because these small dishes from Spain work so well with so many wines. Marinated anchovies with Belgian endive, a garlicky dish of olives and manchego cheese, ratatouille, and marinated skirt steak with Argentine chimichurra sauce are typical and cost from $4 to $6; main courses are pricier. Moorish-looking glass lamps and a Mexican-style hammered tin ceiling set the tone. No lunch on weekends. ~ 829 Main Street, Napa; 707-224-8555. MODERATE.

COPIA's organic garden is a cornucopia of fresh ingredients for Julia's Kitchen; in summer, up to 90 percent of the restaurant's produce is harvested onsite.

Pilar opened in 2004 to offer some of the finest dining in town. Co-owner Pilar Sanchez, formerly chef at both Greystone and Meadowood, puts her talents to work on dishes such as rabbit with spaetzle, stuffed quail and rack of lamb. The restaurant's ambience is refined, with linen-topped tables, a recessed ceiling, gray flooring and abstract paintings. Closed Sunday and Monday. ~ 807 Main Street, Napa; 707-252-4474. DELUXE TO ULTRA-DELUXE.

The Restaurant Pearl serves "world-mix" cuisine, from tacos to pastas, either outdoors or in the high-ceilinged dining room. The seasonal menu is all over the map—a bit of Asia, a bit of Mexico—and yes, they do serve oysters along with other seafood. The industrial-looking decor is unusual for Napa, as is the gem of a restaurant. Closed Sunday and Monday. ~ 1339 Pearl Street, Napa; 707-224-9161. MODERATE.

On the east side of town, hunt for the **Old Adobe Bar and Grille**. Housed in an 1840 adobe with original thick walls and exposed beams, this restaurant serves fish, pasta, steaks and prime rib. A full bar adds to the ambience. ~ 376 Soscol Avenue, Napa; 707-255-4310, fax 707-255-8568. MODERATE.

HIDDEN ►

The cooking's not French but the cuisine is definitely "haute"—and so are the prices at **Julia's Kitchen**, the restaurant on the ground floor of COPIA. Named for the legendary Julia Child, the room has one wall of glass facing onto the gardens, whence so many goodies come. The changing menu is long on seafood—pan-roasted Atlantic cod, sautéed day boat scallops—but includes heavier fare like grilled Angus ribeye steak, roasted lamb and duck breast. No dinner Monday through Wednesday. Closed Tuesday. ~ 500 1st

Street, Napa; 707-265-5700; www.juliastable.com. DELUXE TO
ULTRA-DELUXE.

Farther east, just on the other side of the Silverado Trail,
Monticello Deli is the saving grace of vacationers who just want   ◀ *HIDDEN*
something to eat, not a five-star dining experience. An ultra-casual
favorite with locals, this deli serves up breakfast, sandwiches, salads and hot dishes like chicken. You can tote your meal out or
enjoy it here on bistro tables. ~ 1810 Monticello Road, Napa; 707-
255-3953, fax 707-255-3624; www.monticellodeli.com. BUDGET.

Fume Bistro is an easygoing place just off Route 29 also on   ◀ *HIDDEN*
the north side of Napa. You can make a meal of small plates such
as wasabi-infused ahi tuna and duck confit spring roll, or get serious with pizza, seafood, lamb, steak or chicken. The light and
airy bistro has a well-chosen wine list and a full-service bar.
Sunday brunch. ~ 4050 Byway East, Napa; 707-257-1999, fax
707-257-1115. MODERATE.

The majority of Napa's retailers can be found on the perimeter   **SHOPPING**
in a variety of large shopping centers. Specialty shops tend to be
found downtown.

Copperfield's Books is the local branch of a regional chain that
has shops in Sonoma and one up in Calistoga. It's an invaluable
source for local authors and guidebooks and carries a very good
selection of magazines. ~ 3600 Bel Air Plaza, Napa; 707-252-8002;
www.copperfields.net.

Fiction, nonfiction, children's books and regional guides fill
the shelves at the friendly **Bookends Book Store**. ~ 1014 Coombs
Street, Napa; 707-224-1077 or 707-254-7323.

Though not well known outside of foodie circles, **Shackford's**
has been catering to cooking fanatics for a quarter of a century.
Inside this plain-looking store is an array of equipment and gadgets,
from Cuisinarts to cookbooks to cake-decorating supplies to talking snack dispensers. Most shoppers are astounded to discover
things they never knew they needed. Closed Sunday. ~ 1350 Main
Street, Napa; 707-226-2132.

Napa's Premium Outlets is home to major retailers like Ann
Taylor, Calvin Klein and Timberland, among many others. (Take
the 1st Street exit off Route 29.) ~ 629 Factory Stores Drive,
Napa; 707-226-9876.

Across the river from downtown, the **JV Warehouse** is where   ◀ *HIDDEN*
wallet-watching wine lovers know to look for ongoing bargains.

The stock, discounted because bought in bulk, changes over time, but there are always deals. Sometimes a particular bottle is only a couple of dollars cheaper than at the grocery store, but it's worth the effort if you're buying half a case or more. ~ 426 1st Street, Napa; 707-253-2624; www.jvwine.com.

NIGHTLIFE The **Ring's Lounge**, an upscale lounge at the Embassy Suites Napa Valley, is a pleasant spot for quiet conversation. ~ 1075 California Boulevard, Napa; 707-253-9540.

Jazz singers, classic dramas, lighthearted musicals and one-man shows are all part of the extensive repertoire presented throughout the year at the historic **Napa Valley Opera House**. ~ 1030 Main Street, Napa; 707-226-7372; www.nvoh.org.

Downtown Joe's features rock, pop and blues bands nightly except Monday and Tuesday; open-mic on Wednesday. Cover on Friday and Saturday during the summer. ~ 902 Main Street, Napa; 707-258-2337.

Since 1933, the **Napa Valley Symphony** has been entertaining with classics as well as a handful of modern pieces and pops concerts. From mid-October through April, the group presents multiple performances of five programs at the Lincoln Theater in Yountville. Call for programs. ~ 707-226-8742; www.napavalley symphony.org.

Among its unusual offerings, the **Jarvis Conservatory** presents, during the last weekend of June, programs of *zarzuella*, the seldom-performed Spanish opera form, in addition to regularly scheduled "open opera" the first Saturday of each month, when it's first come, first sing. ~ 1711 Main Street, Napa; 707-255-5445.

PARKS **JOHN F. KENNEDY MEMORIAL PARK** 🚶 🛶 🚤 With hiking trails along the Napa River, this is one of the valley's best parks.

AUTHOR FAVORITE

Some of my favorite movies are foreign ones with a good dose of travelogue. These—along with other independent films and appearances by filmmakers—are typical fare at the **Friday Night Flicks** held at the 278-seat theater at COPIA: The American Center for Wine, Food & the Arts. Admission. ~ 500 1st Street, Napa; 707-259-1600, 888-512-6742; www.copia.org.

You'll also find softball fields, an 18-hole golf course and playgrounds in this 340-acre parcel. Boating is allowed. Picnic areas may be reserved for a fee. ~ 2291 Streblow Drive, Napa; 707-257-9529, fax 707-257-9532.

SKYLINE WILDERNESS PARK 🚶 🚴 🐎 ⛴ With 35 miles of trails good for hiking, mountain biking and horseback riding, this 850-acre park is a bit of wilderness just two miles from downtown Napa. From its oak-studded hills, you can see San Francisco on clear days. A small lake, once used as the water supply for Napa State Hospital, is favored for bass, crappie and bluegill fishing. Facilities include restrooms, showers and barbecue pits. Day-use fee, $5. ~ 2201 East Imola Avenue, Napa; 707-252-0481; www.skylinepark.org.

▲ There are 30 RV sites, $25 and $27 per night; a handful of tent sites are $15 per night.

WESTWOOD HILLS WILDERNESS PARK 🚶 On the west side of Route 29, this 111-acre park is home to the modest Carolyn Parr Nature Center (707-255-6465) and three miles of hiking trails. The museum is closed Monday through Thursday except by appointment. ~ Browns Valley Road at Laurel Street, Napa; 707-257-9529.

▾▾▾▾▾▾▾▾▾▾
Yountville to Rutherford

The village of Yountville thrives in a postcard setting, flanked by vineyards with the Mayacamas Mountains off to the west. (If you really want to get an overview, take one of the hot-air balloon flights offered here.) Formerly known as Sebastopol (now the name of a Sonoma city), it got its current name around 1860, after North Carolinian George C. Yount settled here on the 11,000-acre land grant known as Rancho Caymus. Lately the town has been on a building spree, with several inns built in the past few years along with some of the valley's best-known dining palaces. It's home to only about 3500 people, meaning there's a restaurant for roughly every 400 citizens.

A couple of miles north along Route 29 is Oakville, established in the 1870s as soon as the train line was extended that far from Napa. There is no real town center here; its raison d'être is the presence of notable wineries such as Robert Mondavi and Opus One.

Rutherford, due north, got its start as a railroad station that, in the 1880s, was named for Thomas L. Rutherford, who had married a granddaughter of George Yount. The town is even smaller than Oakville but boasts, among other things, Beaulieu Vineyard, which recently celebrated its 100th anniversary.

SIGHTS

Oakville and Rutherford are even smaller than Yountville, but they are home to some of the country's top wineries. But in all three towns you'll find excellent restaurants and, in Yountville, great inns as well as an important museum. Washington Street is the main artery of the latter, running parallel to Route 29 one block to the east.

HIDDEN ►

The Napa Valley Museum, which is practically next door to Domaine Chandon, is not your mother's museum. Far from stuffy, it's a vibrant center for the arts. But its most stunning attribute is the high-tech permanent exhibit, "California Wine: The Science of an Art." The museum celebrates the history, culture and lifeblood of the area with changing exhibits of arts and crafts. Closed Tuesday. Admission. ~ 55 Presidents Circle, Yountville; 707-944-0500, fax 707-945-0500; www.napavalleymuseum.org, e-mail info@napavalleymuseum.org.

Domaine Chandon, owned by France's fabled champagne producer Moët & Chandon, sits on a knoll west of town. Producing some of California's foremost sparkling wines, this winery provides a close look into the production and bottling of the bubbly. It's housed in a modernistic building with barrel-vaulted ceilings and contains exhibits by local artists as well as a gourmet restaurant. There's a tasting salon and terrace. Tasting fee. ~ 1 California Drive, Yountville; 707-944-2280, fax 707-944-1123; www.chandon.com, e-mail info@chandon.com.

Vintage 1870, the highest-profile structure in all of Yountville, began life as the Groezinger Winery. A multistory red-brick building, it's now home to a slew of boutiques and specialty shops. ~ 6525 Washington Street, Yountville; 707-944-2451.

In the late 1990s, **Cardinale Estate** transformed an existing tasting room with lots of marble and natural light, and now offers tastings of its cabernet sauvignon, cardinale (a bordeaux blend) and merlot in a room evocative of the Mediterranean countryside. The views from the top of the knoll encompass nearly 360 degrees; visitors can see some of the winery's vineyard sources on Howell Mountain and Mount Veeder from the chairs and tables set on a small balcony. No tours. Tasting fee. ~ 7600 Route 29, Oakville; 707-948-2643, 800-588-0279; www.cardi nale.com, e-mail info@cardinale.com.

Cabernet sauvignon fanatics wait in long lines to get their hands on the latest release from **Silver Oak Cellars**. It's an obsession, partly because this is one of the few ultra-premium wine producers that: a) make only cabernet and b) age the wines long enough to make them immediately drinkable. Both the Napa Valley and the Alexander Valley wines are released at both estates simultaneously—the Napa Valley on the Saturday in February nearest February 1 and the Alexander Valley on the Saturday in

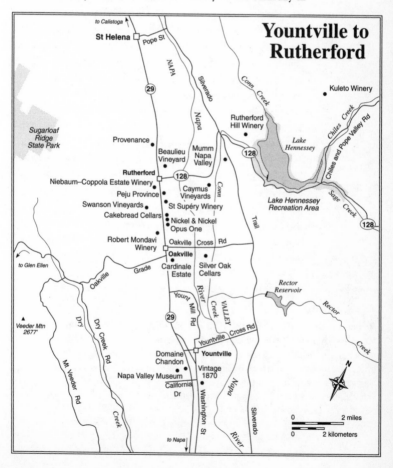

Yountville to Rutherford

August nearest to August 1. Closed Sunday. Tasting fee. ~ 915 Oakville Cross Road, Oakville (second location in northern Sonoma: 24625 Chianti Road, Geyserville); 707-944-8808, 800-273-8809, fax 707-944-2817; www.silveroak.com, e-mail info@silveroak.com.

HIDDEN ▶   Thirteen extensively landscaped gardens envelop the winery at **Far Niente**, which is reached by a private road off the Oakville Grade. Redwoods, acacias, dogwoods, gingko trees and some 8000 Southern azaleas decorate the property, which was founded in 1885 by John Benson. The old winery, constructed by noted architect Hamden McIntyre and now on the National Register of Historic Places, was abandoned at the beginning of Prohibition but resuscitated in 1979 by the Nickel family. It opened to the public in 2004, when it instituted a tour-and-tasting program that includes a stop in a barn housing classic racing automobiles and concludes with a seated tasting of Far Niente's acclaimed cabernet sauvignon and chardonnay, plus a dessert wine called Dolce. (By the way, the winery's name derives from an Italian phrase for "how sweet it is to do nothing.") Open by appointment only. Tasting fee. ~ 1350 Acacia Drive, Oakville; 707-944-2861, fax 707-944-2312; www.farniente.com, e-mail info@farniente.com.

Among the most well-known in the Napa Valley, **Robert Mondavi Winery** is a Spanish mission–style building offering a variety of informative tours by reservation. They range from a basic production tour with tasting to a three-hour look at the entire process from vineyard to laboratory to winery. The chardonnay and fumé blanc are excellent, and you can sample reserve wines by the glass. Tasting fee. ~ 7801 St. Helena Highway, Oak-

◆◆

ALL ABOARD

An unusual option for touring the Wine Country is to climb aboard the **Napa Valley Wine Train**, which runs daily between the city of Napa and the vineyards slightly north of St. Helena. Travelers may choose the lunch, brunch or dinner trip, each of which takes three hours and smoothly chugs past some of the most scenic parts of the valley. The 1915–47 Pullman cars have been beautifully restored; the dining car is straight out of a romance novel. ~ 1275 McKinstry Street, Napa; 707-253-2111, 800-427-4124, fax 707-251-5264; www.winetrain.com.

ville; 707-963-9611; www.robertmondavi.com, e-mail info@
robertmondavi.com.

They charge an arm and a leg (okay, $25) for tastings at **Opus
One**, but then, you can be pretty confident you'll enjoy the experience. At least if you love red wine. The futuristic edifice is worth
a peek at any rate; its enormous semicircular barrel cellar is mod-
eled after the one at the Château Mouton Rothschild winery in
France. ~ 7900 St. Helena Highway, Oakville; 707-963-1979, fax
707-948-2497; www.opusonewinery.com.

While many new wineries are embracing ultra-contemporary,
almost futuristic architecture, **Nickel & Nickel** looked in the other
direction to re-create an elegant homestead setting, circa 1880.
Opened in 2003, the collection of buildings includes an original
Queen Anne–style farmhouse (now the welcome center), a 1770s
barn imported from New Hampshire in pieces and rebuilt on the
site, and a new fermentation barn structured from century-old fir
beams. Nickel & Nickel produces ten 100-percent varietal, single-
vineyard wines, including cabernet sauvignon, merlot, syrah and
zinfandel. Open by appointment only. Tasting fee. ~ 8164 Route
29, Oakville; 707-967-9600. fax 707-967-0918; www.nickeland
nickel.com, e-mail info@nickelandnickel.com.

Continuing along Route 29 you'll drive through the tiny town
of **Rutherford**, passing a patchwork of planted fields. The family-
run **Cakebread Cellars** is known not only for its cabernet sauvignon, chardonnay, pinot and syrah, but also for its cooking classes
and other food-related events. Most of the latter are held in a
gracious barbecue area behind the winery, near the extensive gardens that produce flowers as well as herbs and vegetables for the
winery's chefs. In summer, leftover produce is sold at a cute little
stand near the parking lot. All visits by appointment only.
Tasting fee. ~ 8300 Route 29, Rutherford; 707-963-5221, 800-
588-0298, fax 707-963-1067; www.cakebread.com, e-mail cellars
@cakebread.com.

For those who think they've seen it all, a visit to **Swanson
Vineyards** will prove them wrong. There's no tasting bar at this unusual property, which looks like a family-owned winery in the
French countryside, complete with red-tile roofing and faded blue
shutters. Tastings are conducted in a coral-walled "salon" decorated with local artwork, with a maximum of eight guests seated
at an octagonal table, where they are served elegant cheeses and

wines, while a "salonnier" guides the conversation as if this were a Parisian living room. By appointment only. Closed Monday and Tuesday. Tasting fee. ~ 1271 Manley Lane, Rutherford; 707-967-3500; www.swansonvineyards.com, e-mail salon@swansonvineyards.com.

Just across the highway is **St. Supéry Winery**, which features a first-rate gallery with numerous exhibits on Napa Valley winemaking. Three-dimensional displays include a replica of an actual grapevine growing out of deep soil, smell-a-vision (a contraption that enables you to smell eight of the aromatic components of wine), and topographical maps that show why the valley is good for grapes. Daily guided tours available An educational vineyard display and a restored Victorian add spice to the winery tour. Tasting fee. ~ 8440 St. Helena Highway, Rutherford; 707-963-4507, 800-942-0809, fax 707-963-4526; www.stsupery.com, e-mail divinecab@stsupery.com.

HIDDEN ▶   **Long Meadow Ranch** offers a trio of unusual tours at its hillside property, which is known for producing robust red wines. The wine and olive oil tour (including a visit to the valley's oldest olive grove) is offered Saturday mornings May through October; an excursion in an open-sided Swiss Army cross-country all-terrain Pinzgauer culminates with a wine and olive oil tasting; and an invigorating hike through the vineyards that, depending on the season, concludes with a sampling of LMR's garden produce and grass-fed beef. The winery also prepares picnic lunches and even arranges for weekend stays. These activities are available for a fee by reservation only. All tours begin at the winery's gardens (see below). ~ 1796 Route 29, Rutherford; 707-963-4555 ext. 161; www.longmeadowranch.com.

Long Meadow Ranch's Rutherford Gardens and roadside stand are open Saturdays from 10 a.m. to 3 p.m. to sell fresh veg-

WHERE THE WINERIES ARE

If you set out for a morning or afternoon of winetasting—a full day is not recommended—a good approach, logistically speaking, is to drive north on Route 29 and south on the Silverado Trail. The bulk of the wineries can be found on one road or another, with a handful up in the hills or along some of the narrow roads that run east–west between the two main thoroughfares.

etables, fruits, eggs, grass-fed beef, and flowers and offer a walk through the beautiful gardens. ~ 1796 Route 29, Rutherford; 707-963-4555; www.longmeadowranch.com.

One of the prettiest wineries in Rutherford is the **Rubicon Estate Winery**, where movie great Francis Ford Coppola and his wife Eleanor have been making wine since 1975. In 1995 they purchased the adjacent Inglenook Château and vineyard, unifying the original 1879 estate of winemaker Gustave Niebaum. The ivy-draped château houses the Centennial Museum, where the history of winemaking at the estate is chronicled. Specialties here include rubicon, cabernet franc, merlot and zinfandel. Steep admission includes wine tasting. ~ 1991 St. Helena Highway, Rutherford; 707-968-1100, 800-782-4226, fax 707-963-9084; www.rubicon estate.com, e-mail info@rubiconestate.com.

Founded in 1900 by Frenchman Georges de Latour, **Beaulieu Vineyard** remains one of the most appealing wineries in Napa Valley, thanks to its old ivy-covered stone structures. BV owes a lot to the late winemaking genius Andre Tschelistcheff; the current winemaker was among his protegés. In his honor, you could hoist a glass of cabernet sauvignon. An elegant reserve room was added in 2005. Tasting fee. ~ 1960 Route 29, Rutherford; 707-967-5233; www.bvwines.com, e-mail bv.feedback@guinnessudv.com.

Peju Province stands out from its neighbors thanks to a copper-topped tasting room tower, accessible via a footbridge arching over a reflection pool filled with colorful *koi*. The winery grounds are extensively landscaped, with a series of garden "rooms" interspersed with marble sculptures all flanked by towering trees. Tours by appointment. Tasting fee. ~ 8466 Route 29, Rutherford; 707-963-3600, 800-446-7358; www.peju.com, e-mail info@peju.com.

Provenance, housed in a huge red building, produces cabernet sauvignon, merlot and sauvignon blanc. The historic estate vineyards date to the mid-19th century and are prized for the quality of their soil. The brightly lit tasting room sports lots of bare wood and a floor made of old barrel staves that still bear legible coopers' marks. Tasting fee. ~ 1695 Route 29, Rutherford; 707-968-3633; www.provenancevineyards.com, e-mail info@provenance vineyards.com.

To reach the wineries along the Silverado Trail, take the Rutherford Cross Road, which leads east to meet the trail.

The Silverado Trail

The Silverado Trail, an old stagecoach road, parallels Route 29 on the east and links with it via a succession of cross-valley roads as it runs 29 miles from Napa to Calistoga. Fully paved, this route is a favorite among cyclists as well as leisurely drivers. In addition to glimpses of Napa Valley as it was in the 1960s, it's an excellent place to search out small wineries. All along this rural stretch are family-owned vineyards, set on the valley floor or tucked into nearby hills. To reach it, you can follow Trancas Street east from Route 29 through Napa and turn left onto the Silverado Trail. Or better yet, head north from Napa on Route 29 to Oak Knoll Avenue and turn right, which will take you past **Monticello** (page 40), a winery in a replica of Thomas Jefferson's mansion, before crossing the Napa River and intersecting the trail. Here's a sampling of the wineries you'll find along the route:

SHAFER VINEYARDS   About two miles north of the Oak Knoll intersection on the Silverado Trail, Shafer Vineyards lies at the base of a rocky outcropping surrounded by fields of cabernet sauvignon grapes. Removed from the road, it's a placid spot with views of the fields and the valley. Tours of the winery (which include tastings) and wine cave are by appointment only and should be made four to six weeks in advance. Closed weekends. ~ 6154 Silverado Trail, Napa; 707-944-2877, fax 707-944-9454; www.shafervineyards.com, e-mail info@shafervineyards.com.

CAYMUS VINEYARDS   Nine miles north of Shafer Vineyards, after skirting the town of Yountville, the Silverado Trail brings you to this unpretentious winery run by Chuck Wagner. The winery was established by his parents, who were Napa winemakers in the early 1900s. Caymus focuses exclusively on it's delicious cabernet sauvignon. Tastings by appointment only. ~ 8700 Conn Creek Road, Rutherford; 707-967-3010, fax 707-963-5958; www.caymus.com.

A winery with an old French name, **Mumm Napa** is a good place to see *methode champenoise* production via daily tours. Located on an oak-shaded hillside, the pitched-roof winery is housed in a redwood barn. In the tasting room you can sample flutes of sparkling wine. Don't miss the permanent exhibit of Ansel Adams photographs. Tasting fee. ~ 8445 Silverado Trail, Rutherford; 707-967-7700, 800-686-6272, fax 707-967-7796; www.mumm napa.com, e-mail info@mummnapa.com.

HIDDEN ►   On the hill beyond the Auberge du Soleil resort, **Rutherford Hill Winery** beckons with one of the largest wine-aging cave sys-

STERLING VINEYARDS   In a few more miles you'll pass the turnoff to the village of St. Helena. Another seven miles will bring you to Sterling Vineyards near the outskirts of Calistoga. Set atop a knoll near the head of Napa Valley, this Greek monastery–style winery is reached via an aerial tramway (fee). The gondolas carry visitors to a multitiered, brilliant white building that commands sentinel views of the surrounding valley. Once atop this lofty retreat, a self-guided tour leads through various winemaking facilities to an elegant tasting room. It also has 18th-century church bells that add an exotic element to this unusual winery. ~ 1111 Dunaweal Lane, Calistoga; 800-726-6136, fax 707-942-3467; www.sterlingvineyards.com, e-mail info@svclub.com.

MOUNT ST. HELENA   If you continue north after arriving in Calistoga, the Silverado Trail trades the warm, level terrain of the valley for the cool, rugged landscape of the mountains. It climbs and winds through thick coniferous forests and past bald rockfaces. In touring Napa, you've undoubtedly noticed the stately mountain that stands sentinel at the north end of the valley. Mount St. Helena, named by 19th-century Russian explorers for their empress, rises 4343 feet, dominating the skyline.

ROBERT LOUIS STEVENSON STATE PARK   Perched on the side of Mount St. Helena is Robert Louis Stevenson State Park. The Scottish writer and his wife honeymooned in these parts, camping in the hills and enjoying the recuperative air. Here he wrote sections of *The Silverado Squatters* and studied settings later used in *Treasure Island.* Today the Memorial Trail leads through this undeveloped park one mile to an old mine and a monument commemorating the spot where Stevenson spent his honeymoon. Then a fire road continues four more miles to the top of Mount St. Helena. From this impressive aerie the entire Napa Valley lies before you, with views stretching from the Sierra Nevada to San Francisco. Bring your own water; there is none in the park. ~ Route 29, about eight miles north of Calistoga; 707-942-4575, fax 707-942-9560.

tems in the wine country. A mile long, the caves can hold more than 8000 barrels in constant cool temperatures and low humidity. Although the winery makes cabernet sauvignon, chardonnay, gewürztraminer, port, sangiovese, sauvignon blanc and zinfandel, it is best known for its merlot. Tasting and touring fee. ~ 200 Rutherford Hill Road, Rutherford; 707-963-1871, fax 707-963-1878; www.rutherfordhill.com, e-mail info@rutherfordhill.com.

The **Yountville Inn** has 51 rooms distributed among seven buildings alongside Hopper Creek are attractive, with fieldstone fire-

LODGING

places; many have French doors, small patios or decks, wood-beamed ceilings and refrigerators. Continental breakfast is included. ~ 6462 Washington Street, Yountville; 707-944-5600, 800-972-2293, fax 707-944-5666; www.yountvilleinn.com. DELUXE TO ULTRA-DELUXE.

Practically next door to Vintage 1870, the diminutive **Napa Valley Railway Inn** consists of restored boxcars and cabooses. The result is an assortment of appealing, if a bit too rectangular, guest accommodations, which are roomier than you might think. ~ 6503 Washington Street, Yountville; 707-944-2000, fax 707-944-1701. DELUXE.

Five distinctive rooms comprise **Petit Logis**, a single-story inn in the heart of town. Five rooms sport jacuzzis, fireplaces, lovely murals and high ceilings. Breakfast can be included in the room rate; guests have a choice of two nearby restaurants. ~ 6527 Yount Street, Yountville; 707-944-2332, fax 707-944-2338; www.petit logis.com, e-mail jay@petitlogis.com. DELUXE TO ULTRA-DELUXE.

For a dash of history with your evening glass of wine, consider the **Maison Fleurie**. A lodging place since 1873, this stone building is still a fashionable country inn. There are seven rooms in the old ivy-covered structure and six others in two adjacent buildings, each room crowded with antiques. Quilts and teddy bears adorn the beds, while chandeliers and brass lamps illuminate the historic setting; all have private baths and many have fireplaces and spa tubs. As a contemporary touch, there is a swimming pool, a hot tub and bikes available for guest use.

AUTHOR FAVORITE

My favorite place to stay in this neighborhood is the **Vintage Inn Napa Valley**, where all the rooms have cross-ventilation and the pool and hot tub are a blessing at the end of a strenuous day of winetasting. Rose gardens and trickling fountains surround smart-looking, two-story villas with brick facades and wood shingles on the roof. The 80 rooms are like mini-suites, adorned with fireplaces and shuttered windows, marble wet bars and baths—all in all, some of the most desirable rooms in the valley. The complimentary breakfast buffet is quite extensive. An Olympic-sized pool and tennis courts are also found here, and Yountville's exclusive shops and eateries are but a short stroll away. ~ 6541 Washington Street, Yountville; 707-944-1112, 800-351-1133, fax 707-944-1617; www.vintageinn.com. ULTRA-DELUXE.

Breakfast is buffet style, and afternoon wine and tea are served daily. ~ 6529 Yount Street, Yountville; 707-944-2056, 800-788-0369, fax 707-944-9342; www.foursisters.com, e-mail maison fleurie@foursisters.com. DELUXE TO ULTRA-DELUXE.

Perched on a hillside studded with olive trees, **Auberge du Soleil** is a curious blend of French Mediterranean–style cottages named after French winegrowing regions and decorated in breezy California/Southwest style. Bare Mexican tile floors, louvered doors, fireplaces and private terraces are a refreshing change from the cluttered feel of older hotels in the valley. Thirteen cottages stagger down the hill, all but three of them containing four rooms. There's also a pool and spa to relax in. ~ 180 Rutherford Hill Road, Rutherford; 707-963-1211, 800-348-5406, fax 707-963-8764; www.aubergedusoleil.com, e-mail info@aubergedusoleil.com. ULTRA-DELUXE.

Crafted from white oak, the Spanish Colonial **Rancho Caymus Inn** is a romantic retreat with stained-glass windows, a colonnade, a courtyard and gardens. There is a total of 26 rooms; in the split-level rooms you'll find queen-sized carved wooden beds, private balconies, and charming adobe beehive fireplaces. Five master suites have king-sized beds and jacuzzi tubs. ~ 1140 Rutherford Road, Rutherford; 707-963-1777, 800-845-1777, fax 707-963-5387; www.ranchocaymus.com, e-mail info@rancho caymus.com. ULTRA-DELUXE.

The reputations of some of the restaurants in this neighborhood are in inverse proportion to the size of the towns. The gamut ranges from haute cuisine to hot dogs, priced accordingly.

DINING

E'toile at Domaine Chandon has undergone a renaissance with a new chef and menu and has maintained itself as a dependable choice for outstanding Wine Country cooking. This is a grown-up restaurant, where seasonal entrées arrive as complete dinners such as Alaskan halibut with forbidden rice, chorizo, manila clams and saffron foam, and beef tenderloin with cream potatoes, seasonal vegetables and carmelized shallot sauce. Prices are steep, but in keeping with modern surroundings, sophisticated food and ultra-smooth service. There's an outdoor patio for more-casual lunch dining. Closed Tuesday and Wednesday from November through March. ~ 1 California Drive, Yountville; 707-944-2892, fax 707-944-1123; www.chandon.com. e-mail maryann_vangrin@chandon.com. ULTRA-DELUXE.

HIDDEN ► Richard Reddington, former chef at Auberge du Soleil and other prestigious destination restaurants, opened his own place on Yountville's Restaurant Row in 2005. The menu at **Redd** expresses his global thinking through main courses such as butternut squash ravioli, rabbit mole and Alaskan halibut saltimbocca, as well as via sensational desserts like banana cake with coconut ice cream, Meyer lemon panna cotta and caramel chocolate mousse with espresso cognac sorbet. In a contemporary, uncluttered setting, patrons can order à la carte or avail themselves of the five- and nine-course tasting menus. ~ 6480 Washington Street, Yountville; 707-944-2222; www.reddnapavalley.com. DELUXE TO ULTRA-DELUXE.

Philippe Jeanty runs a classic French bistro on Yountville's main drag. Escargot, pâtés, lamb tongue, kidneys, sweetbreads, salad Niçoise and the inevitable *haricot verts* are typical offerings at **Bistro Jeanty**, along with seafood and some heavier dishes. As far as appearance goes, this two-room wonder is right out of the French countryside. ~ 6510 Washington Street, Yountville; 707-944-0103, fax 707-944-0370; www.bistrojeanty.com, e-mail bistrojeanty@earthlink.net. MODERATE TO DELUXE.

For Mexican dining—breakfast, lunch and dinner—cruise into **Compadres**. The brick-lined restaurant is an unusually pretty setting for Americanized south-of-the-border specials. It's especially popular for its margaritas. ~ 6539 Washington Street, Yountville; 707-944-2406, fax 707-944-8407; www.compadrestaurants.com, e-mail compadresytv03@aol.com. MODERATE.

Set in a two-story 1890s building, the **French Laundry** features contemporary American cuisine with a classic French influence. Fare may include sirloin of young rabbit, veal sweetbreads with lobster ravioli, pan-seared duck breast, and monkfish fricassée. The award-winning food is excellent, the wine list extensive, and the prix-fixe menu changes nightly. Owner Thomas Keller is considered one of the top chefs in the world due to his innovative and ever-changing creations. It's very popular; reservations must be made two months in advance. No lunch Monday through Thursday. ~ 6640 Washington Street, Yountville; 707-944-2380; www.frenchlaundry.com. ULTRA-DELUXE.

Gordon's Café and Wine Bar is adored by devoted locals who love the easy-going ambience as much as the food. To get to know some of the regulars, take a seat at one of the large community tables after you place your order for breakfast or a light lunch (soup, salad, sandwich or a daily special). ~ 6770 Washington Street, Yountville; 707-944-8246. BUDGET.

Mustards Grill is an ultramodern brass-rail restaurant complete with track lighting and contemporary wallhangings. There's an attractive wooden bar and paneled dining room, but the important features are the woodburning grill and oven. Here the chefs prepare rabbit, grilled pork chops, smoked duck, and hangar steak. This eatery specializes in fresh grilled fish like sea bass, ahi tuna and salmon. ~ 7399 St. Helena Highway, Yountville; 707-944-2424, fax 707-944-0828; www.mustardgrill.com. MODERATE TO DELUXE.

A capacious room, with a wall of windows overlooking herb gardens and the Mayacamas Mountains and an inviting outdoor patio, sets the tone for the flavorful menu at **Brix**. The cuisine here is decidedly Californian, featuring primarily local produce and an on-site vegetable garden. Its seasonal menu might offer grilled Atlantic salmon with saffron-scented rice, roasted Sonoma duck breast with ginger-mushroom ravioli, or Szechuan pepper-crusted ahi tuna. Dessert includes the likes of warm apple *tarte tatin* with maple gelato or meyer lemon cheesecake with mint sorbet. ~ 7377 St. Helena Highway, Yountville; 707-944-2749. DELUXE.

Auberge du Soleil, a hillside dining room overlooking the vineyards, has been revered as a destination restaurant for more than two decades. Modern in design, this gourmet hideaway is a curving stucco structure with a wood-shingle roof. The circular lounge is capped by a skylight-cum-cupola and the dining area is an exposed-beam affair with an open fireplace. Even architecture

MIDNIGHT MUNCHIES

Bouchon is a glamorous and glorified bistro, with lots of sparkle in the decor and on the menu. Entrées lean to *coq au vin, entrecote avec frites*, marinated leg of lamb, sole meuniere, onion soup, roast chicken, sautéed seasonal vegetables, fruit tarts and soufflés. Yet its most unusual feature may be its late-night dining—as late as 12:30 a.m. as a courtesy to night owls such as workers from area restaurants. ~ 6534 Washington Street, Yountville; 707-944-8037, fax 707-944-2769; www.bouchonbistro.com. MODERATE TO DELUXE.

such as this pales in comparison with the menu, which changes seasonally. Lunch might begin with the fois-gras terrine and *torchon* with a cherry compote and candied pistachios, then move on to wild King salmon with corn pudding, zucchini and toasted almond broth. Dinner entrées include quail with smoked ham, lobster risotto, or herb-basted lamb loin. There's also an extensive wine list. ~ 180 Rutherford Hill Road, Rutherford; 707-963-1211, 800-348-5406, fax 707-963-8764; www.aubergedusoleil. com, e-mail info@aubergedusoleil.com. ULTRA-DELUXE.

SHOPPING   Vintage 1870 is living proof that shopping malls can be charming. Housed in the historic Groezinger Winery, a massive brick building smothered in ivy, it contains several dozen fashionable shops. Wooden corridors, designed with an eye to antiquity, lead along two shopping levels. There are clothing stores galore and several restaurants, as well as galleries and specialty shops offering arts-and-crafts products. ~ 6525 Washington Street, Yountville; 707-944-2451, fax 707-944-2453; www.vintage1870.com.

Across the street, the **Groezinger Wine Company** features hard-to-find premium wines from California, Oregon and Washington. Closed Sunday. ~ 6484 Washington Street, Suite E, Yountville; 707-944-2331, 800-356-3970.

The restaurant **Brix** has room for one of the best wine shops in the area, with hundreds of choices (all the whites are available chilled) at prices not much above what you'd pay in a grocery store—that is, if you could find Grgich Hills chardonnay and some lesser-known sangioveses in your average Safeway. ~ 7377 St. Helena Highway, Yountville; 707-944-9350.

You can sample the goods before making a purchase at the **St. Helena Olive Oil Company**. This manufacturer and retailer of

AUTHOR FAVORITE

When I'm heading out for a picnic, I like to stop by the **Oakville Grocery** for supplies. This falsefront country store on the National Register of Historic Places sells wines and cheeses, fresh fruits, specialty sandwiches, and baked goods, as well as a host of gourmet and artisanal items. In addition, there's a coffee and espresso bar for a pick-me-up. ~ 7856 St. Helena Highway, Oakville; 707-944-8802, 800-973-6324; www.oakvillegrocery.com, e-mail napavalley@oakville grocery.com. BUDGET TO MODERATE.

extra-virgin oil is located in the historic Peddler's Pack building, where occasional seminars are offered on their favorite topic. ~ 8576 Route 29, Rutherford; 800-939-9880; www.sholiveoil.com.

NIGHTLIFE

On Thursday night **Compadres** restaurant features regular entertainers. ~ 6539 Washington Street, Yountville; 707-944-2406.

The place to be with the in crowd is at the piano bar at the posh **Auberge du Soleil**. Sooner or later, everyone who is anyone shows up. The bar offers an excellent selection of ports and other after-dinner drinks and the fireplace adds a cozy note on chilly evenings. ~ 180 Rutherford Hill Road, Rutherford; 707-963-1211, 800-348-5406.

PARKS

LAKE HENNESSEY RECREATION AREA Located about ten miles south of Rutherford, this lake provides water to the city of Napa. You can fish here but you can't rent a boat. There are picnic grounds and the scenery—lots of oak trees blanketing the surrounding hills—is wonderful. ~ West of the Silverado Trail along Route 128.

Outdoor Adventures

WATER SPORTS

Napa River Adventures rents one- and two-person kayaks for exploring the river and marshlands. A two-hour guided cruise aboard a luxury, electric-motor launch is also available. By appointment only. ~ Launches from Kennedy Park Dock, Napa; 707-224-9080; www.napariveradventures.com.

Wine Country Yacht Charters give up to six cruisers a gull's-eye view of the Napa River as well as San Francisco Bay from the ridge of a 42-foot motor yacht, with options such as onboard wine tastings and meals, with sailings out of the Napa Valley Marina. ~ 866-440-2428; www.wineyacht.com.

GOLF

As you might expect in this agricultural preserve, there are a number of golf courses. Golf is a year-round sport in this temperate valley, and while the resort courses are always expensive, public and semiprivate courses tend to be affordable. You should make reservations for weekend play.

The 18-hole **Napa Golf Course at Kennedy Park** is surrounded by the park and rents clubs and carts. ~ 2295 Streblow Drive, Napa; 707-255-4333; www.playnapa.com.

The **Chardonnay Club** has 27 championship holes arranged Scottish links-style on a par-72 course. You'll find a driving range, pro shop and club house. ~ 2555 Jameson Canyon Road, Napa; 707-257-8950; www.chardonnaygolfclub.com.

TENNIS

Tennis courts are far and few between outside of the big resorts. However, public courts can be found in the city of Napa.

There are six tennis courts at the centrally located **Napa High School**, but they are not lighted for night play. ~ 2474 Jefferson Street, Napa; 707-253-3715.

On the north side of Napa, **Vintage High School** maintains eight courts for public use. ~ 1375 Trower Avenue, Napa; 707-253-3715.

BALLOON RIDES

A hot-air balloon ride is the best way to get a bird's-eye-view of the Napa Valley. These rides depart daily at the crack of dawn, weather permitting, and usually conclude with a champagne brunch. Expect to pay about $185 for most outings.

Adventures Aloft, the oldest company of its kind in Napa, departs from Vintage 1870. If you've ever considered renewing your wedding vows aloft, these are the folks for you. ~ 6525 Washington Street, Yountville; 707-944-4408; www.napavalley aloft.com. **Napa Valley Balloons** has a flotilla of seven balloons so there's almost always room for a couple more people. ~ 6795 Washington Street, Yountville; 707-944-0228; www.napavalley balloons.com.

BIKING

The flat terrain that characterizes most of this area is ideal for cycling. If you like hills, head out Route 128 to Pope Valley Road; you'll work up a sweat. If you like the looks of the Oakville Grade linking Napa with Sonoma, think again. It's a rugged climb up from the Napa side.

A bike ride through the Lower Chiles Valley will give you quite a workout. A tough 48 miles (roundtrip) if you start in Yountville, this one's best done in the early morning hours before the sun and the traffic heat things up. It's a hilly, scenic ride but one that will take you perilously close to Lake Berryessa. Head over to the Silverado Trail and go north until you turn east on Route 128 East. Then it's north on Chiles and Pope Valley Road and southwest on lower Chiles Valley Road. Return via Route 128 West.

For something easier, try the **14-mile loop** around Yountville and the Stag's Leap district. Though you can pick up the route anywhere, you might begin at Route 29 and Oak Knoll Avenue. Pedal east across Big Ranch Road to the Silverado Trail, then head left and up to Yountville Cross Road, which zigzags to Yountville. Hook up with Washington Street and take it south to California Drive. Go west, under the highway, then south on Solano Avenue, which leads back to Oak Knoll Avenue. By heading east again, crossing Route 29, you will shortly arrive back where you started. There is a bike lane along most of the Silverado Trail.

Fans of mountain biking are welcome at **Skyline Wilderness Park**. Most of its 25 miles of trails are open to both hiking and mountain biking. Elevation ranges from 130 feet to 1100.

HIKING

With most open space devoted to vineyards, you won't find a lot of formal trails in this portion of Napa. Your best bet is in the parks; walking along major thoroughfares is a really bad idea. All distances listed for hiking trails are one way unless otherwise noted.

One easily accessible trail is the Trancas to Lincoln segment (2.5 miles roundtrip) of the **Napa River Trail**. From Route 29, turn east on Trancas Street and travel 1.5 miles (or go half a mile east of the Silverado Trail). There is a hiker access sign on the west side of the Napa River, where you will start your hike, all of it easy and almost all of it level. This is not a wild trail; you're never far from houses but you can find blackberry, ivy and wild grape as well as other flora thriving under live oak and bay trees. Get out your camera as you approach the end (before your return trip); there are some wonderful photo ops on the trail not far from an RV park.

Skyline Wilderness Park has about 25 miles of hiking trails, ranging in elevation from 130 to 1100 feet. One of the most popular here is **Lake Marie Road** (2 miles). To reach the trailhead, take Imola Avenue east to where it ends at 4th Avenue. From the south corner of the parking lot, a signed trail turns to the right (just before a native plant garden); follow the grassy path west, turning left at the road. You will pass between two small lakes before the road begins to climb. Along this trail are fruit trees once cared for by patients at Napa State Hospital. Remain on the trail until you reach Lake Marie.

THREE

Northern Napa Valley

Napa Valley's residents have gone to extreme lengths to preserve their slice of heaven. At least 90 percent of the arable land is zoned for agricultural use, and almost every single possible acre has already been planted in vineyards. The result is an almost unbroken stretch of wineries that lines Route 29 from Yountville—where the four-lane highway shrinks to two lanes—all the way to Calistoga, except for a few blocks in downtown St. Helena. On either side, from the Howell Mountains on the east to the Mayacamas on the west, rows upon rows of grapevines provide a vista that evolves through the seasons, from the green of spring and summer to the rust and gold of fall. Even in winter, the gnarled vines are picturesque, more so when wild mustard comes into bloom, carpeting the valley in brilliant yellow blossoms in January and February.

Locals call the area north of Rutherford "up valley," an area that encompasses two towns—St. Helena and Calistoga—engulfed by prize real estate. Especially if you're a vintner. This is where some of the country's famed wine pioneers made their name—Louis Martini, Charles Krug, and the Beringer Brothers among them. You can visit these wineries today, as well as a plethora of newcomers. The area is also home to two state parks, the valley's best shops and some of Wine Country's premier restaurants. Visitors can feast on freshly baked bread and pick up deluxe supplies for a picnic in the park or at any of a number of wineries that provide tables for expressly this purpose.

With millions of dollars sunk into vineyards and Napa Valley wines fetching record prices in retail stores as well as at auctions (especially the prestigious local auction each June), there are of course plenty of millionaires in the area. Yet at one level, this is farm country. When the scene threatens to become just a bit too precious, try to remember: these are farmers. And there are plenty of regular folks living here as well.

The Wappo Indians got here first, and though white explorers came across present-day Napa as early as 1823, the influx of pioneers did not begin until a British surgeon named Edward Bale arrived and built a flour mill near present-day St. Helena in 1846. He married into General Mariano Vallejo's family and received a Spanish land grant of some 20,000 acres, practically the entire acreage of the upper valley. Today, visitors picnic beside the Bale Grist Mill, now a state historic park three miles north of St. Helena.

Nearby is the oldest continuously operating winery in the valley, bonded in 1876. Frederick Beringer founded the winery and built the Rhine House, virtually a shrine to his German home. Another former Beringer home, the Hudson House, is now home to the winery's Culinary Arts Center.

Long before becoming famous as a wine region, Napa was a sought-after tourist destination for quite another reason. We have Sam Brannan to thank for that. In 1859, he founded Calistoga, at the northern end of the Napa Valley, envisioning it, correctly, as a resort that would rival those on the East Coast. A century and a half later, however, Calistoga remains resolutely un-chic, despite counting numerous swank wineries among its chief attractions. The same underground hot springs that supply the bathwater for numerous day spas in Calistoga also fuel another of the town's quirky charms: its own version of Old Faithful Geyser that continues to live up to its name.

Up the hill from Calistoga is another attraction right out of *Ripley's Believe It or Not!* A petrified forest sits a stone's throw from the highway, an intriguing destination for an afternoon stroll in the shade. Created by mighty eruptions from nearby Mount St. Helena, the forest is a natural wonder that brings to life the rich geological history of the region.

▼▼▼▼▼▼▼▼▼▼

St. Helena

In St. Helena, Route 29 becomes known as Main Street, but this is no Mayberry. The four central blocks are lined cheek-to-cheek with boutiques and restaurants and the occasional store selling hardware or books. A pretty street lined with 19th-century stone buildings, it becomes a virtual parking lot in the high season. The town, named for nearby Mount St. Helena, evolved after British surgeon Edward Bale arrived in California aboard a whaling vessel, virtually penniless. He received a Spanish land grant of about 20,000 acres, built a flour mill in

1896 some three miles north of present-day St. Helena and probably died a very, very rich man.

One of Napa's most famous visitors was the prolific author Robert Louis Stevenson. A couple of blocks from the heart of town is a museum devoted to the Scottish writer, who traveled through the area in 1880 en route to the hills beyond Calistoga.

SIGHTS

Dozens of wineries are located to the north, south, east and west, but visitors owe it to themselves to get out of their cars and meander through the heart of town. It's the only way to get a feel for the regional lifestyle and, after all, it's one of only three actual "downtowns" in the whole Napa Valley.

HIDDEN ▶

A scenic 761-acre hillside ranch on the eastern edge of the Napa Valley is home to the **Kuleto Family Estate Winery**. Pat Kuleto, acclaimed for designing Farallon, Postrio and other high-profile Bay Area restaurants, established his vineyards in 1992 to produce cabernet sauvignon, chardonnay, pinot noir, rosato, sangiovese and syrah. Tours and tastings by appointment only. Tasting fee. Closed Sunday. ~ 2470 Sage Canyon Road; 707-963-9750; www.kuletoestate.com, e-mail info@kuletoestate.com.

An array of special tasting opportunities is the calling card at **Franciscan Oakville Estate**. Fronted by a landscaped fountain area, the winery offers standard tastings as well as private sessions on blending and sensory evaluations. Be sure to sample the chardonnay produced with wild (instead of commercially grown) yeasts. Tasting fee. ~ 1178 Galleron Road; 707-967-3830, 800-529-9463, fax 707-967-3876; www.franciscan.com.

In a contemporary building, painted ocher and lavender to soften its strong geometric lines, **Whitehall Lane** makes cabernet sauvignon, chardonnay, merlot, sauvignon blanc and dessert wines from six Napa Valley vineyards. The yellow-walled tasting room has a white beamed ceiling that makes the cozy space seem larger. No tours. Tasting fee. ~ 1563 Route 29; 800-963-9454; www.white halllane.com, e-mail greatwine@whitehalllane.com.

Heitz Wine Cellars was established on this site in the early 1960s but soon moved two miles away to a larger, historic property off the Silverado Trail. In 2002, the winery opened this small but high-ceilinged tasting room. Visitors may enjoy their wines in the shade of a pergola behind the native stone building. The specialty is vineyard-designated cabernet sauvignon, particularly

Northern Napa Valley

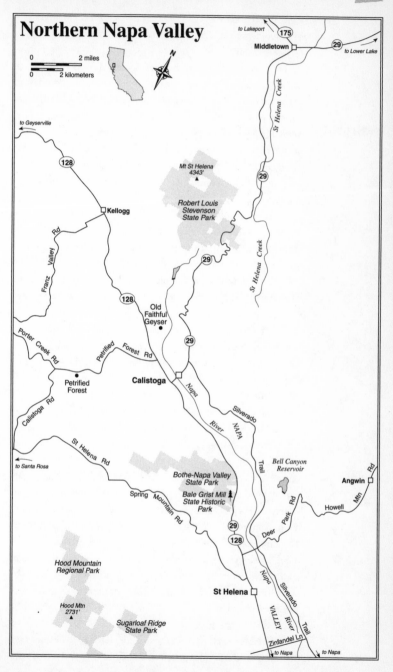

0   2 miles
0   2 kilometers

to Geyserville

to Lakeport
175
Middletown
29
to Lower Lake

St Helena Creek

128

Mt St Helena
4343'

Kellogg

Robert Louis
Stevenson
State Park

29

St Helena Creek

Franz Valley Rd

128

Old
Faithful
Geyser

29

Porter Creek Rd

Petrified Forest Rd

29

Petrified
Forest

Calistoga

Napa River

Silverado

NAPA

Calistoga Rd

St Helena Rd

to Santa Rosa

Bothe-Napa Valley
State Park

Bell Canyon
Reservoir

Angwin

Howell Mtn Rd

Spring Mountain Rd

Bale Grist Mill
State Historic
Park

Deer Park Rd

Howell

29
128

Hood Mountain
Regional Park

Hood Mtn
2731'

Sugarloaf Ridge
State Park

St Helena

Napa River

Silverado Trail

VALLEY

Zinfandel Ln

to Napa   to Napa

from prestigious Martha's Vineyard in Oakville. Winery tours by appointment only. ~ 436 Route 29; 707-963-2047; www. heitzcellar.com.

Founded in San Francisco in 1885 and moved to St. Helena in 1976, **V. Sattui Winery** is one of the most popular destinations in the valley. The wines—which are sold only here—draw happy crowds who sample some of the 35 varieties and pick up deli items for a picnic in the shade by the highway. The enormous tasting room is in a barn-like building almost obscured by vines; aging cellars and the winery itself are housed in a historic stone building. ~ 1111 White Lane; 707-963-7774, fax 707-963-4324; www.vsattui.com.

HALL is small but easy to locate thanks to its bright red awning and collection of contemporary sculpture. In addition to the winery's Bordeaux varietals, visitors may sample wines from a sister property, Kathryn Hall Vineyards. A shaded arbor beside the old building is ideal for picnicking. Tours by appointment. Tasting fee. ~ 401 Route 29; 866-667-4255; www.hallwines.com, e-mail info@hallwines.com.

The **Sutter Home Winery** made white zinfandel famous, but makes many other wines intended for mass consumption as well. The winery is an attractive bevy of beautiful Victorian buildings, and its gift shop is one of the busiest in town. Founded in 1874 by a Swiss-German immigrant, it was bought by the Sutters in 1906 and is now owned by the Trinchero family, which produces an eponymous line of premium wines. ~ 277 St. Helena Highway; 707-963-3104, fax 707-967-9184; www.sutterhome.com.

HIDDEN ▶ Not much port is made in this part of the world, but you can sample several versions at **Prager Winery and Port Works**. Obscured by the infinitely larger Sutter Home Winery, this cozy warren of barrel cellars, tasting room and spider webs is as different from mainstream wineries as merlot is from chenin blanc. The Prager family make their ports a little drier than the Portuguese do, so it's a great place to learn more about this underappreciated treat, which you're unlikely to find anywhere else but here and in a few Napa Valley restaurants. Tasting fee. ~ 1281 Lewelling Lane; 707-963-7678, 800-969-7678, fax 707-963-7679; www.pragerport.com.

A formal courtyard welcomes visitors into the cavernous tasting room at **Merryvale**, which is housed in one of the first winery buildings constructed after Prohibition. It boasts an extensive lineup of tasting experiences. Wine seminars ($15) are held every weekend morning; reservations are required. The elaborate schedule also includes component and barrel tastings, and wine and food pairing basics. Fee for tasting and seminars. ~ 1000 Main Street; 707-963-2225, 800-326-6069 ext. 439; www.merryvale. com, e-mail tastingroom@merryvale.com.

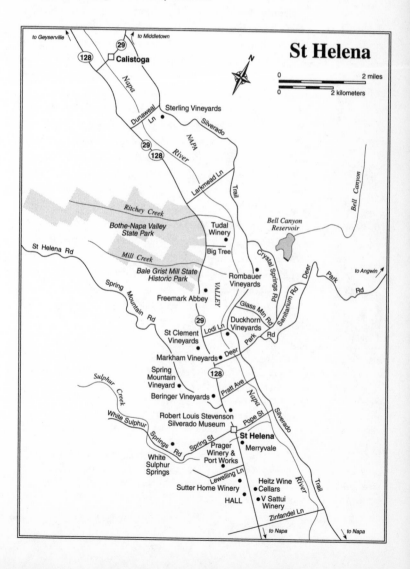

St Helena

In the Victorian-style downtown area, the brick-and-stone IOOF Building looms several stories above the pavement, as it has for a century. ~ 1352 Main Street.

The cynosure of St. Helena is the **Ritchie Block**, a stone structure with brick-and-wood facade. Featuring more frills and swirls than a wedding cake, it is a study in ornate architecture. ~ 1331 Main Street.

Beringer Vineyards, which was established in 1876, occupies a huge, landscaped parcel of land on the north side of St. Helena. While there is much to be said for visiting boutique producers, only a winery as large and historic as Beringer can offer visitors so many different experiences. Its crowning glory is the 1884 Rhine House, a Queen Anne–style mansion embellished with spires, turrets, gables and a mansard roof. The interior is illuminated through stained glass and paneled in hand-carved hardwoods. Also of interest are 1000 feet of tunnels handcut into the neighboring hillside by 19th-century Chinese laborers. The adjacent historic bottling room has been converted into a gift shop/tasting room. Fees for tours and tastings. ~ 2000 Main Street; 707-967-4412, fax 707-963-8129; www.beringer.com.

HIDDEN ▶   Visitors to **Spring Mountain Vineyard** may do a double-take when they see the picturesque, white Miravalle House. If so, it's because they remember it as the fictional home of an extremely dysfunctional winemaking family on *Falcon Crest*, the popular 1980s nighttime soap opera starring Jane Wyman. But there is

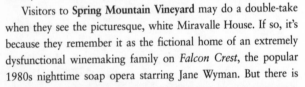

AUTHOR FAVORITE

A good place to get a dose of literature and California history is at the **Robert Louis Stevenson Silverado Museum**. It houses a collection of artifacts from Robert Louis Stevenson's life and his sojourn in the Napa Valley. Having visited Monterey and San Francisco, the Scottish author arrived in Calistoga in 1880. (Stevenson was en route to Hawaii and the South Seas, seeking a salubrious environment in which to escape his lifelong illnesses.) Among the memorabilia at the museum are manuscripts, letters, art, photographs and first editions (as an English major, I like to look at them, even if I can't touch them), as well as personal effects left behind by the globe-girdling Victorian. Closed Monday. ~ 1490 Library Lane; 707-963-3757, fax 707-963-0917; www.silveradomuseum.com, e-mail rlsnhs@calicom.net.

much more to see on the tour here, which covers only a fraction of the 845-acre property that has been vineyards since the 1800s. The guided tours visit a demonstration vineyard, gardens planted with citrus and bamboo trees, and a Victorian horse barn with a photo gallery of 19th-century winemakers and antique winemaking equipment; they end with a sit-down tasting where visitors can get a taste of the winery's specialty, mountain-grown cabernet sauvignon. Open by appointment only. Fee for tours and tastings. ~ 2805 Spring Mountain Road; 707-967-4188, 877-769-4637; www.springmountainvineyard.com, e-mail office@springmtn.com.

Founded by a Frenchman in 1879, **Markham Vineyards** is less famous than such contemporaries as Charles Krug and Schramsberg, perhaps because it changed hands (and names) over its first century of operation. Now, with 330 acres of vineyards on the Napa Valley floor, Markham produces nine varietals, notably reserve merlot. The winery has an exceptional tasting room with quality gifts as well as frequent art exhibits. Private wine and food pairing sessions are available for a fee. Tasting fee. ~ 2812 St. Helena Highway North; phone/fax 707-963-5292; www.markhamvineyards.com, e-mail admin@markhamvineyards.com.

St. Clement Vineyards is headquartered on the historic estate of Fritz Rosenbaum, a German immigrant who began making wines in the cellar in 1878. The pretty green knoll-top Victorian has been restored and now houses the tasting room, where visitors can sample chardonnay, sauvignon blanc, merlot and blended wines as well as cabernet sauvignon, the house specialty and Oroppas, their signature wine. A pretty patio offers tables and chairs for visitor picnicking in full view of vineyards. Winery tours are available by appointment. Tasting fee. ~ 2867 Route 29 North; 800-331-8266, fax 707-963-1412; www.stclement.com.

Duckhorn Vineyards' tasting room is in a lovely contemporary farmhouse painted taupe with white trim and rimmed with a furnished porch. Inside, the tasting room has a club-like ambience, with windows on three sides and small, square tables where visitors are served the day's selections. Look for the impressive display of vintage duck decoys in the lobby beyond the tasting room, and don't miss the merlot. Tasting fee. ~ 1000 Lodi Lane; 707-963-7108, 888-354-8885, fax 707-963-7595; www.duckhorn.com, e-mail welcome@duckhorn.com.

HIDDEN ►

A long, landscaped driveway winds into the woods that surround **Rombauer Vineyards**, one of the few fine Napa wineries that still offer complimentary tastings. Rombauer makes one of California's best chardonnays (from Carneros grapes) and an unusually perky zinfandel (made from grapes grown in the Sierra foothill counties of El Dorado, Amador and Lake). The views from the ranch-style winery building take in nothing but the forested hills on the horizon. Tours by appointment. ~ 3522 Silverado Trail; 707-963-5170, 800-622-2206; www.rombauer vineyards.com, e-mail sheanar@rombauervineyards.com.

There's nothing monastic about **Freemark Abbey**; the winery got its name from three former partners, Charles Freeman, Markquand Foster and Albert "Abbey" Ahern. But the most important name to remember is Josephine Marlin Tychson, who, following her husband's death in 1886, became the first woman to build and operate a winery in California. The wines not to miss are the vineyard-designated cabernet sauvignons, the chardonnays and a late-harvest riesling called Edelwein Gold. Visitors can sip wine on the patio. Tasting fee. ~ 3022 St. Helena Highway North; 800-963-9698, fax 707-963-0554; www.free markabbey.com, e-mail wineinfo@freemarkabbey.com.

North of St. Helena, **Bale Grist Mill State Historic Park** is a picturesque stop. Sitting beside a tumbling stream, an 1846 waterwheel mill creates a classic scene. It was built for a Mexican land grantee and served as an early gathering place for farmers throughout the area. The mill is now restored and there are guided tours. There's a visitors center plus a pair of raw wood buildings that housed the mill and granary. Admission. ~ Route 29; 707-942-4575, fax 707-942-9560.

Not far past the old mill stream, a side road leads from Route 29 to **Tudal Winery**. Touted as one of the world's smallest wineries, it consists of a cluster of contemporary buildings surrounded by luxurious grape arbors. Tours and tasting at this family affair are by appointment. A walk around the entire winery will probably take a grand total of ten minutes, after which the owner may regale you for hours with tales of the Wine Country. Closed weekends. ~ 1015 Big Tree Road; 707-963-3947, fax 707-968-9691; www.tudalwinery.com, e-mail tudalwinery@aol.com.

HIDDEN ►

It's easy to find **Litto's Hubcap Ranch**. Just take Howell Mountain Road east from the Silverado Trail in St. Helena to the hamlet of Pope Valley. Head north three miles until you see at least a thousand points of light. Those are Litto Damonte's hubcaps, more than 5000 strong, adorning houses, barns, fences and pastures. Just to make sure you know who's responsible, Damonte has plastered his name on the barn in—what else—hubcaps.

LODGING

The only decent motel—in fact, apparently the only motel—in the area is **El Bonita**, a pretty little complex that sports window boxes and nicely landscaped grounds. The 41 rooms (some are in two-story buildings in the rear) are done up in pastels and florals more befitting a country inn. The pool is a rarity in these parts. Continental breakfast included. ~ 195 Main Street; 707-963-3216, 800-541-3284, fax 707-963-8838; www.elbonita.com. MODERATE TO DELUXE.

◄ *HIDDEN*

The **Inn at Southbridge** is just off the main drag in a complex that includes a restaurant, a winery and the Health Spa of Napa Valley. Spacious second-story accommodations are done in soothing Tuscan colors such as mustard and olive. Handcrafted furnishings bring some life to these somewhat lonely rooms. Room rates include continental breakfast and use of the adjacent health club. ~ 1020 Main Street; 707-967-9400, 800-520-6800, fax 707-967-9486; www.innatsouthbridge.com, e-mail sbres@meadowinn.com. ULTRA-DELUXE.

The **Harvest Inn**, one of the few places to stay within walking distance of downtown, occupies eight extensively landscaped acres amid a working vineyard; several lowrise buildings are linked by a network of pretty brick walkways. The 74 rooms are decorated in bright colors and feature amenities such as fireplaces and refrigerators. Two 24-hour swimming pools and hot tubs make this a good choice if you are looking for a place to really unwind between winery excursions. Top of the line are three townhouse spa suites that command vineyard views. Continental breakfast is included, as is complimentary wine. ~ 1 Main Street; 707-963-9463, 800-950-8466, fax 707-963-4426; www.harvestinn.com, e-mail reservations@harvestinn.com. ULTRA-DELUXE.

> Dating to 1852, White Sulphur Springs Inn & Spa is the oldest hot-springs resort in California.

In the center of town, **Hotel St. Helena** is a traditional false-front building dating to 1881. It features 18 guest rooms, all but four of which have private baths (the four share two European-style bathrooms down the hall). Many rooms include such decor as caneback chairs, brass beds, antique armoires, marbletop vanities, and bent-willow headboards. Each is painted in warm pastel colors and plushly carpeted. Guests share an indoor reading room and sitting room with fireplace, plus other facilities like the hotel's wine bar. Continental breakfast is included. ~ 1309 Main Street; 707-963-4388, 888-478-4355, fax 707-963-5402; www. hotelsthelena.com. MODERATE TO ULTRA-DELUXE.

A gracious Victorian topped with a fanciful cupola affording 360° views of the Napa Valley, **Ink House Bed & Breakfast** offers a pleasant and serene place to stay. The 1884 house is encircled by a wide veranda with white wicker chairs and offers seven antique-filled guest rooms, five with private bath. In addition to a full gourmet breakfast, wine and appetizers are served in the afternoon. There's a gameroom with an antique pool table; mountain bikes are available for guests. ~ 1575 St. Helena Highway; 707-963-3890, fax 707-968-0739; www.inkhouse.com, e-mail inkhouse bb@aol.com. MODERATE TO ULTRA-DELUXE.

HIDDEN ► Spread across 45 acres is **White Sulphur Springs Inn & Spa**. A deeply shaded creek runs through the property, which also contains a redwood grove and a natural sulphur spring and pool. The cottages (five small, four large) and carriage house possess a rustic charm. The former have private baths, while the latter share a bathroom, lounge and kitchenette with a fireplace. There are also "inn rooms" with private baths available at moderate cost. In the spa you can treat yourself to a massage, an herbal facial, a body wrap, or stone therapy. Or you can hop into the swimming pool, jacuzzi or sulphur soaking pool. ~ 3100 White Sulphur Springs Road; 707-963-8588, 800-593-8873, fax 707-963-2890; www. whitesulphursprings.com. MODERATE TO DELUXE.

Secluded at the end of a tree-shaded country road, **Meadowood** comprises 85 accommodations, a top-tier restaurant, a nine-hole golf course, two croquet lawns, two pools, tennis courts, a fitness center, a spa and hiking trails. Guests may choose to stay in cozy cottages or in the Croquet Lodge; either way, they'll have comfortable furnishings and serene views of the grounds. ~ 900 Meadowood Lane; 707-963-3646, 800-458-8080, fax 707-963-3532; www.meadowood.com, e-mail info@meadowood.com. ULTRA-DELUXE.

Soaring ceilings, unusual lighting, and festive displays of peppers
and garlic make **Tra Vigne**'s setting as exciting as its menu. The
theme here is regional Italian: chewy breads, bold pizzas, hearty
salads, rabbit, chicken and grilled seafood dishes, and a first-rate
wine list. This dramatic restaurant also specializes in unusual an-
tipasti such as melon with shaved prosciutto and parmesan gelato.
~ 1050 Charter Oak Avenue; 707-963-4444, fax 707-963-1233;
www.travignerestaurant.com, e-mail travigne@napanet.net. MOD-
ERATE TO ULTRA-DELUXE.

Located within the Tra Vigne complex, **Cantinetta** is an upscale Italian deli with a wood-paneled bar serving espresso, cam-
pari and wines by the glass. In addition to panini (Italian for sandwich), focaccia and the like, you'll find a changing array of picnic
and heat-at-home items. You'll also probably find local vinters at
the bar. ~ 1050 Charter Oak Avenue; 707-963-8888, fax 707-963-
1233; www.travignerestaurant.com e-mail travigne@napanet.net.
BUDGET.

Pizzeria Tra Vigne is a terrific place to bring the family. It's   ◄ HIDDEN
kid-friendly as well as budget-friendly, with thin-crust Neopolitan-
style pizzas, pasta, salads and other easy-to-eat fare in an upbeat
setting. Inexpensive wines are sold by the glass. ~ 1016 Main
Street; 707-967-9999, fax 707-967-0495; www.pizzeriatravi-
gne.com. BUDGET TO MODERATE.

Chef Cindy Pawlcyn, best known for her benchmark
Mustards Grill, now runs **Cindy's Backstreet Kitchen** in a pretty,   ◄ HIDDEN

AUTHOR FAVORITE

I love the coziness of the California Craftsman–style bungalow
that is home to the **Martini House**. In addition, no other Wine Country
restaurant does such a great job of acknowledging Napa Valley history. This
is one of the surest bets in the Wine Country. Partner/designer Pat Kuleto
(who created Boulevard and Farallon in San Francisco) blended American
Indian accents (acorns and baskets) into the beautifully lit main-floor
dining room. Tables surround an open stairwell that leads down to the
wine bar, which showcases Napa Valley winemaking history. Chef Todd
Humphries turns out inventive dishes like seared mahi with celery
root purée, sautéed venison loin and killer desserts. ~ 1245 Spring
Street; 707-963-2233; www.martinihouse.com. ULTRA-DELUXE.

white, two-story building just a block from Main Street. Everything she makes is good, a combination of comfort food and rock-solid flavor. The spice-rubbed quail and slow-smoked pork chops are especially fine choices. ~ 1327 Railroad Avenue; 707-963-1200; www.cindysbackstreetkitchen.com. MODERATE TO DELUXE.

HIDDEN ► Terra, St. Helena's leading restaurant for the past decade, serves an exotic blend of French, California and Asian cuisine. You might be treated to appetizers such as fried rock shrimp, foie gras tortellini, and *tataki* of tuna on the seasonally changing menu. Entrées feature exotic preparations of seafood, beef and squab. By way of ambience there are stone walls, terra-cotta features, and a wooden trim that lends an Asian overtone to this comfortable, Tuscan farmhouse–style dining room. Dinner only. Closed Tuesday. ~ 1345 Railroad Avenue; 707-963-8931, fax 707-963-0818; www.terrarestaurant.com. DELUXE TO ULTRA-DELUXE.

Unlike most Napa Valley restaurants, **Market** specializes in well-made American food such as fried chicken and macaroni and cheese. This is one of the best bargains, aside from ethnic establishments, in the Napa Valley, and the wine list is surprisingly extensive given the reasonable menu prices. ~ 1347 Main Street; 707-963-3799. MODERATE.

HIDDEN ► **Silverado Brewing Co. and Restaurant** is the only brewpub in town, serving blonde ale, amber ale, pale ale, oatmeal stout and a variety of seasonal brews. Everything on the menu goes with beer (wines and a full bar are also available): hamburgers, barbecued ribs and chicken, flatiron steak, and beer-battered prawns. The entrance is off a parking lot shared with Freemark Abbey. ~ 3020 North Route 29; 707-967-9876. MODERATE.

The **Wine Spectator Greystone Restaurant** at the Culinary Institute of America—just call it Greystone—is a cavernous res-

ST. HELENA STANDBY

Taylor's Refresher is a blast from the past that has been turning out burgers and dogs since 1949. Now you can get homemade tacos and salads and see how they taste with chocolate malts. Take your order to one of the picnic tables. ~ 933 Main Street; 707-963-3486; www.taylors refresher.com. BUDGET TO MODERATE.

taurant in an 1889 National Historic Landmark in north St. Helena. The complex includes a top-notch cooking school, but not to worry—the chefs are for real. The inspired seasonal menu ranges from crabmeat mariposa to a carmelized red snapper paella. "Street food of the world" is a lunchtime specialty. It's great fun to match dishes with different wines. Flanked by century-old stone walls, the restaurant is large enough to have cooking, baking and grilling stations in full view, which provide a terrific distraction for fidgety kids. Closed two weeks in January. ~ 2555 Route 29; 707-967-1010, fax 707-967-2375; www.ciachef.edu, e-mail wsgr@culinary.edu. DELUXE TO ULTRA-DELUXE.

Napa Valley's chief destination for high-end shopping is downtown St. Helena.

SHOPPING

If you consider to-die-for footwear a necessity, not a luxury, you'll beat a path to **Amelia Claire Shoes** and check out the bargains in the back room. ~ 1230 Main Street; 707-963-8502.

Diva Perfumes, tucked into a tiny, apothecary-style shop, sells an intoxicating array of perfumes, colognes and eau de toilettes. ~ 1309 Main Street; 707-963-4057.

Feel guilty about leaving Junior at home? The shop for newborns to first-graders is **Freckles**, which has some offbeat clothing you're unlikely to find at the mall. ~ 1309 Main Street #5; 707-963-1201.

Main Street Books stocks used books. Closed Sunday. ~ 1315 Main Street; 707-963-1338.

Even if you have no immediate need for a tiara, it's fun window shopping at **Patina, Estate & Fine Jewelry**. ~ 1342 Main Street; 707-963-5445.

Art on Main features original works by primarily Northern California artists as well as sculptures, bronze work and limited-edition etchings and serigraphs. ~ 1359 Main Street; 707-963-3350.

Exquisite morsels handmade with fresh nuts, cream and spices (but no preservatives) are packaged, Tiffany-style, in pale blue boxes at **Woodhouse Chocolate**. ~ 1367 Main Street; 707-963-8413.

You can decorate your home with all manner of Wine Country accessories from **Vanderbilt and Company**, a chic house-and-garden store with disposable supplies for a gourmet picnic as well as

Italian handblown wine glasses, majolica pottery and other fine goods. ~ 1429 Main Street; 707-963-1010.

On the north side of town, you can find everything for the home cook (or the professional one) at the **Spice Islands Marketplace,** where you can purchase specialty spices that aren't available in any supermarket. Located on the ground floor of the Culinary Institute of America at Greystone. ~ 2555 Main Street; 707-967-2309.

The **Napa Valley Olive Oil Manufacturing Co.** is more than a gourmet shopping spot: it's a sightseeing adventure as well. Housed in a former oil manufacturing plant, it contains the original press and crusher. Wagon tracks run along the cement floor, and posters of old Italia cover the walls. Today this tiny factory sells its own olive oil, along with delicious cheeses, salami, pasta and condiments. ~ 835 Charter Oak Avenue; phone/fax 707-963-4173.

An extensive wine department, gourmet-to-go, exquisite produce, and every type of trendy condiment imaginable fills the cavernous **Dean & Deluca** store, a West Coast offshoot of the original in New York. ~ 607 Route 29; 707-967-9980; www.dean deluca.com.

At **St. Helena Premier Outlets** you will find a shopping mall with clothing stores and an assortment of other shops. ~ 3111 North St. Helena Highway.

NIGHTLIFE   If they could roll up the sidewalks in St. Helena after dark, no doubt they would. There are few things to do at night in this town other than enjoy a fabulous meal.

PARKS   **BOTHE–NAPA VALLEY STATE PARK** 🚶 🏊 Rising from the valley floor to about 2000 feet elevation, this outstanding park is fully developed along one side, wild and rugged on the other. Until 1960, the park was a private resort called Paradise Park, owned by Reinhold Bothe. For those seeking to escape the Wine Country

AUTHOR FAVORITE

My dog forgives me instantly for leaving her at home when I surprise her with Char-dog-nay bones from **Fideaux.** This precious shop is devoted to products and accessories for the upscale dog and cat. ~ 1312 Main Street, St. Helena; 707-967-9935.

crowds, there are ten miles of hiking trails leading along sloping hillsides through redwood groves. More than 100 bird species inhabit the area, including hawks, quail and six types of woodpecker. There are also coyotes, bobcats, deer and fox here. The park's developed area, much of it wheelchair-accessible, features spacious picnic groves, campgrounds, a swimming pool open in the summer, restrooms and showers (fee). Day-use fee, $6 per vehicle. ~ On Route 29 about five miles north of St. Helena; 707-933-1600, fax 707-942-9560; www.napanet.net/~bothe, e-mail bothe@silverado.cal-parks.ca.gov.

▲ There are 40 tent/RV sites and 9 walk-in sites; $25 per night. Reservations are recommended: 800-444-7275 or visit www.parks.ca.gov.

Calistoga

Founded in 1859, Calistoga owes its origin and name to Sam Brannan. Brannan was the shrewd Mormon journalist and entrepreneur who first alerted San Francisco to the gold discovery. A decade later he saw liquid gold in Napa Valley's mineral springs and geysers. Determined to create a California version of New York's famous Saratoga spa, he named the region Calistoga. Indeed, its hot springs and underwater reservoirs were perfectly suited to a health resort.

Today Brannan's idea is carried on by numerous spas and health resorts. After imbibing at vineyards throughout the valley, visitors arrive in Calistoga to luxuriate in the region's mineral waters. I highly recommend that you sign up for "the works" at one of the local spas. You'll be submerged in a mud bath, led into a whirlpool bath then a steam room, wrapped head to toe in a blanket, and finally given a massage. By the end of the treatment, your mind will reside somewhere in the ozone and your body will be completely loose. (For a rundown on rubdowns, please see "The Spas of Calistoga" feature in this chapter.)

The same geological factors that created the hot springs and other unusual features in this part of the Napa Valley also influence the landscape in another way.

In the surrounding countryside are some of the top vineyards in the state. The volcanic soil and climate are different here than in the lower portions of the Napa Valley, meaning the wines are unique. Days tend to be hotter and nights cooler than elsewhere, thanks to the inland setting sheltered from most of the cold Pacific

winds. And Calistoga is much farther from the tempering atmosphere of the San Francisco Bay that infiltrates the landscape
around, say, Yountville. Two of the state's leading producers of
sparkling wine are located here. For an overview, sign up for a
hot-air balloon ride on a calm, fog-free morning. Almost all the
points of interest around here relate, in some way, to towering
Mount Helena.

SIGHTS   Though it's been tamed considerably, **downtown** Calistoga still
looks like a backdrop for a movie about the Wild West. Falsefront
buildings dominate the streetscape on the main drag, interspersed
with century-old brick buildings. The town's proximity to Mount
St. Helena has given rise to a booming industry based on hot
springs and mud baths and the attendant spa treatments.

Historic points of interest are the **Sharpsteen Museum** and adjacent **Sam Brannan Cottage**. Dedicated to Calistoga's original settlers, the museum displays tools from a blacksmith's shop and an
early California kitchen. Sam Brannan's cottage is furnished in period fashion with Victorian furniture and a glorious old piano. The
highlight of the entire display, however, is an elaborate diorama
portraying Brannan's health resort in miniature. Representing Calistoga circa 1865, it contains everything from railway station to
racetrack, hotel to distillery. ~ 1311 Washington Street; 707-942-
5911, fax 707-942-6325; www.sharpsteen-museum.org, e-mail
museum@napanet.net.

On the east side of the valley is an unusual small winery run
by physician Ralph Wermuth. (When people ask him why he gave
up medicine, he likes to tell them, "The medicine didn't work.")
Not for **Los Flores**, with his Rancho de Los Flores label, is the endless chasing of this season's hottest new varietals. Instead, sample
the colombard, gamay and other less-familiar wines. And get
Ralph to sign your bottle. Since the winery's a small affair, Ralph's
mantra remains: "If the sign says 'open,' come down the drive."
Tasting fee. ~ 3942 Silverado Trail; 707-942-5924.

The imposing 1884 stone building that once housed the Hans
HIDDEN ►   Kornell Champagne Cellars is now home to the **Frank Family
Winery**. Highly regarded for the cabernet sauvignon produced
from estate vineyards in Rutherford, the winery is also known
for its chardonnay, pinot noir, sangiovese and zinfandel, plus a
small amount of sparkling wine. The laid-back tasting room here

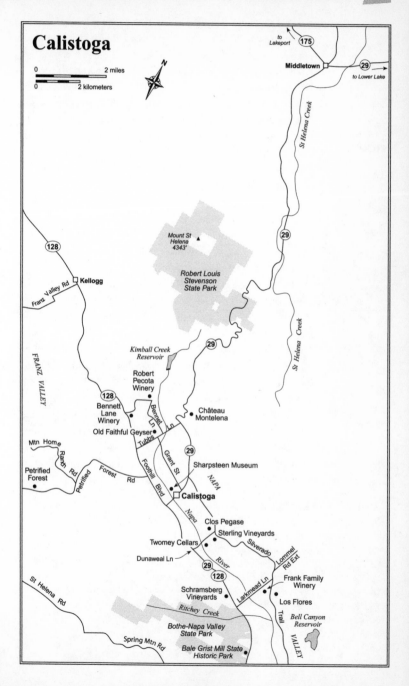

Calistoga

0 ————— 2 miles
0 ————— 2 kilometers

N

to
Lakeport
175

Middletown
29
to Lower Lake

St Helena Creek

128

Mount St
Helena
4343'

Robert Louis
Stevenson
State Park

Franz Valley Rd □ Kellogg

29

St Helena Creek

FRANZ VALLEY

Kimball Creek
Reservoir

29

Robert
Pecota
Winery

128

Bennett
Lane
Winery

Bennett Ln

Château
Montelena

Old Faithful Geyser

Tubbs

Mtn Home

Ranch Rd

Grant St

29

Sharpsteen Museum

NAPA

Petrified Forest Rd

Petrified
Forest

Foothill Blvd

□ Calistoga

Napa

Clos Pegase

Sterling Vineyards

Twomey Cellars

Silverado

Lommel
Rd Ext

Dunaweal Ln

29

River

128

Larkmead Ln

Frank Family
Winery

St Helena Rd

Schramsberg
Vineyards

Trail

Los Flores

Bell Canyon
Reservoir

Ritchey Creek

Bothe-Napa Valley
State Park

VALLEY

Spring Mtn Rd

Bale Grist Mill State
Historic Park

is one of the few in Napa Valley to offer complimentary samples. A few steps away, visitors can find picnic tables in the shade of old oak trees. ~ 1091 Larkmead Lane; 800-574-9463; www.frank familyvineyards.com, e-mail info@frankfamilyvineyards.com.

On the west side of the valley, you'll soon encounter a winery that makes some of the state's most cherished sparkling wines. When Robert Louis Stevenson visited the **Schramsberg Vineyards**, he tasted 18 different wines. Today you'll have to settle for a tour (by appointment) of this historic facility, founded in 1862. The road up to Schramsberg burrows through a dense forest before arriving at the original owner's home. The winery has added several buildings since Stevenson's day and now specializes in sparkling wine, but the old tunnels and cellars remain. Tasting available only on the tour. ~ Schramsberg Road; 707-942-4558, 800-877-3623, fax 707-942-5943; www.schramsberg.com, e-mail info1@schramsberg.com.

Twomey Cellars is one of the few wineries of note devoted almost exclusively to a single varietal—merlot—let alone a single vineyard source. The winemaker at Twomey (pronounced "too-mee") uses only grapes from a vineyard in the southeastern Napa Valley and employs elaborate, time-honored techniques used by classified growths in Bordeaux to create his wine. Closed Sunday. Tasting fee. ~ 1183 Dunaweal Lane; 800-505-4850, fax 707-944-2817; www.twomeycellars.com, e-mail info@twomeycellars.com.

Art and architecture vie with the fine wines at **Clos Pegase**. Designed by noted architect Michael Graves, the winery's tasting room features Honduran mahogany flourishes and antique glass decorations. There's a sculpture garden and fine works of art

THAR SHE BLOWS!

It's corny but decidedly wonderful to visit the **Old Faithful Geyser** about two miles northwest of town. It's only a pale resemblance to the huge one in Wyoming by the same name, but this version spews a satisfying jet stream of boiling water as high as 60 feet in the air. The show recurs about every 15 to 30 minutes, depending on varying tidal, lunar and tectonic conditions. It's a vivid reminder of the power of nearby Mount St. Helena. Admission. ~ 1299 Tubbs Lane, Calistoga; 707-942-6463, fax 707-942-6898; www.oldfaithfulgeyser.com, e-mail geyser@oldfaith fulgeyser.com.

shown throughout the premises. A glass wall exposes the upright tank room where vintners make cabernet sauvignon, merlot and chardonnay. Tasting fee. ~ 1060 Dunaweal Lane; 707-942-4981, 800-366-8583, fax 707-942-4993; www.clospegase.com, e-mail cp@clospegase.com.

It's worth going a little off course to find the charming **Chateau Montelena**, where the attractions include a lake sur-   ◄ *HIDDEN* rounded by classic Chinese landscaping. Established in the 1870s, the castle-like winery became the seventh-largest in the Napa Valley by 1896. Its main claim to fame, however, came at the legendary Paris Tasting of 1976, when its 1973 chardonnay was one of the top whites in the contest that pitted California's best against France's finest. Current releases of chardonnay, cabernet sauvignon and zinfandel are available in the tasting room. Tasting fee. ~ 1429 Tubbs Lane; 707-942-5105, fax 707-942-4221; www.montelena.com.

On the northwest side of Calistoga, **Bennett Lane Winery** be-   ◄ *HIDDEN* longs to Lisa and Randy Lynch (who, by the way, claim to be the first California vintners to sponsor a NASCAR team). You can taste four wines—two Napa Valley cabernet sauvignons, a Napa Valley chardonnay ($28) and a blend of cabernet, merlot and syrah dubbed "Maximus," a real palate-pleaser referred to as "a red feasting wine." Picnic tables available. Tours available. Tasting fee. ~ 3340 Route 128; 707-942-6684; www.bennettlane.com, e-mail info@bennettlane.com.

Robert Pecota Winery is a family-run operation in what is   ◄ *HIDDEN* probably Napa's northernmost wine-growing parcel, 37 acres highly suited to red wines. Pecota and two of his daughters are in charge, turning out 8000 cases a year of cabernet sauvignon, sauvignon blanc, syrah and moscato—premium Bordeaux varietals. Tours by appointment only. ~ 3299 Bennett Lane; 707-942-6625, fax 707-942-6671; www.robertpecotawinery.com, e-mail info@robertpecotawinery.com.

Three and a half million years ago, a volcano near Mount St. Helena exploded. Evidently, eruptions from this firepit leveled an entire redwood grove, which transformed over the ages into a **Petrified Forest**. Located six miles up the mountain southwest of Calistoga, this eerie spot contains a succession of fallen giants. Redwoods measuring over 100 feet long and 8 feet in diameter lie along the forest floors, perfectly preserved in stone. Unfortunately, the place has the trappings of a tourist trap. Admission. ~ 4100 Petrified Forest Road; 707-942-6667, fax 707-942-0815; www. petrifiedforest.org, e-mail pforest@sonic.net.

LODGING   This unpretentious town has relatively few stuffy digs, at least compared to the rest of the Napa Valley. It's home to many modest lodgings that offer mineral baths as well as numerous bed and breakfasts.

Tucked into a hilly canyon where old oak groves, a lake and a rock-strewn stream create a cozy hideaway, the 46-room **Calistoga Ranch** is the fanciest place to stay in northern Napa (considering it's a sister property to Auberge du Soleil down the road, is that any wonder?). With its own vineyard, a private lakeside restaurant, a spa, a fitness center and a yoga deck (as well as a swimming pool), Calistoga Ranch offers guests many places to unwind and enjoy the pristine natural setting. The accommodations have enclosed decks and lots of glass that incorporate as much of the outdoors as possible, even in cool or rainy weather; some have outdoor fireplaces and hot tubs. ~ 590 Lommel Road; 707-254-2800, 800-942-4220, fax 707-254-2888; www.calistoga ranch.com. ULTRA-DELUXE.

The **Calistoga Inn & Brewery** has reasonably priced rooms that include a continental breakfast. This 18-room hostelry sits atop a restaurant and pub that serve their own Napa Valley

AUTHOR FAVORITE

When I need to balance my chakras (or just clear my head), I head for **Harbin Hot Springs**, the perfect place to hike in the hills, eat vegetarian, and bask naked (optional, of course) in a steaming pool full of New Agers. Although it may not be for everyone, it's a popular place, as witnessed by the weekend crowds. Natural springs feed the warm, hot and cold mineral-water pools of this New Age retreat center. You may stay in a dormitory, a retreat room, an ultra-deluxe-priced cabin, or camp out and enjoy quiet conversation with the other guests. There's a restaurant serving breakfast and dinner, or you can bring your own vegetarian food to cook in the communal kitchen. Also on the vast property are a health food store, bookstore, temple and garden. Massage and Watsu available. ~ Harbin Springs Road, Middletown; 707-987-2477, fax 707-987-0616; www. harbin.org, e-mail reception@harbin.org. MODERATE TO DELUXE.

Brewing Company beer. The European-style accommodations are small but tidy, carpeted wall-to-wall, and plainly decorated. The furniture is simple and baths are shared, but each room has its own sink. ~ 1250 Lincoln Avenue; 707-942-4101, fax 707-942-4914; www.calistogainn.com, e-mail info@calistogainn.com. MODERATE.

Several Calistoga spas also provide overnight accommodations. One of the most accommodating is the two-story **Golden Haven Hot Springs Spa**, where the 28 rooms are standard-issue but attractive and spanking clean. All have refrigerators and some have microwaves. They are within a few steps of the resort's indoor-outdoor swimming pool and outdoor hot tubs, all heated with natural hot springs mineral water. Golden Haven deeply discounts its accommodations on weekdays and from November through March 15, and features bargain-rate spa packages on its website. ~ 1713 Lake Street; 707-942-8000; www.goldenhaven.com. MODERATE.

◄ HIDDEN

Built in 1914, the renovated **Mount View Hotel** has the aura and feel of a classic small-town hotel. It's a 32-room affair with a dining room and lounge downstairs and Victorian flourishes throughout. The spacious lobby features a fireplace and contemporary artwork. Guest rooms are nicely decorated with a mix of Victorian and modern touches. In addition, there are three cottages, each with a private hot tub. Guests are free to use the hotel's pool and spa. Continental breakfast is delivered to your room. ~ 1457 Lincoln Avenue; 707-942-6877, 800-816-6877, fax 707-942-6904; www.mountviewhotel.com, e-mail info@mount viewhotel.com. DELUXE TO ULTRA-DELUXE.

Cosseted by elm trees, the 16 bungalows at the **Cottage Grove Inn** are the most chic in Calistoga, with luxurious touches like front porches, two-person hot tubs, mini-refrigerators, DVD players and wi-fi, as well as skylights. Furnishings are plush and thoughtfully arranged. Continental breakfast is included, as are afternoon wine and cheese. ~ 1711 Lincoln Avenue; 707-942-8400, 800-799-2284, fax 707-942-2653; www.cottagegrove.com, e-mail cottage@sonic.net. ULTRA-DELUXE.

Calistoga Spa Hot Springs is a jewel disguised as a plain old motel. The 57 rooms are contemporary and quite attractive, with well-equipped kitchenettes. (Try to book a corner room on the

Text continued on page 94.

The Spas of Calistoga

The town of Calistoga is ground zero for the warm mineral-bath industry in California. A mixture of ash from nearby Mount Helena and natural water bubbling up hot from beneath the earth make for some very relaxing mud baths. Sitting in a tub of piping hot lava with a whiff of sulfur in the air may sound odd to the uninitiated, but to the converted, there's nothing better in terms of relaxation and detoxification. The spas in this small town in northern Napa Valley have more than mud baths. They offer just about every kind of body treatment known to man.

Calistoga Spa Hot Springs is a dream for water babies. Four outdoor pools of varying sizes and temperatures share a spacious courtyard to one side of the treatment rooms. All are filled with naturally heated mineral water, from the 18-inch deep wading pool to the L-shaped swimming pool to the large octagonal hot tub shaded by a pretty gazebo roof. If you're booking a treatment, you can use the pools for only $5 extra. Other day visitors are welcome for a modest fee on weekdays (a little more on weekends). House specialties are the mud and mineral baths, available in combination with a steam bath and blanket wrap and/or massage. The complex is built on the site of Dr. Aalder's Hot Mud Baths, dating from the 1920s and pictured in photographs that line the hallway to the spa section. Today the place has a vaguely art deco ambience that perfectly suits its off-the-main-drag location. This is one of the few spots where night bathing is offered. ~ 1006 Washington Street; 707-942-6269; www.calistogaspa.com.

Calistoga Village Inn and Spa is another possibility. They offer the unique powdered mustard bath as well as the more standard steam baths, blanket wraps, massages, salt scrubs and facials. ~ 1880 Lincoln Avenue; 707-942-0991, fax 707-942-5306; www.greatspa.com, e-mail greatspa@napanet.net.

Housed in a mid-19th-century bank building, the **Lincoln Avenue Spa** made some big changes in late 2006 to appeal to an increasingly sophisticated spa-going public. Custom oils and creams have upgraded the product line. The lobby has been expanded and furnished with charcoal-colored leather sofas and love seats, and two treatment rooms were reconfigured to accommodate couples. As always, the spa has a certain panache thanks to details such as beautiful woodwork and green tile in the steam room. The spa offers salt scrubs, which are full body scrubs that culminate in a jacuzzi or steam bath. There are several other nice touches here, such as mint, green tea, wine, sea mud and herbal wraps and a number of facial treatments. ~ 1339 Lincoln Avenue; 707-942-5296; www.lincolnavenuespa.com.

The Mount View Spa has just room for one love seat in the pretty little waiting room, where sponged blush walls create the illusion of a glow (watch out for those prices). Located in the back of the Mount View Hotel, between the lobby and the pool area, the European-style spa is the most elegant in town, perhaps because it has no traditional mud baths. ~ 1457 Lincoln Avenue; 707-942-5789, 800-816-6877, fax 707-942-6904; www.mountviewhotel.com, e-mail info@mountviewhotel.com.

Dr. Wilkinson's Hot Springs is the granddaddy of Calistoga mud bathing. Facilities here are not glamorous—except for the nearby salon adjunct—but travelers familiar with some of the no-frills European-style spas will feel at home. Skin-care treatments available on the weekend. ~ 1507 Lincoln Avenue; 707-942-4102; www.drwilkinson.com.

Indian Springs looks like a motor court you might have found in the desert in the 1950s—a wonderful mix of white, blue and red-orange that sets it apart from every other place in town. Neat bungalows march around the horseshoe driveway, evoking road trips from childhood. But this is a savvy place with some truly cool touches such as old-fashioned bathing suits displayed in Plexiglas frames and white beadboard walls in the treatment rooms. The mud at Indian Springs is not mixed, so it's startlingly black. The property, which has been here since the 1860s, is situated on three thermal geysers on 16 acres of ancient volcanic ash and has been welcoming guests to this very bathhouse since 1913. Along with the mud and mineral baths, Indian Springs offers treatments such as facials, body polishes and Swedish massage, most available à la carte or as part of a package. The fantastic raised pool, estimated to be two times Olympic size, is open only to spa and overnight guests. ~ 1712 Lincoln Avenue; 707-942-4913, fax 707-942-4919; www.indiansprings calistoga.com.

upper level if you like a little extra space.) The pull here is a multitude of pools of varying sizes and temperatures as well as a bathhouse featuring a volcanic ash mud bath and mineral and steam bath. Two-night minimum stay required on weekends and during summer months, three on holiday weekends. ~ 1006 Washington Street; 707-942-6269, fax 707-942-4214; www.calistogaspa.com. MODERATE TO DELUXE.

If you like your lodgings intimate, check into the aptly named **Foothill House** in the foothills on the north side of town. Accommodations include three suites that have been carved out of an early-20th-century farmhouse and two freestanding cottages. All have private entrances, small refrigerators and woodburning stoves or fireplaces. Most rooms have whirlpool tubs. Full breakfast is included. ~ 3037 Foothill Boulevard; 707-942-6933, 800-942-6933, fax 707-942-5692; www.foothillhouse.com, e-mail info@foothillhouse.com. DELUXE TO ULTRA-DELUXE.

Meadowlark Country House is a beautiful 19th-century home with 20 acres of wooded grounds that feature an enclosed mineral pool (clothing optional), hot tub and sauna. Each of the seven rooms features contemporary or English country antique furniture, comforters and a view of forest or meadow. There is also a luxurious poolside guesthouse with a whirlpool tub, kitchen and private deck. A generous breakfast is served each morning and you will find the serene veranda a great place to catch up on your reading. Gay-friendly. Not recommended for families with young children. ~ 601 Petrified Forest Road; 707-942-5651, 800-942-5651, fax 707-942-5023; www.meadowlarkinn.com, e-mail info@meadowlarkinn.com. ULTRA-DELUXE.

DINING   For its size, Calistoga has the most varied restaurant scene of any town in the Napa Valley. You'll find a wide range of moderately priced places to dine, as well as a couple of budget choices.

The **Flatiron Grill** is a classic steakhouse that also offers some alternatives, such as smoked chicken pasta, beef brisket and grilled salmon. The decor is an uncluttered blend of bare wood floors, cedar-colored plaster walls, suede-covered booths and cow paintings by Lowell Herrero. Newcomers are welcome to mix with locals who like dining at the wine bar. ~ 1440 Lincoln Avenue, Calistoga; 707-942-1220; www.flatirongrill.com, e-mail info@flatirongrill.com. MODERATE TO DELUXE.

Wappo Bar Bistro dishes up dazzling food that spans the globe with Asian noodles with shiitake mushrooms, Thai shrimp curry, Ecuadorean braised pork, osso buco, chiles rellenos with walnut pomegranate sauce, and Turkish mezze (that hard-to-find treasure that in this case includes herb-and-cheese-stuffed eggplant sandwich, white bean salad, carrots, golden beets, shaved fennel, cracked green olives, hummus, yogurt sauce and, believe it or not, more). Everything tastes even better on the sun-dappled patio. ~ 1226 South Washington Street; 707-942-4712, fax 707-942-4741; www.wappobar.com, e-mail wappo@napanet.net. MODERATE TO DELUXE.

The **All Seasons Bistro** is a Wine Country classic—a little bit bistro, a lot California. White-tableclothed marble tables set on a black-and-white checkerboard floor seem small once you pile them up with organic greens, local game birds, wild mushrooms and various pastas and imaginative main courses (their wonderful desserts are all housemade). The wine list, like the adjacent wine shop, is chock-full of regional. Lunch available on weekends. ~ 1400 Lincoln Avenue; 707-942-9111, fax 707-942-9420; www.allseasonsnapavalley.com, e-mail allseasons@att.net. MODERATE TO DELUXE.

The setting is informal and the menu Italian. Day or night at **Bosko's** you'll find fresh pasta dishes like bay scallops, mushrooms and pesto cream over fettuccine, linguine with bay shrimp and asiago cream sauce and spaghetti with meatballs. Or you can have a meatball, sausage, or Italian ham sandwich on their homemade focaccia. The wine list is extensive and the meals they offer are good and filling. ~ 1364 Lincoln Avenue; 707-942-9088, fax 707-942-9661; www.boskos.com. MODERATE.

With an eclectic menu and little fanfare, **Stomp** installed itself on the ground floor of the historic Mount View Hotel after

BETTER IN A BOOTH

If you want a place where you will feel instantly at ease, slide into a booth in the bar at **Brannan's Grill**. In a great big dining room softened by mica light shades and skylights, American regional cuisine is served up in hearty and handsome portions. Expect seasonally themed dishes using local ingredients as well as vegetarian options. ~ 1374 Lincoln Avenue; 707-942- 2233, fax 707-942-2299; www.brannansgrill.com. DELUXE.

Catahoula closed. The Louisiana theme has been replaced with a color scheme of soft green and yellow, illuminated by large cylindrical ceiling lights wrapped in grapevines. The short, seasonal menu is long on meat entrées such as a grilled boneless rib eye accompanied by potato croquettes and an English pea purée, although most nights you'll find several seafood options like seared striped bass with a crab-filled squash blossom or focaccia-crusted Alaskan halibut with black truffle purée. Closed Monday. ~ 1457 Lincoln Avenue; 707-942-8272, fax 707-942-6846; www.stomprestaurant.com, e-mail stomprestaurant@earthlink.net. DELUXE TO ULTRA-DELUXE.

Hot dishes such as beef teriyaki, vegetable tempura and gyoza (pot stickers), along with raw food, are on the menu at **Kitani Sushi**. Softly lit by paper lanterns, this cozy spot has only 12 tables inside, but there are six stools at the sushi bar plus patio dining in good weather. ~ 1631 Lincoln Avenue; 707-942-6857. BUDGET TO MODERATE.

SHOPPING   Virtually all the stores in Calistoga are lined up along Lincoln Street. It's a mixed bag that includes some women's and children's clothing boutiques, a bookstore and two top-notch places to buy regional and international wines.

The historic **Calistoga Depot** has been converted to a mall. Within this former railway station are assorted stores, including the **Calistoga Wine Stop** (707-942-5556, 800-648-4521), housed in an antique railroad car. ~ 1458 Lincoln Avenue.

At **Attitudes**, both men and women will find labels such as Royal Robbins, Hanky Panky, Johnny Was, Mac & Jac and Prana on almost everything from bathing suits to fancy pumps. ~ 1333B Lincoln Avenue; 707-942-8420.

◆◆

MINDING YOUR BEESWAX

Hurd Beeswax Candles has, since 1954, elevated candlemaking to the level of art. The waxworks resemble statues rather than tapers; fashioned by hand, they are formed into myriad intricate shapes (some are also hand-painted). There's also a demonstration beehive and winetasting on the premises. ~ 1255 Lincoln Avenue, Calistoga; 707-942-7410, fax 707-942-7415; www.hurdbeeswaxcandles.com.

The Main Element showcases Northern California artists as well as hand-crafted furniture, jewelry, art glass and women's accessories. ~ 1333 Lincoln Avenue; 707-942-6347.

Copperfield's Books and Music, the privately owned, Sonoma-grown chain of bookstores, now has a branch in the "other valley," where specialties include fiction, food and wine, regional interest and a used-book section. ~ 1330 Lincoln Avenue; 707-942-1616.

Italian-born artist Carlo Marchiori, known for the dazzling trompe l'oeil murals at his nearby villa, now sells Roman-style bas relief stone plaques, cleverly painted pictures, vases and other ceramics and even small pieces of furniture at his **Ca'Toga Galleria D'Arte.** ~ 1206 Cedar Street; 707-942-3900. www.catoga.com.

NIGHTLIFE The northern end of the Napa Valley is quite a bit less chi-chi than the southern part. What nightlife there is tends to be more down-home—sometimes actually loud.

Wednesday is open-mic night and Friday and Saturday nights bring live rock-and-roll to the pub at the **Calistoga Inn, Restaurant and Brewery.** ~ 1250 Lincoln Avenue; 707-942-4101.

PARKS **ROBERT LOUIS STEVENSON STATE PARK** ☆ On the slopes of Mount St. Helena northeast of Calistoga, this sprawling parcel inspired many scenes in Stevenson's *The Silverado Squatters.* This is where the author and his bride spent their honeymoon in 1880, in an abandoned bunkhouse that belonged to the Silverado Mine. Few of the park's 3300 acres are developed, except for a couple of lengthy hiking trails. It's worth the climb to one of two summits for one of the best vantage points in the Wine Country. ~ Route 29; 707-942-4575.

Outdoor Adventures

There's not much in the way of golf courses in this neck of the woods.

GOLF Duffers will have to settle for the nine holes at the **Mount St. Helena Golf Course.** It's a par-34 public course with a snack bar and golf shop. The 2670-yard course is flat and easy to walk; fairways are narrow and lined with trees; only one hole has water. Closed for five days over the Fourth of July weekend. ~ Napa County Fairground, Calistoga; 707-942-9966.

A nine-hole course where oak trees and wandering streams provide a rustic backdrop, **Aetna Springs Golf Course** is hidden ◀ HIDDEN away in a valley northeast of Calistoga. ~ 1600 Aetna Springs Road, Pope Valley; 707-965-2115.

RIDING STABLES

Triple Creek Horse Outfit offers one- to three-hour guided rides in Bothe-Napa Valley State Park. Riders must be at least eight years old and weigh no more than 240 pounds to ride through open meadows, across creeks and into redwood forests. Similar outings are available at two Sonoma Valley parks. Rides by reservation. ~ Route 29, about five miles north of St. Helena; 707-933-1600.

BIKING

The key to happy pedaling in the Napa Valley is to keep away from Route 29. There are side roads that go virtually straight up hillsides as well as flat places on lightly trafficked roads. A couple of bike shops can give you their own suggestions; rentals run usually about $7 an hour or $30 for the whole day.

A bike trail runs along the Silverado Trail from Soscol Avenue all the way to Calistoga, but the only safe riding is north of Trancas Street.

Bike Rentals   **St. Helena Cyclery** rents 24-speed hybrid bikes, ideal for comfortable rides, by the hour or by the day. The helpful staff can tailor outings to suit your needs, from winery tours to short, flat rides in a nearby residential area. Closed Monday in winter. ~ 1156 Main Street, St. Helena; 707-963-7736.

Getaway Adventures offers guided bike (as well as hike and kayak) tours throughout the Wine Country. ~ 2228 Northpoint Parkway, Santa Rosa; 707-568-3040, 800-499-2453; www.getawayadventures.com.

HIKING

Some strenuous hiking is required to get the most stunning Wine Country views, but there are a number of moderate trails as well. Poison oak is a consideration almost everywhere in warm weather, as are ticks, so dress accordingly. All distances listed for hiking trails are one way unless otherwise noted.

The best hiking destination in the St. Helena vicinity is Bothe–Napa Valley State Park. The moderate **History Trail** (1.2 miles) begins at the picnic area and passes the Pioneer Cemetery, where members of the Tucker family are buried beyond a white picket fence. At a three-way junction, the middle path heads up sharply through a mixed forest of madrone, tan oak, black oak and Douglas fir. From the peak of the trail, you descend to Mill Creek and pass a stone dam built by Edward Bale's daughter. The trail leads to the historic Grist Mill, from which you can return to the start.

The moderately difficult **Coyote Peak Trail** (1.5 miles) heads away from Ritchey Creek, then climbs up to 1170 feet elevation for scenic views of the Napa Valley.

Ritchey Canyon Trail (3.9 miles) starts off easy on an 1860 roadbed that wanders beside a stream and is shadowed by redwoods and firs. Farther along, the trail becomes moderate and leads past a small cascade that flows into a small canyon.

A tranquil hike along Ritchey Creek can also be found on **Redwood Trail** (1 mile). In spring, redwood orchids and trilliums add to the beauty of this tree-shaded pathway.

The **South Fork Trail** (.9 mile) is a moderately strenuous hike that circles the rim of Ritchey Creek and arrives at a vista point overlooking the canyon.

The **Ritchey Canyon Trail** and **Upper Ritchey Canyon Trail** (4.2 miles total) combine for a moderate hike. Ritchey Creek flows beside the early part of the trail, which leads to the old Hitchcock house (home to the family of San Francisco's famed Lily Hitchcock Coit). You can venture off the trail along small paths that lead to the creek; keep an eye out for the crayfish that thrive here. Trees flower in the springtime, making it one of the loveliest times for a visit. The trail leads to the state park boundary, where you will make an about-face for the return trip.

For an easy walk, much of which is wheelchair-accessible, examine the **Petrified Forest Loop** inside the only petrified redwood forest in the world. The trail is a quarter-mile long; a meadow walk is open for tours by appointment. Admission. ~ 4100 Petrified Forest Road, Calistoga; 707-942-6667.

FOUR

Sonoma Valley

 A temperate climate, plentiful agricultural potential, numerous hot springs, abundant wildlife and access to a bay create a natural wonderland that has been attracting people to this area for thousands of years. The Wappo Indians were the first humans to arrive and the influx continues to this day. Grapes have been grown in the valley since the early 1800s, setting the stage for the birth of the California wine industry in a crescent-shaped valley only 50 miles from the city of San Francisco.

Human settlement in the Sonoma Valley has been traced back some 12,000 years, following the great migration from Asia across the Bering land bridge and then southward from Alaska. Among them were the Wappo, Mayakmahs and Wintuns in the north portion, closest to the Mayacamas Range; Miwoks along the coast; Pomos in the southern portion of the valley; Patwins in the southeast; and Koskiwok closest to San Francisco Bay. The population of these tribes probably approached 5000. They lived in tule-thatched huts, traded among each other, cleared land to ferret out more game and found restoration in the natural hot springs.

As the missionaries and explorers came north from Mexico in the early 19th century, they found an ideal mission site that they named San Francisco Solano de Sonoma. Founded in 1823, the settlement was the last and northernmost of the 21 California missions. It took the Franciscan fathers a scant few years to convert the locals to their religion, but the harshness of the regime led to unrest. The Mexican government decided to secularize the mission and sent one of their top men, General Mariano G. Vallejo, to carry out the assignment. Vallejo was successful in transforming the settlement into a pueblo; he laid out the central plaza, built barracks and wound up acquiring a great amount of land, money and influence.

By the 1840s, however, an influx of American settlers from the other side of the Sierra Nevada led to the end of Mexican power. By 1848, Mexico ceded all of California to the United States. By 1850, California became a state, with Vallejo elected to the state senate. Despite his efforts to retain Sonoma as the county seat, Santa Rosa won out in 1854 (a result still challenged by some historians). Adding insult to injury, residents of the current county seat removed all the county records in the middle of the night, and many Sonomans today feel that was the end of their town's political clout.

But the valley had other resources. The Franciscan fathers had planted, among other things, mission grapes. The history of premium grapes, however, follows a different plot. The behemoth that is the modern California wine industry has its roots in the Sonoma Valley, but while mission grapes were grown here and elsewhere in the state, the first European varietals were introduced in Sonoma by Count Agoston Haraszthy. He arrived here in 1857, established the Buena Vista Winery and, in the early 1860s, returned to Europe to tour wine-producing regions there. He sent hundreds of premium grape cuttings back to be planted in his extensive acreage on the east side of the valley.

As more Europeans, especially Italians, arrived in Sonoma, they carried on their traditions from the old country. By 1876, Sonoma Valley was turning out more than two million gallons of wine a year. In 1904, Samuele Sebastiani, who had emigrated from Tuscany in 1895 at the age of 21, purchased a small Sonoma wine cellar, married a local girl and dreamed up the concept of shipping volumes of wine in railroad tank cars—an improvement over shipping it in freight cars. Little did he know that he was beginning a dynasty that would lead to the present, when the fourth generation of Sebastianis are likewise occupied in the family business. However, like everywhere else in the Wine Country, phylloxera threatened to completely douse the burgeoning industry in the valley. The coup de grace came in 1919 with Prohibition, although many locals found ways to circumvent the restrictions against producing alcoholic beverages.

It was around this time that Jack London, the most prolific and best-paid author of his era, arrived in the valley and put it on the map in *The Valley of the Moon*, a novel that mythologizes the region. Remains of his fantastic Glen Ellen estate are now part of a California historical park.

By the early 1930s, two men found another agricultural product that would thrive in Sonoma—cheese. Celso Viviani and Tom Vella were among the pioneers; their scions run successful cheese businesses in downtown Sonoma to this day. Along with an increasing number of artisanal bakers, the cheesemakers and winemakers with shops in downtown Sonoma make it easy to assemble a picnic to enjoy on the grounds of the historic plaza, where more than 200 species of trees provide bountiful summertime shade and duck ponds delight generation after generation.

Begin your tour on Route 12/121, the two-lane road that leads into town from San Francisco and other points south. (If by chance you are arriving from Napa or other points east, your first stop should be at the Visitors Bureau, located within the plaza on 1st Street East.)

▼▼▼▼▼▼▼▼▼▼▼▼▼▼▼
Southern Sonoma Valley

Even if there were no wine industry, Sonoma would make a worthwhile destination because of its historical significance and small-town charm. The 19th-century structures built by General Vallejo now form a portion of a multi-part state park, most of which face the downtown plaza. It was Vallejo who laid out the eight-acre plaza, still in existence today, that defines the city's core. Many of the adobe and falsefront buildings dating from that era have evolved into shops, restaurants, offices and hotels that help make the town one of northern California's premier tourist destinations.

SIGHTS

If you're not familiar with the Sonoma Valley, make your first stop the **Sonoma Valley Visitors Bureau.** Located at Cornerstone Gardens, it's a well-stocked outpost of the main bureau downtown, and can help you select brochures, maps and books. ~ 23570 Route 121, Sonoma; 707-935-4747; www.sonomavalley. com, e-mail info@sonomavalley.com.

The Tuscan-style **Viansa Winery & Italian Marketplace** sits atop a small hill with a commanding view north to much of the valley. Viansa produces a variety of wines made from well-known Italian grapes such as sangiovese and pinot grigio along with lesser known varieties such as arneis, aleatico and primitivo, as well as several California varietals, including cabernet sauvignon, cabernet franc, chardonnay and merlot. The marketplace is the size of a dining hall and is stocked with all kinds of California-Italian comestibles and condiments (many set out for sampling) as well as wines available for tasting. Tasting and touring fee. ~ 25200 Arnold Drive (Route 121), Sonoma; 707-935-4700, 800-995-4740, fax 707-996-4632; www.viansa.com, e-mail tuscan@viansa.com.

HIDDEN ►

Within plain sight of the winery and, to a lesser extent, the highway, the **Viansa Wetlands** are testimony to Viansa winery founder Sam Sebastiani's commitment to the environment. The 90-acre

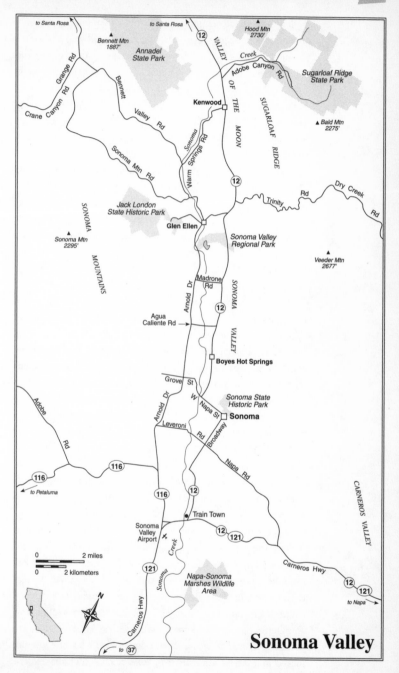

Sonoma Valley

preserve attracts all manner of waterfowl—great blue herons, cinnamon teal, widgeons, mallards, pintails, geese, egrets and swans among them—as well as snipe, dowitchers, sparrows, turkey vultures, hawks and eagles, depending on the time of year. Ninety-minute tours (fee) are offered on alternate Sundays from February through June, weather permitting. Closed July through January. ~ 25200 Arnold Drive (Route 121), Sonoma; 707-935-4700, 800-995-4740, fax 707-996-4632; www.viansa.com, e-mail tuscan@viansa.com.

Across the highway from Viansa, the tasting room at **Cline Cellars** is housed in an award-winning restored farmhouse dating to the mid-19th century. The winery is known for its zinfandels and Rhone varietals, including mourvedre, viognier and syrah. Picnic tables are set in the shade beside the nearby duck ponds and rose gardens. ~ 24737 Arnold Drive (Route 121), Sonoma; 707-940-4030, 800-546-2070, fax 707-940-4034; www.clinecellars.com, e-mail info@clinecellars.com.

It would take weeks to visit all the sites where Spanish padres built missions along the 650-mile-long El Camino Real from San Diego to Sonoma between 1769 and 1823. Not only that, all 21 of them were razed or at least seriously threatened—if not by enemies of the Catholic Church or natural disaster, then by secularization or the toll of time and the elements. Fortunately, scale models of these historic buildings have been collected, restored **HIDDEN ▶** and put on display in the **California Mission Models Museum** behind the tasting room at Cline Cellars. ~ 24737 Arnold Drive (Route 121), Sonoma; 707-939-8051; www.californiamissions museum.com, e-mail missionmodels@yahoo.com.

About a mile north, **Gloria Ferrer Champagne Caves** can be glimpsed from the highway. This sparkling wine facility, an American sister to the Ferrer family holdings in Spain, was an instant hit with its first wines. The Ferrers carved caves (typical in their native country) out of the hillside for storing premium sparkling wines. The wines are available for purchase or for tasting either indoors or on a wide patio with lovely views of the surrounding countryside. Tasting fee. ~ 23555 Carneros Highway (Route 121), Sonoma; 707-996-7256, fax 707-996-0720; www.gloriaferrer.com, e-mail info@gloriaferrer.com.

Schug Carneros Estate Winery looks like a bit of Germany tucked into the hills of Carneros. Walter Schug had long experi-

ence making pinot noir for other wineries before he opened his
own in 1990, using the post-and-beam architecture of his native
Rhine River Valley. While best known for that varietal, which, like
chardonnay, does so well in the cool, windy conditions of the appellation, Schug also produces cabernet sauvignon, merlot, sauvignon blanc and sparkling wines. Visitors are welcome to play
some *petanque*, the French version of lawn bowling. Tours by appointment. ~ 602 Bonneau Road, Sonoma; 707-939-9363, 800-

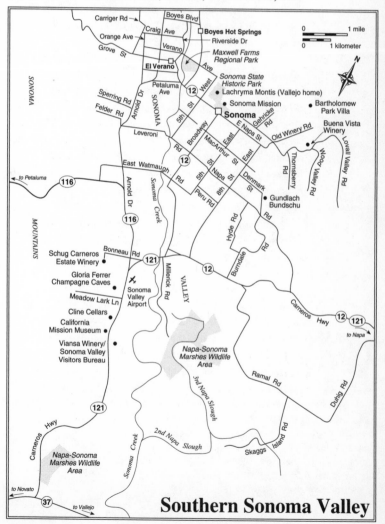

Southern Sonoma Valley

966-9365, fax 707-939-9364; www.schugwinery.com, e-mail schug@schugwinery.com.

Reynaldo Robledo spent decades learning how to tend grapevines, toiling in other people's vineyards. Over time, he and his wife Maria purchased 30 acres in the Carneros and ultimately became one of the first Latino families to open their own winery in the region. Several of their children work at **Robledo Family Winery**, making and marketing chardonnay, merlot, pinot noir, sauvignon blanc and other wines. ~ 21901 Bonness Road, Sonoma; 707-939-6903, fax 707-939-6978; www.robledofamily winery.com.

HIDDEN ►

It's about a ten-minute drive to downtown **Sonoma**, a Spanish-style town of 9200 people. And the spot to begin this tour-within-a-tour is the **Plaza**, bounded by 1st Street East, 1st Street West, Spain and Napa streets. The center of Sonoma for more than 150 years, this shady park is an excellent picnic place. The largest plaza in the state, it contains a playground, an open-air theater, a duck pond and a rose garden. At the **Sonoma Valley Visitors Bureau** there are maps and brochures of the area. They also provide recommendations for local restaurants and lodgings. ~ 453 1st Street East, Sonoma; 707-996-1090, fax 707-996-9212; www.sonomavalley.com, e-mail info@sonomavalley.com.

After you check out the plaza but before you tour the nearby historical structures, head south on Broadway (Route 12) about a block.

Works by local, national and international artists in all media, including video, architecture and crafts, appear in changing exhibits at the **Sonoma Valley Museum of Art**. Some of the art is borrowed from private collections and museums and combined in off-

sights

AUTHOR FAVORITE

If you're traveling with children, here's a trick that might make your trip a little easier: Kids who tire of all the dusty history can be bribed with a visit to **Train Town**. Miniature steam engines chug around a ten-acre park, passing over trestles and bridges, through two tunnels, and arriving at a scale-model Western town. Also visit the petting zoo, antique carousel, Ferris wheel and cabooses. Closed Monday through Thursday during winter. Admission. ~ 20264 Broadway, Sonoma; 707-938-3912; www.traintown.com.

beat groupings. Closed Monday and Tuesday. Admission (free on Sunday). ~ 551 Broadway, Sonoma; 707-939-7862, fax 707-939-1080; www.svma.org, e-mail admin@svma.org.

Spanish adobes, stone buildings, and falsefront stores surround the historic square. Mission San Francisco Solano, or **Sonoma Mission**, stands at the northeast corner. Founded in 1823, this was the last and most northerly of the 21 California missions. With its stark white facade, the low-slung adobe houses a small museum. There are dozens of paintings portraying other California missions; the chapel has also been painted brilliant colors and adorned with carved wood statues. ~ 1st Street East and East Spain Street, Sonoma.

The **Sonoma Barracks**, across the street, were built with Indian labor during the 1830s to house the troops of Mexico's General Mariano Guadalupe Vallejo. A two-story adobe with sweeping balconies, it's now a museum devoted to early California history. ~ 1st Street East and East Spain Street, Sonoma.

Next door, the **Toscano Hotel** is furnished in 19th-century fashion with wood-burning stoves, brocade armchairs, and two gambling tables. Dating to 1852, this wood-frame structure was built as a general store but later used to house Italian workers. ~ 20 East Spain Street, Sonoma.

The only remains of General Vallejo's 1840 house, **La Casa Grande**, is the servant's house with its sagging adobe facade. ~ West Spain Street between 1st Street East and 1st Street West. Together with the mission and other historic buildings encircling the plaza, it is part of **Sonoma State Historic Park**; all these noteworthy places can be toured for a single admission price. ~ Sonoma; 707-938-1519, fax 707-938-1406; www.napanet.net/~sshpa.

Just north of the plaza stands the **Depot Park Museum**, where the displays commemorate railway history and the Bear Flag uprising when Americans revolted against General Vallejo in 1846. You can also see Sonoma as it was at the turn of the 20th century. Closed Monday and Tuesday. ~ 270 1st Street West, Sonoma; phone/fax 707-938-1762; www.vom.com/depot, e-mail depot@vom.com.

About three-quarters mile west of the town square, you'll find another antique structure. **Lachryma Montis** was the home General Vallejo built in 1852, after the United States had assumed control of California. Vallejo successfully made the change to

American rule, becoming a vintner and writing a five-volume history of early California. Something was lost in the transition, however, and this yellow Carpenter Gothic Victorian house with pretty green shutters fails to evoke images of a Mexican general.

Nevertheless, it's well worth touring. Every room is appointed in 19th-century style, as though Vallejo were expected to arrive any moment. The old pendulum clock still swings and the dinner table is set. Out back, the cookhouse contains personal effects of the Chinese cook, and ducks flap around the turtle pond. Part of Sonoma State Historic Park, it also features a cactus garden, a mini-museum and a picnic area. Admission. ~ At the north end of 3rd Street West, Sonoma; 707-938-9559, fax 707-938-1406.

HIDDEN ▶

What started in 1976 as a cult winery famous for its spicy zinfandels, **Ravenswood Winery** has evolved into a mega-business producing some 750,000 cases of wine a year. Ravenswood, housed in a charming stone building, makes cabernet franc, cabernet sauvignon, chardonnay, merlot, carignane and petite sirah, but the bulk of its production is devoted to 13 different zinfandels. The patio outside the tasting room is a popular picnic spot, especially for bicyclists who like pedaling up the gradual slope to the winery. Tasting and touring fee (reservations required for once-daily tours). ~ 18701 Gehricke Road, Sonoma; 707-938-1960, 888-669-4679; www.ravenswood-wine.com, e-mail rwwine@ravenswood-wine.com.

While Vallejo was settling into his American-style home, Count Agoston Haraszthy, a Hungarian aristocrat, moved to Sonoma and founded **Buena Vista Carneros Winery** in 1857. Popularly known as the "father of the California wine industry," he eventually imported 100,000 vines from Europe. Today the actual winemaking occurs at the vineyard estate in the Carneros area, but you can taste sample vintages in the old stone winery and take a self-

GETTING AWAY

For those wanting to enjoy the Wine Country air, **Getaway Adventures** operates one-day, weekend and six-day biking trips through the Napa, Sonoma and Alexander valleys, as well as kayak trips on the Russian River. ~ 1718 Michael Way, Calistoga; 707-568-3040, 800-499-2453, fax 707-568-3055; www.getawayadventures.com, e-mail info@getawayadventures.com.

guided tour around the grounds. Now a historical monument, the winery also has picnic tables for the crowds that visit. Tasting fee. ~ 18000 Old Winery Road, Sonoma; 707-938-1266, 800-926-1266, fax 707-939-0916; www.buenavistacarneros.com, e-mail tastingroom@buenavistacarneros.com.

The white, Pompeian-style **Villa** in Bartholomew Park houses an astonishing, largely unsung collection of memorabilia and artifacts relating to local winemaking history. Here you can see a replica of Buena Vista Winery founder Agoston Haraszthy's mansion, which burned down; the Villa was built in the early 1990s by the widow of Frank Bartholomew, the pioneering war correspondent who bought 500 acres of Haraszthy's abandoned vineyards in 1943 and helped revitalize the Sonoma Valley wine industry. Closed Monday-Friday and weekend mornings except by appointment. ~ 1695 Castle Road, Sonoma; 707-938-2244.

◀ *HIDDEN*

A short drive south and east leads to another of the oldest wineries in California. Six generations have worked at **Gundlach Bundschu** since 1858, though there was a long hiatus from Prohibition until the 1970s. Cabernet and merlot are some of G-B's best products, aside from a series of hilarious wine posters. Cave tours are offered on weekends; picnic grounds are open year-round. Tasting fee. ~ 2000 Denmark Street, Sonoma; 707-938-5277, fax 707-938-9460; www.gunbun.com, e-mail wino@gunbun.com.

At **Bacchus Glass**, visitors get to watch artisans spin steel tubes laden with a shapeless blob of molten glass in red-hot ovens to create works of art. How hot are the furnaces? Up to 2470°F. Working in the Venetian style, the young men here perform as a team, with each one responsible for a different step. As the glass cools, a form emerges. An entirely separate process involves the addition of color. Closed Saturday and Sunday. ~ 21707 8th Street East, Sonoma; 707-939-9416; www.bacchusglass.com.

◀ *HIDDEN*

Small historic hotels can be found on and near the plaza, as can bed-and-breakfast inns. From the Carneros to the northern edge of town is a smattering of very nice motels with comfortable furnishings and quirky charm. While the top places cost well over $200 a night, you can find happiness for half that at some smaller establishments, especially from January through March, when demand is down. That's the only time any budget accommodations are available.

LODGING

Claiming a corner of a busy intersection near the Gloria Ferrer Champagne Caves, the **Vineyard Inn** is a classic Mission Revival–style motor court. It has 24 adjoining bungalows, each with a private entrance off the landscaped courtyard. The suites have a wetbar and refrigerator; some have whirlpool tubs. Extras include a small pool and continental breakfast. ~ 23000 Arnold Drive, Sonoma; 707-938-2350, 800-359-4667, fax 707-938-2353; www. sonomavineyardinn.com. DELUXE.

A massive remodeling of a historic mansion led to the creation of **MacArthur Place**, which features 64 rooms and suites in a series of contemporary cottages and two-story buildings. All rooms are outfitted with DVD players; suites have fireplaces and whirlpool baths. Decor throughout is chic country, with sophisticated color schemes in shades such as olive and lemon. A full-service spa is located near a swimming pool amid the extensively landscaped grounds. The inn's restaurant specializes in top-quality steak. ~ 29 East MacArthur Street, Sonoma; 707-938-2929, 800-722-1866, fax 707-933-9833; www.macarthurplace.com, e-mail info@macarthurplace.com. ULTRA-DELUXE.

HIDDEN ►   **Les Petits Maisons** are four cozy, freestanding cottages a mile east of the Sonoma Plaza that are well-suited to travelers who prefer to prepare their own food and enjoy a bit of residential-style privacy. Chic, cleverly designed and decorated in Provencal colors, the little houses with the French names all have fully equipped kitchens, small private patios, sitting rooms and TV/DVDs. The grounds include an enclosed yard for visiting pets plus a private garden with a fountain, picnic tables and market umbrellas. Bicycles, propane barbecue grills and light breakfast are included. Housekeeping available. Pet fee. Two-night minimum. ~ 1190 East Napa Street, Sonoma; 707-933-0340, 800-291-

A STUCCO STANDOUT

The **El Dorado Hotel**, located on the square, is a small gem. Originally an adobe built in 1843, this refurbished stucco establishment offers 27 small- to moderate-size rooms as well as a full-service bar and restaurant. Appointed with four-poster beds, down comforters, Mexican tile floors, and California/Spanish–style furniture, each has a private balcony. There's also a heated swimming pool and complimentary morning coffee. ~ 405 1st Street West, Sonoma; 707-996-3220, 800-289-3031, fax 707-996-3148; www. hoteleldorado.com, e-mail info@hoteleldorado.com. DELUXE.

8962; www.thegirlandthefig.com/lespetitsmaisons, e-mail lespetits maisons at thegirlandthefig.com. DELUXE.

When the **Ledson Hotel** opened in the summer of 2003, people were impressed with how well the graceful two-story stone structure suited the site facing the historic Sonoma Plaza. No one was happier than Steve Ledson, owner of Ledson Winery and a fifth-generation Sonoman, who had purposely designed it to look like an early-19th-century structure. Upstairs, six guest rooms, all with fireplaces and balconies, are appointed with period furniture and accessories along with contemporary conveniences such as whirlpool tubs and computer hook-ups. The attention to detail, particularly in the elaborate woodwork, makes this place worth its prices. (The ground floor is occupied by a restaurant, the Harmony Club.) ~ 480 1st Street East, Sonoma; 707-996-9779; www.ledsonhotel.com. ULTRA-DELUXE.

The **Swiss Hotel**, an adobe building circa 1840 and a State Historical Landmark, is a five-room hostelry that features rooms with private baths and a refrigerator. One has a four-poster bed and pine furniture, others have a variety of antique and modern pieces. The hotel rests on the town's central plaza and contains a bar and restaurant downstairs. ~ 18 West Spain Street, Sonoma; 707-938-2884, fax 707-938-3298; www.swisshotelsonoma.com, e-mail swisshotel@vom.com. DELUXE TO ULTRA-DELUXE.

Sonoma's plaza boasts another historic hostelry, the **Sonoma Hotel**, which dates to around 1879 and is a 16-room facility decorated entirely with French Country furnishings. The lobby has a stone fireplace and the adjoining restaurant features a hand-carved bar. Combining history with comfort, this vintage hotel is worth a visit. Continental breakfast is included, as is complimentary wine service. ~ 110 West Spain Street, Sonoma; 707-996-2996, 800-468-6016, fax 707-996-7014; www.sonomahotel.com, e-mail sonomahotel@aol.com. MODERATE TO ULTRA-DELUXE.

The **Thistle Dew Inn**, located a half-block west of the town plaza, is a dream-come-true for fans of the Craftsman bungalow style. Arts and Crafts furniture looks like it came with the house; an 1869 cottage in the rear adds another four rooms. An outdoor hot tub can be used almost year-round. Full breakfast is included. ~ 171 West Spain Street, Sonoma; 707-938-2909, 800-382-7895, fax 707-938-2129; www.thistledew.com, e-mail info@thistledew.com. DELUXE TO ULTRA-DELUXE.

DINING

There are a dozen places to eat on or just off the Sonoma plaza. A handful of decent establishments are scattered throughout the area, though as yet you won't find any restaurants in the Carneros district in the southern part of the valley.

HIDDEN ▶

One of the few places to eat in southernmost Sonoma Valley, the **Market Café** is an important adjunct to the Cornerstone Gardens complex. Glass walls, high ceilings and retail displays create a cheery setting for light breakfasts and lunch fare such as roasted beet or Cobb salads, paninis, fresh sandwiches and desserts. ~ 23584 Route 121, Sonoma; 707-935-1681 or 707-935-3823; www.cornerstonegardens.com. BUDGET.

Deuce is an American bistro housed in a rambling Victorian cottage with an elegant art nouveau interior and tasteful ambiance. Start with pumpkin squash ravioli or sautéed Dungeness crab cakes, and move on to filet mignon with bone marrow and potato cake, lamb steak with white beans and wild mushrooms or seafood options such as Maine lobster risotto. Patio seating is delightful in decent weather, and always an option to consider early in the evening before moving indoors. Desserts are scrumptious, especially the chef's special tiramisu or crème brûlée. ~ 691 Broadway, Sonoma; 707-933-3823, fax 707-933-9002; www.dine-at-deuce.com. MODERATE TO DELUXE.

Small plates—lots of them, mostly innovative and all tasty—are the order of the day at the ritzy **Harmony Club**, on the ground floor of the Ledson Hotel. The menu changes frequently but typical choices include pork tenderloin and seared scallops. Some 25 wines are available by the glass. Service is offered at inside tables as well as those outside beneath a metal and glass awning that ex-

AUTHOR FAVORITE

On the west side of the valley is a local hangout known as **Juanita Juanita**, a place that redefines ambience to mean children's drawings on the wall, plastic cutlery and plates, and dozens of small bottles of all kinds of hot sauces lined up along the counter. This is where I head for cheap, ultra-fresh Mexican food. The super quesadilla and the daily dinner specials are the best deals, though you really can't go wrong regardless. ~ 19114 Arnold Drive, Sonoma; 707-935-3981 or 707-938-4025; www.juanitajuanita.com. BUDGET TO MODERATE.

tends to the curb. ~ 480 1st Street East, Sonoma; 707-996-9779; www.ledsonhotel.com. MODERATE TO DELUXE.

Sonoma Cheese Factory is *the* spot to visit on the way to the picnic grounds. In addition to a grand assortment of cheeses, it sells wines, sandwiches and gourmet specialty foods. There's also a small outdoor patio for diners. ~ 2 West Spain Street, Sonoma; 707-996-1931, 800-535-2855, fax 707-935-3535; www.sonoma cheesefactory.com, e-mail retailstore@sonomacheesefactory.com. BUDGET.

The Girl & The Fig occupies most of the ground floor of the historic Sonoma Hotel, which has seen half a dozen restaurants come and go in as many years. The muted color scheme of ivory and moss green takes a back seat to "country food with a French passion" such as steak and *frites*, Liberty duck confit, regional seafood with local produce and the bistro's signature fig salad with arugula and local goat cheese. The large brick patio out back is the best place to sample the brasserie menu between lunch and dinner. ~ 110 West Spain Street, Sonoma; 707-938-3634, fax 707-938-2064; www.thegirlandthefig.com, e-mail info@thegirlandthe fig.com. MODERATE TO DELUXE.

The most convivial restaurant in town (as evidenced by the predominance of local patrons at both lunch and dinner), **Sonoma-Meritâge Martini Oyster Bar & Grill** is also one of the prettiest. Typical dishes include free-range chicken breast sautéed in a kalamata olive sauce and served over vegetable couscous risotto, seafood stew and seared duck breast served over potato risotto with a blood orange sauce. Chef Carlo Cavallo's southern French and northern Italian cuisine is based on fresh local ingredients that inspire seasonal changes to the menu. Closed Tuesday. ~ 165 West Napa Street, Sonoma; 707-938-9430, fax 707-938-9447; www.sonomameritage.com. MODERATE TO DELUXE.

The **Red Grape** is best known for thin-crusted, New Haven–style pizzas, but it is also a favorite for its outstanding fresh pastas, most available with either red or white sauce. The high-ceilinged room features glass walls on three sides and an open kitchen; there's also patio seating. ~ 529 1st Street West, Sonoma; 707-996-4103; www.theredgrape.com. BUDGET TO MODERATE.

In 2005, **El Dorado Kitchen** opened on the ground floor of the Hotel El Dorado to serve up-to-the-minute California food like pumpkin risotto, Pacific salmon in a white bean cassoulet, and forest mushroom–goat cheese pizza. ~ 405 1st Street West, Sonoma; 707-996-3030, 800-289-3031, fax 707-996-3148; www.eldoradosonoma.com, e-mail info@eldoradosonoma.com. MODERATE TO DELUXE.

When no one in your dining party can agree on where to eat, it may be time to try a place that serves African, Brazilian and Portuguese dishes. **LaSalette** is the masterpiece of chef Manuel Azevedo, whose heritage and wide-ranging travels have inspired an unusual menu. Salt cod with onions, oven-roasted salmon, Mozambique prawns with tomatoes, and grilled plantain are usually on a menu that changes slightly with the seasons. There's patio seating for balmy evenings. Closed Monday. ~ 452 1st Street East, Suite H, Sonoma; 707-938-1927; www.lasalette-restaurant.com.

If you prefer Mexican cuisine, try **La Casa**. Located just off the plaza, this colorful restaurant offers a full menu from south of the border. There are margaritas and other tequila drinks at the bar, plus a bill of fare ranging from fish tacos to chile verde to chimichangas. Enjoy your meal on their outdoor patio. ~ 121 East Spain Street, Sonoma; 707-996-3406, 800-766-2832, 707-938-0285; www.lacasarestaurant.com, e-mail lacasafood@aol.com. BUDGET TO MODERATE.

If you dine at **Della Santina** on a mild day, head to a table on the brick-lined back patio. This Italian favorite is the only place in town to order petrale sole (occasionally available). There are other daily fish and veal specials as well as classic northern Italian dishes: lasagna, tortellini, cannelloni and so on; rabbit, duck, turkey, pork and chicken rotate on the rotisserie. Della Santina's is especially known for its gnocchi; here a bowl of the little dumplings runs less than $14. The wine list, of course, incorporates Italian as well as California vintages. ~ 133 East Napa Street, Sonoma; 707-935-0576, fax 707-935-7046; www.dellasantinas.com, e-mail ndellasantina@mindspring.com. MODERATE TO DELUXE.

Don't let the simplicity of the decor or menu fool you. The half-dozen or so main courses at **Cafe La Haye** are the result of a sophisticated chef who manages to create delectable dishes in a postage stamp–size kitchen. Chicken, beef, pasta and daily fish and risotto selections get the deluxe treatment in this split-level storefront restaurant just off the Sonoma plaza. Dinner only. Closed Sunday and Monday. ~ 140 East Napa Street, Sonoma; 707-935-

5994; www.cafelahaye.com, e-mail cafelahaye@vom.com. MODER-
ATE TO DELUXE.

The Fig Pantry, an offshoot of The Girl & The Fig restaurant,
is jam-packed with premium condiments, wines, cheeses and gifts.
The deli offers upscale, ready-to-eat food such as grilled meats,
imaginative salads, bread pudding and the like, and also has a
bakery section. ~ 1190 East Napa Street, Sonoma; 707-933-
0340, 800-291-8962. DELUXE TO ULTRA-DELUXE.

The Breakaway Café is way above your average shopping-
center eatery. It's the love child of a chef who once ran an upscale
restaurant in Glen Ellen and now contents himself with preparing
simpler food with the occasional flourish. Mostly it's comfort food
along the lines of meatloaf, gourmet hamburgers, steaks, pasta and
seafood, as well as brunch specials, but daily specials keep regulars from getting bored. Open for breakfast, too. ~ 19101 Route
12, Sonoma; 707-996-5949, fax 707-996-0410; www.breakaway
cafe.com. BUDGET TO MODERATE.

SHOPPING

The old Spanish town of Sonoma contains a central plaza around
which you'll find its best shops. Stroll the square (bounded by 1st
Street East, 1st Street West, Spain and Napa streets) and encounter
gourmet stores, boutiques, a designer lingerie company, antique stores, poster galleries, and a brass
shop. Many of these establishments are housed in
historic Spanish adobes.

> In 1911, Agostino Pinelli
> sacrificed a thousand
> gallons of his red wine
> to put out the great
> Sonoma fire that
> burned a chunk
> of downtown
> property.

Villa Terrazza stocks an eclectic assortment of furnishings and accessories for indoor-outdoor living, including Italian urns, hand-painted ceramic tables, wicker
rocking chairs and pizza ovens. ~ 869 Broadway, Sonoma;
707-933-8286.

Readers Books stocks fiction, nonfiction, travel and other titles
and hosts frequent author appearances. ~ 130 East Napa Street,
Sonoma; 707-939-1779; www.readersbooks.com.

Robin's Nest specializes in discount kitchen accessories and
gifts such as Italian bowls and platters. ~ 116 East Napa Street,
Sonoma; 707-996-4169.

One place to consider is the Arts Guild of Sonoma, containing
works by local artisans. Here are paintings, ceramics, sculptures
and mixed-media art. Closed Tuesday. ~ 140 East Napa Street,
Sonoma; 707-996-3115.

A nearby mall, **El Paseo de Sonoma** contains more off-street shops. ~ 414 1st Street East, Sonoma.

Baksheesh is chockablock with gifts, toys, clothing and home accessories imported from Third World countries around the globe. ~ 423 1st Street West, Sonoma; 707-939-2847.

The Sign of the Bear celebrates the pleasures of life in the Wine Country. The shop sells a huge selection of gadgets, cookware, cookbooks, bakeware, ceramics, linens and tools for the wine enthusiast. ~ 435 1st Street West, Sonoma; 707-996-3722.

You don't have to live in town to find something elegant (and small enough to pack in your suitcase) at **Sonoma Home**, an enticing corner store decked out with furnishings, decorative pieces and accessories such as candles, linens and potpourri. ~ 497 1st Street West, Sonoma; 707-939-6900.

Chateau Sonoma is a tony boutique specializing in unusual European antiques and objets d'art such as ornate French bird cages, 19th-century Swedish wooden tables, vintage wine baskets, and Parisian garden stone balls. ~ 153 West Napa Street, Sonoma; 707-935-8553.

The chandeliers, lamps, shades and wall sconces created at **Bacchus Glass** are available for sale in the adjacent gallery. Closed weekwnds. ~ 21707 8th Street East, Sonoma; 707-939-9416.

NIGHTLIFE   As in the Napa area, Sonoma Valley nightlife revolves around summer events at the wineries. Check local calendars for concerts, theatrical performances, and other special programs. If that seems uninteresting, or if it's not summertime, you'll have to rely on hotel and restaurant bars for entertainment.

Depending on the night, you may find folk singers, Irish music or open games of Trivial Pursuit at **Murphy's Irish Pub**. ~ 464 1st Street East, Sonoma; 707-935-0660.

HIDDEN ▶

FARM-FRESH FOODS & FUN

You'll find organic produce, flowers and crafts, along with foodstuffs such as cheeses, honey and grass-fed beef, at the **Sonoma Certified Farmers Market**, held every Friday at Arnold Field (1st Street West) from 9 a.m. to noon. From April through October, the farmer's market also takes place Tuesday evenings right on the plaza (Broadway at Napa Street) from 5:30 p.m. until dusk. Expect live music and a festive atmosphere. ~ 707-538-7023, fax 707-538-7023.

With old photos adorning its walls, the bar of the historic **Swiss Hotel** is a favorite meetingplace of locals and travelers alike. You can also get a pretty filling meal here. ~ 18 West Spain Street, Sonoma; 707-938-2884, fax 707-938-3298.

Cucina Viansa has a full wine bar. ~ 400 1st Street East, Sonoma; 707-935-5656.

Northeast of Sonoma's city center, the century-old **Little Switzerland** is where you can dance the polka and waltz and pretend you're in another time and place. There's live music certain nights. Join your partner on the main dancefloor inside or in the beer garden outside. Dinners of steak, pasta and chicken are also served. Reservations recommended; call ahead for details. Cover. ~ Corner of Riverside Drive and Grove Street, El Verano; 707-938-9990, fax 707-938-3606; www.lilswiss.com.

MAXWELL FARMS REGIONAL PARK A paved path encircles most of this centrally located park, where early morning finds many older people taking their constitutionals, some with dogs in tow. There are five tennis courts and a skateboard park. Parents bring their offspring to burn off energy in the playground and the grassy infield is ideal for games of Frisbee. Parking fee, $5. ~ Route 12 at Verano Avenue, Sonoma; 707-565-2041, fax 707-579-8247.

PARKS

▼▼▼▼▼▼▼▼▼▼▼▼▼▼▼▼▼▼▼▼
Northern Sonoma Valley

From the northern Sonoma city limits to Santa Rosa, a ribbon of two-lane road runs through the scenic Valley of the Moon. The farther north you drive, the fewer commercial buildings and the more open space, with vineyards in the foreground and Sonoma and the Mayacamas mountains forming the borders. This is prime grapegrowing country and has been even before the days that Jack London lived and farmed here, when he was writing some of his best-selling novels.

Due north of Sonoma's city limits at Verano Avenue, **Boyes Hot Springs** blossomed as a summer resort area popular with San Franciscans who traveled by train from the city. Now this unincorporated town is experiencing a mini-renaissance, thanks in large part to the expansion of the Sonoma Mission Inn. If the Napa Valley is Stevenson country, however, Sonoma Valley belongs to Jack London. A world adventurer and self-described

SIGHTS

"sailor on horseback," London was not the type to settle down. Illegitimate son of an astrologer, he was in turn an oyster pirate, socialist, gold prospector, and internationally renowned author. But settle he did, a few miles northwest of Sonoma in the town of **Glen Ellen**.

Calling this area "the valley of the moon," London and his wife Charmian acquired a 1400-acre ranch and began construction of the Wolf House, an extraordinary mansion with 26 rooms and nine fireplaces. In 1913, when nearly completed, London's dream house burned, probably the result of a spontaneous combustion caused by oil-soaked rags left inside the house. Three years later, after producing 51 books and becoming America's first millionaire author, he died of kidney failure at age 40.

Today, at **Jack London State Historic Park**, you can wander what London called his Beauty Ranch. At the east end of the park, the House of Happy Walls, built by Charmian in 1919 after her husband's death, is a museum containing first editions and original manuscripts. London's study is adorned with the original artwork for his stories, and many keepsakes from his world adventures are here. A half-mile path leads past the author's grave, simply marked by a stone boulder, to the west side of the park and the tragic ruins of the Wolf House, a monument to a lost dream. Nearby, the cottage where London lived and wrote from 1911 until his death in 1916 still stands. Admission. ~ 2400 London Ranch Road, Glen Ellen; 707-938-5216, fax 707-938-4827; e-mail jacklondonshp@aol.com.

A bit of history awaits at the **Valley of the Moon Winery**, which sits on 60 acres that were once part of General Vallejo's 48,000-acre land grant. A winery has operated at this location since 1876, and portions of the farmhouse-style winery still possess the original stone and concrete walls. Two picnic areas are open for guest use. Tours of the winery are available daily at 10:30 a.m. and 2 p.m., while tasting runs all day. ~ 777 Madrone Road, Glen Ellen; 707-996-6941, fax 707-996-5809; www.valleyofthemoon winery.com, e-mail luna@valleyofthemoonwinery.com.

HIDDEN ►   Set on 61 acres of rolling hills, the **Quarryhill Botanical Garden** houses one of the world's largest collections of scientifically documented plants from China, Japan, India, Nepal and Taiwan. It is open to the public for docent-led tours on the third Saturday of each month from March through October. The tours last approximately two hours and require advance reservations. Fee. ~ Off Route 12, Glen Ellen; 707-996-3802, fax 707-996-3198; www.quarryhillbg.org, e-mail info@quarryhillbg.org.

Children and wine connoisseurs alike will enjoy the 45-minute tractor-pulled tram tour (fee) through the 85-acre **Benziger Family Winery**. This scenic facility, just to the east of Jack London State Historic Park, also boasts a peacock aviary and a lovely terraced picnic area. Tastings of their chardonnays, cabs, merlots and sauvi-

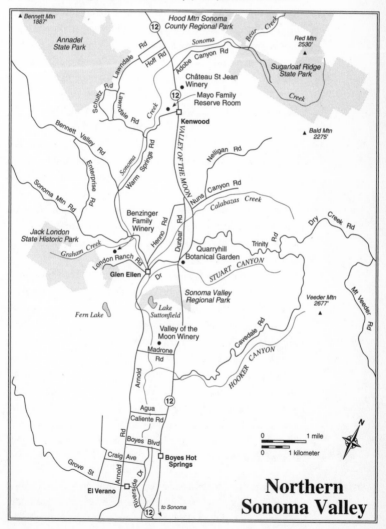

Northern Sonoma Valley

gnon blancs, among others, are available in the tasting room and private estate wine room. Tasting fee. ~ 1883 London Ranch Road, Glen Ellen; 707-935-3000, 888-490-2739, fax 707-935-3016; www.benziger.com, e-mail greatwine@benziger.com.

Kenwood, a residential community straddling the highway, has no real downtown to speak of. A few stores and top-notch wineries line the scenic highway.

The hottest trend in the Wine Country is food pairings in tasting rooms. The **Mayo Family Winery Reserve Room** has one of the best programs going: seven small plates of extremely inventive treats matched with seven wines. Available from 10:30 a.m. to 6:30 p.m. Thursday through Monday, it's one of the best deals in the whole region—and an educational experience to boot. Reservations recommended. Tasting fee. ~ 9200 Route 12, Kenwood; 707-833-5504; www.mayofamilywinery.com.

The strikingly beautiful **Château St. Jean Winery** sits beside a colonnaded mansion built during the 1920s. The winery has added several similar buildings. Wine, not extraordinary vistas, is the business here, and the winery has won several awards for its chardonnays and cabernet sauvignons. You can taste these and other varietals, explore the gardens and set out a picnic on one of the redwood-shaded tables. ~ 8555 Sonoma Highway, Kenwood; 707-833-4134, 800-543-7572, fax 707-833-4200; www.chateaustjean.com.

Gray and almost brooding in the shadow of the Mayacamas Mountains, **Ledson Winery & Vineyards** was originally intended as a residence. Plans changed midway, however, and the sprawling Normandy-style château now houses the winery. Steve Ledson claims he used more than two million bricks in constructing what locals refer to as "the castle." The winery is best-known for its estate-grown merlot and zinfandel and its Russian River chardonnay. The well-stocked Marketplace sells old dishes, fresh sandwiches and some 100 cheeses, which may be enjoyed at oak-shaded picnic tables. Tasting fee. ~ 7335 Route 12, Kenwood; 707-833-2330, fax 707-537-3026; www.ledson.com, e-mail hospitality@ledson.com.

LODGING   This area offers some unusual choices, from full-service resorts to small B&Bs. You certainly won't come across any chain lodging in this part of the Valley of the Moon. Some quasi-legal B&Bs

operate on a word-of-mouth basis, but you won't find them reviewed here.

The **Fairmont Sonoma Mission Inn & Spa** lives up to its excellent reputation. The pale pink stucco facade on this gracious Mission Revival–style hotel harks back to the days when American Indians enjoyed the natural mineral waters of this area. The 228 accommodations are appointed in earthy tones, with wooden shutters and ceiling fans adding a hint of the plantation; some rooms have fireplaces. A full-service spa, two restaurants, two swimming pools and an 18-hole golf course nearby add up to one of the best retreats in the Wine Country. ~ 100 Boyes Boulevard, Boyes Hot Springs; 707-938-9000, 800-441-1414, fax 707-938-4250; www.fairmont.com/sonoma, e-mail smi@smispa.com. ULTRA-DELUXE.

With a nod to the motor courts of the 1930s and 1940s, the 16-room **Sonoma Creek Inn** is perkily decorated with accessories such as handcrafted bathroom tiles, lampshades featuring vintage scenes and original artwork. The entire structure was built in 2001 next door to a café that will do take-out for breakfast or lunch. All rooms have cable TV and refrigerators; some feature balconies or patios. ~ 239 Boyes Boulevard, Boyes Hot Springs; 707-939-9463, 888-712-1289, fax 707-938-3042; www.sonomacreekinn. com, e-mail info@sonomacreekinn.com. MODERATE TO DELUXE.

◄ *HIDDEN*

A short drive from downtown Glen Ellen leads to the **Glenelly Inn**, one of the few properties around here that was actually built,

AUTHOR FAVORITE

One of the pleasures of living in or visiting the Wine Country is to gaze out over the vineyards. I've found few views to equal those of the **Ranch at Sonoma**. The ultra-private quarters allow visitors to experience, if briefly, the idyllic life of a landowner way up on Moon Mountain. The 2.6-mile drive up from Route 12 leads through prestigious vineyards before depositing you at a one-bedroom cottage with a kitchen, a woodburning stove, and views of vineyards and the San Francisco skyline. Chairs abound: on the wide porch, on the oak-shaded patio and on the hot tub deck. With red-tailed hawks for company, guests can hike beside a stream to a secluded redwood grove. Breakfast included. ~ Moon Mountain Road, Sonoma; 707-996-1888, fax 707-996-3838; www.staysonoma.com, e-mail wendy@staysonoma.com. ULTRA-DELUXE.

in 1916, to serve as an inn. Most of the inn's seven rooms are on the small side, but touches like a hot tub, a common room with a cobblestone fireplace and breakfast tables in the shade of old oak trees lure guests out of their quarters. There are two one-bedroom garden cottages with whirlpool tubs and private patios. The inn also runs 14 off-site rental cottages and homes that are more expensive. ~ 5131 Warm Springs Road, Glen Ellen; 707-996-6720, fax 707-996-5227; www.glenelly.com, e-mail glenelly@glenelly. com. DELUXE TO ULTRA-DELUXE.

The most elegant accommodations in Glen Ellen can be found at the **Gaige House Inn**, built as a private residence in the 19th century. Most of the 15 rooms and suites are done up in chic fashion with Asian accents. A full country breakfast is served in the large, bright dining room on the ground floor or on the terrace near a large pool flanked with white umbrellas and magnolia trees. ~ 13540 Arnold Drive, Glen Ellen; 707-935-0237, 800-935-0237, fax 707-935-6411; www.gaige.com, e-mail gaige@ sprynet.com. ULTRA-DELUXE.

The **Beltane Ranch** is an 1892 farmhouse converted into an easygoing inn. Backed by hundreds of acres that climb up the slopes of the Mayacamas Mountains that border the Napa Valley, the five rooms in this pretty yellow B&B are furnished with well-worn antiques as well as some swings and hammocks on the two-story wraparound porches. There's also a two-room cottage with its own patio. Tennis courts and private hiking trails beckon after the full breakfast, which is included. Two-night minimum from April through December. ~ 11775 Route 12, Glen Ellen; 707-996-

SPORTY SONOMA

Morton's Warm Springs Resort has three naturally heated mineral pools (the small one is perfect for kids) that attract a crowd on weekends and after 1 p.m. most weekdays. The low-key hideaway also has courts for volleyball and basketball, horseshoe pits, ping-pong tables and large playing fields for baseball, frisbee, bocce ball and soccer. There's a snack bar on the premises. Closed Monday and from November through April. Admission. ~ 1651 Warm Springs Road, Kenwood; 707-833-5511, fax 707-833-1839; www.mortonswarmsprings.com, e-mail mortonwarm springs@comcast.net.

6501, fax 707-833-4233; www.beltaneranch.com. DELUXE TO
ULTRA-DELUXE.

Wonderfully located for visiting wineries in Kenwood, Glen
Ellen and Sonoma, **Birmingham Bed & Breakfast** offers four upstairs accommodations in a 1913 Sonoma County Historic Landmark. Established on what was a 40-acre fruit orchard, the inn
is within walking distance of wineries and restaurants. ~ 8790
Route 12, Kenwood; 707-833-6996, 800-819-1388, fax 707- 833-
6398; www.birminghambb.com, e-mail info@birminghambb.com.
DELUXE TO ULTRA-DELUXE.

The town of Glen Ellen has emerged as the culinary star of this   **DINING**
neighborhood, with a cluster of excellent choices along down-
town's "restaurant row." Less fancy fare, usually Mexican or
Italian, is also available; true bargains can be found at *taquerías*
in Boyes Hot Springs.

The bargain-priced tacos, burritos and tostadas are freshly
made and served by a friendly staff at **Taqueria La Hacienda**. But
the restaurant, which is the most upscale *taquería* in town, even
though service is at bare-topped tables, also offers more elaborate
fare such as Shrimp Diablo and other full dinners. ~ 17960 Route
12, Boyes Hot Springs; 707-939-8226. BUDGET TO MODERATE.

Santé Restaurant presents innovative but unpretentious fare in
an elegant dining room of dark, highly polished woods. Prepared
with local produce, entrées may include salmon with udon noodles, bok choy, wild mushrooms, and vegetable broth; ostrich
medallions; and dijon-marinated rack of lamb. Resortwear for
men and women is required. Dinner and Sunday brunch are
served. ~ Fairmont Sonoma Mission Inn, 18140 Route 12, Boyes
Hot Springs; 707-938-9000, fax 707-938-4250. ULTRA-DELUXE.

A less formal option is **The Big 3 Diner** at Fairmont Sonoma
Mission Inn. This diner-style eatery serves tasty, healthful fare with
a northern Italian influence. You'll find pastas, pizzas and salads
on the lunch and dinner menu, while breakfast features freshly
baked goods, pancakes and egg dishes. ~ Fairmont Sonoma
Mission Inn, 18140 Route 12, Boyes Hot Springs; 707-938-9000,
800-441-1414, fax 707-996-5358. MODERATE TO DELUXE.

For a quick, light lunch, check out the deli department and take-
out cases at the **Glen Ellen Village Market**, which has café seating

inside plus a couple of creekside tables on the far side of the store. ~ 13751 Arnold Drive, Glen Ellen; 707-996-6728. BUDGET.

The Fig Café & Wine Bar is yet another winner from restaurateur Sondra Bernstein, who also has The Girl & The Fig in downtown Sonoma. Here the cuisine is a bit more casual, more like what someone with talent and good French genes would cook at home. Look for charcuterie, salads, pizzas, pasta, sandwiches, artisan cheeses and especially the pot roast. ~ 13690 Arnold Drive, Glen Ellen; 707-938-2130; www.thegirlandthefig.com. MODERATE.

The most consistently good food in the northern Sonoma Valley is served in the dining rooms and on the patio at the **Kenwood Restaurant and Bar**. Management doesn't change the menu much except for specials; everyone must be pleased with the crab cakes, locally raised chicken, lamb and steak dishes, as well as with a longtime favorite, sashimi, which is a rarity in the Wine Country. A fireplace in the long bar room is ideal for a late-afternoon lunch. Closed Monday and Tuesday. ~ 9900 Route 12, Kenwood; 707-833-6326, fax 707-833-2238; www.kenwoodrestaurant.com. MODERATE TO ULTRA-DELUXE.

The strong aroma of garlic envelopes family-owned and -operated **Cafe Citti**, an Italian trattoria set amongst the vineyards of Kenwood that is extremely popular with Sonoma Valley locals, who love its casualness and friendly atmosphere. Flowers and candles on the tables add a bit of romance, while summertime allows patio dining The Italian chef serves up a variety of pastas; rotisserie chicken stuffed with fresh herbs, garlic and rosemary; and weekend specials. He also makes his own mozzarella cheese and biscotti. ~ 9049 Sonoma Highway, Kenwood; 707-833-2690, fax 707-539-6255. BUDGET TO MODERATE.

SHOPPING **The Olive Press** is a unique source of local olive oils, each of them pressed on the premises. In addition to the oils, some of which are always available for sampling, you'll find tabletop merchandise such as plates, platters and bowls. ~ 14301 Arnold Drive, Glen Ellen; 707-939-8900, fax 707-939-8999; www.theolivepress.com, e-mail sales@theolivepress.com.

A wide and pleasing assortment of plants, pet treats, bird baths and other outdoor gifts clutter the indoor-outdoor premises at **Swede's Feeds**. ~ 9140 Route 12, Kenwood; 707-833-5050.

NIGHTLIFE

Out in Jack London country, the **Jack London Saloon** is a pretty, brick-faced bar that draws a mixture of locals and visitors. Fashionably decorated with Tiffany-style lamps and old movie posters, it's a good drinking place. ~ Jack London Lodge, 13740 Arnold Drive, Glen Ellen; 707-996-3100, fax 707-939-9642; www.jacklondonlodge.com.

For weekend jazz, the place to hang out is the **Cellar Cat Café**. Cover. ~ 14301 Arnold Drive, Glen Ellen; 707-933-1465.

PARKS

LARSON PARK Four tennis courts, a softball diamond and an open field are the only attractions at this neighborhood complex. A handful of picnic tables sit in the shade beside little Sonoma Creek. There are restrooms near them. ~ Off Dechene Street, Boyes Hot Springs; 707-565-2041.

JACK LONDON STATE HISTORIC PARK 🏃 Occupying much of a ranch once farmed by the famous author, this park ranges over hilly terrain. The central attractions are a museum, the House of Happy Walls, and the remains of the house that Jack built, Wolf House. Parking fee, $6. ~ 2400 London Ranch Road, Glen Ellen; phone/fax 707-938-5216.

> The Robert Ferguson Observatory at Sugarloaf Ridge State Park boasts a 40-inch telescope and offers public viewing nights. Visit their website for schedules. ~ 2605 Adobe Canyon Road, Kenwood; 707-833-6979; www.rfo.org.

SONOMA VALLEY REGIONAL PARK 🏃 🚴 Both paved and unpaved trails crisscross this parcel, parts of which are shaded. Two miles are paved for bike riding as well as walking. If you hike off the pavement in warm weather, wear boots or keep an eye out for the occasional rattlesnake. Popular with dog owners, the 167-acre park also has a special one-acre play area for off-leash pets near the Route 12 parking lot. Parking fee, $5. ~ 13630 Route 12, Glen Ellen; 707-565-2041, fax 707-579-8247.

SUGARLOAF RIDGE STATE PARK 🏃 🚴 Within this 2820-acre facility lie two different ecological systems as well as 25 miles of hiking trails along which to explore them. There are chaparral-coated ridges (you can see San Francisco and the Sierra Nevada from the top of Bald Mountain), plus forests of maple, laurel, madrone and alder. Sonoma Creek tumbles through the park; you can try for trout here. Spring brings a profusion of wildflowers, and autumn is another popular season in the park. Facilities include picnic areas and restrooms. Day-use fee, $6. ~ Located east off Route 12 between Sonoma and Santa Rosa, the park is at 2605 Adobe Canyon Road in Kenwood; phone/fax 707-833-5712.

▲ There are 49 sites; $20 per site. Camping here is a reasonably priced lodging option for a visit to the Wine Country and is popular with Bay Area families. Reservations: 800-444-7275.

▼▼▼▼▼▼▼▼▼▼▼▼▼▼

Outdoor Adventures

TENNIS

Five public courts are located in a corner of Maxwell Farms Regional Park. They are free and available on a first-come, first-served basis. Parking fee. ~ Route 12 at Verano Avenue, Sonoma; 707-565-2041.

BIKING

A two-mile **bike path** links Route 12 (at Verano Avenue) with Depot Park in downtown Sonoma. Paved and flat, it's too narrow for automobile traffic and thus perfect for cyclists and strollers who only have to cross a few streets along the way.

Although you will see some cyclists on Route 12, they are foolhardy. A better thoroughfare is **Arnold Drive**, which runs parallel to the highway from Petaluma Avenue north through the town of Glen Ellen, where it terminates at Route 12. Near that intersection is a beautiful country lane called **Dunbar Road**. This is a less-traveled route that connects Glen Ellen to Kenwood, on the west side of Route 12.

At Sugarloaf Ridge, try the nine-mile **Bald Mountain Trail** to Gray Pine and then through the meadow loop. You'll pass open meadows sprinkled with oak trees.

Bike Rentals & Tours   The **Good Time Touring Company** offers guided tours of the Wine Country. Choose from a novice-designed 12-mile roundtrip "Winery Lunch Tour" or a more ambitious 20-mile roundtrip "Custom Tour" of the valley's nether regions. For customers staying in the area, Good Time Touring delivers equipment to local hotels and B&Bs. Bike rentals are also available. Book ahead for both tours and rentals. ~ P.O. Box 1955, Sonoma, CA 95476; 707-938-0453, 888-525-0453; www.goodtimetouring.com.

GOLF

Don't worry about wearing the latest fashions to shoot some holes at **Los Arroyos Golf**. This nine-hole course is so laidback you might drift off between tees. ~ 5750 Stage Gulch Road, Sonoma; 707-938-8835.

Thanks to the hills and mountains that define the Sonoma Valley, the hiking here provides some of the best views of any trails in the Wine Country. All distances listed for hiking trails are one way unless otherwise noted.

Trails at Jack London State Historical Park include the walk to the **Wolf House ruins,** a gravel trail (1.5 miles roundtrip) that begins at the House of Happy Walls, the park's visitors center that is located about 350 feet from the parking lot. Along the way you'll see oaks and madrones and a plethora of wildflowers. A much more rigorous outing climbs **Sonoma Mountain** (8 miles roundtrip), takes four or five hours and rises 1800 feet. The trailhead is located off the parking lot.

The trails at **Sugarloaf Ridge State Park** provide opportunities to explore ridges and open fields. Every spring, wildflowers riot throughout the meadows. The park's most popular walk is along **Creekside Nature Trail** (.8 mile roundtrip). This self-guided stroll begins at the day-use picnic area and carries past stands of oak, alder, ash, maple, and Douglas fir. Watch for several species of lichen *and* poison oak! If you are up for a steep climb, try **Bald Mountain Trail** (2.7 miles), which leads to the top of the mountain. At an elevation of 2729 feet, the summit offers spectacular views of the Sonoma and Napa valleys and, on a clear day, San Francisco and the Golden Gate Bridge, the Sierras, and St. Helena. The climb begins at the day-use parking lot near the campground, which is already 1200 feet in elevation.

FIVE

Northern Sonoma County

Covering some 1600 square miles, Sonoma County is too large to tour in a day or even a weekend. It takes less than 15 minutes to drive from Santa Rosa to Healdsburg via Route 101 and only another 20 to reach Cloverdale, but once you veer off into side roads, you will be driving at only about 35 mph.

The secret to touring the area north of Santa Rosa does, after all, lie along country lanes on either side of the highway. At the center of this area is Healdsburg, a country town centered on a plaza and dating back to 1854. The Russian River flowing beside this booming small city long ago inspired many urban types to establish summer homes on its banks, and there are plenty of "river rats" living here full time as well.

Northern Sonoma County extends from Santa Rosa, the county seat located northwest of the Sonoma Valley, north to Cloverdale. The area includes major grapegrowing regions such as the Alexander Valley and the Dry Creek Valley. The Russian River region lies to the west and is covered in Chapter 6. Although Santa Rosa is the county seat and has the biggest urban area in the entire Wine Country, it has very few wineries itself.

Because there is a town of Sonoma, a valley called Sonoma and a county named Sonoma, some visitors become confused. Just as people say "New York" when they should say "New York City," a lot of northern Californians say "Sonoma" and could mean the town, the valley or the entire county. All we can say is, get used to it.

Sonoma is one of the fastest-growing counties in the Bay Area although it has lagged behind San Francisco and the San Jose area. The first people to arrive here were the Miwok and Pomo tribes, who crossed the land bridge from Asia into present-day Alaska. The first white men to arrive came aboard a Spanish ship with the explorer Francisco de Bodega y Cuadro, who was looking for San Francisco Bay. Instead, they hit landfall on the Sonoma coast in the fall of 1775.

But it was the Russians, not the Spanish, who established the first outpost, settling on a bluff to the north and building a fort there in order to protect their lucrative fur trade. They also began moving inland to warmer weather, but after the Mexican missionaries established a mission in the Sonoma Valley in the 1820s, the stage was set for the Mexican to prevail over the Russians as well as the native Indians. Most of Sonoma was still frontier country but, like most of the state, the arable portions were divided into ranchos under Mexican rule. General Mariano Vallejo, who had come to secularize the mission system, cemented his power base through his ability to apportion ranchos in the region. In the process, he convinced his widowed mother-in-law, Dona Maria Carrillo, to join the family. She settled near Santa Rosa Creek in 1837 and built the first European home in the Santa Rosa Valley.

The future town grew up around that adobe home and by 1854—four years after California became a state—wrested the county seat from the town of Sonoma. By the end of that decade, Santa Rosa boasted 100 buildings and 400 citizens. In the process of expanding, the new city boosted the fortunes of the surrounding area. A bit north, Harmon Heald settled on the Sotoyome Rancho, sold lots and helped start the town that bears his name. In 1854, Colonel A. C. Godwin opened Geyserville's first store. Italians, Swiss, British, Irish, Germans and others arrived to develop northern Sonoma. In the process, they established farms and planted vineyards using grapevines brought, by and large, from their native countries. The horticulturist Luther Burbank settled in Santa Rosa; his home and gardens are open to the public today.

Santa Rosa was well-positioned to further its leadership in the world of commerce by the time premium grapes became big business in the area. The valleys on all sides of Santa Rosa are filled with top-notch wineries eager to welcome visitors into their tasting rooms. Today, high technology, in the form of major-league companies such as Hewlett-Packard as well as numerous start-ups, is challenging wine's role as the number-one regional industry. All it takes is one Friday-afternoon rush-hour commute experience to convince anyone of what a boomtown Santa Rosa—along with its satellite communities—has become.

Santa Rosa

Santa Rosa, the largest city in Sonoma County (with over 150,000 residents) and the county seat, is home to a burgeoning high-tech industry that has put it on the list of the country's best places to live and work. The downtown area is a hodgepodge, however. Route 101, which began a widening project in 2006, dissects the city, separating the Historic Railroad Square district from the retail and office complexes of the rest of downtown. The county offices are another neighborhood entirely, located half a mile from the center of town.

SIGHTS

This is not a major tourist destination; it just sits in the middle of one. Still, there are some unusual attractions worth checking out.

HIDDEN ►

Matanzas Creek Winery and Estate Gardens is a gorgeous piece of property in the scenic Bennett Valley, particularly in the spring and early summer when some 4500 lavender plants blossom and fill the air with fragrance. Lavender products such as bath salts and sachets are for sale in the tasting room, along with the winery's lauded cabernet sauvignon, merlot, chardonnay, syrah and sauvignon blanc. Tasting fee. ~ 6097 Bennett Valley Road; 800-590-6464, fax 707-571-0156; www.matanzascreek.com, e-mail info@matanzascreek.com.

Santa Rosa is known worldwide as the home of Luther Burbank, the great horticulturist who worked miracles on plant life, creating the Santa Rosa plum, Shasta daisy, spineless cactus, and hundreds of other hybrids. His legacy remains in full bloom at the **Luther Burbank Home & Gardens**, where visitors can stroll through gardens filled with the descendants of his plant "inventions" and tour the Victorian house where he lived for 20 years. The house is open Tuesday through Sunday from April through October. Admission to tour the house. ~ Santa Rosa and Sonoma avenues; 707-524-5445, fax 707-524-5827; www.lutherburbank.org, e-mail burbankhome@lutherburbank.org.

Two years after his death, the **Charles M. Schulz Museum and Research Center** opened in 2002, a paean to the man, the cartoonist and the craft. Here, his work lives on in a grand scale. In the ground-floor Great Hall, one wall is taken up by Japanese artist Yoshiteru Otani's eye-popping 17-by-22-foot mural that depicts Lucy holding the football for Charlie; a closer view shows it's composed of 3588 "Peanuts" comic strips. Another wall is a sort of bas relief of "Morphing Snoopy," illustrating the evolution of everyone's favorite beagle's appearance. Also here are Schulz's actual studio and various permanent and changing exhibits. Closed Tuesday. Admission. ~ 2391 Hardies Lane; 707-579-4452, fax 707-579-4436; www.schulzmuseum.org, e-mail inquiries@schulz museum.org.

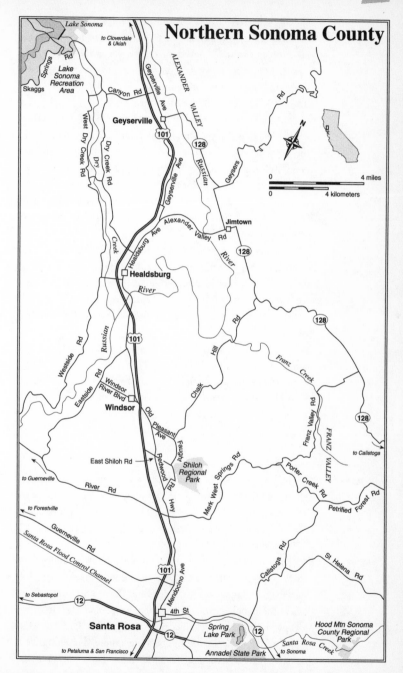

Northern Sonoma County

On the western edge of downtown, **Historic Railroad Square** was once a busy commercial and transport center. Today its buildings, some of which survived the great 1906 earthquake that destroyed much of the city center, contain antique and specialty shops and restaurants. ~ 4th and Wilson streets, located west of Route 101 and east of the railroad tracks.

The old Santa Rosa Depot has been restored and turned into a visitors center and the **Rail Room Gallery**. The museum in the former ticket office has a small display of memorabilia from the depot's past, including photographs and a model train the kids can operate. The **California Welcome Center** provides an overview of the region's wineries and attractions. ~ 9 4th Street; 707-577-8674, 800-404-7673, fax 707-571-5949; www.visit santarosa.com.

Housed in a former 1909 post office, the **Sonoma County Museum** provides a historical and cultural perspective on the region with changing exhibits, some of them designed especially for kids. Closed Monday and Tuesday. Admission. ~ 425 7th Street; 707-579-1500, fax 707-579-4849; www.sonomacounty museum.org.

The prolific creativity of North American Indians—basketry, jewelry, sculpture, beadwork, pottery and textiles—is on display at the **Jesse Peter Museum**, located at Santa Rosa Junior College. Also showcased is art from Africa, Asia, South and Central America, Mesoamerica and the Pacific. Closed mid-May to mid-August. ~ Bussman Hall, Santa Rosa Junior College, 1501 Mendocino Avenue; 707-527-4479, fax 707-527-1861; www.santa rosa.edu/museum.

HIDDEN ▶   Nearby, the **Santa Rosa Rural Cemetery** allows visitors a glimpse of the town's former inhabitants, including victims of the 1906 earthquake. Brochures available at the entrance offer a self-guided tour. ~ Franklin Avenue and Monroe Street; 707-543-3292, fax 707-543-3288.

HIDDEN ▶   **Paradise Ridge Winery** offers visitors a bit of California lore along with its wines, including chardonnay, merlot, cabernet sauvignon and sparkling blanc de blanc. The location adjoins land where the Fountaingrove winery once stood and affords an impressive view. The winemaker there was the first Japanese winemaker in the U.S., the son of a samurai whose fascinating life is the subject of an exhibit at Paradise Ridge. There's also a sculpture grove on the property. Closed weekends January through March. ~ 4545 Thomas Lake Harris Drive (off the Fountaingrove Parkway near Route 101); 707-528-9463, fax 707-528-9481; www.prwinery.com, e-mail info@prwinery.com.

If you've never seen actual airplane engines or ejection seats up close and sans plane, you can't miss them at the **Pacific Coast Air Museum**. This small museum, right next to the airport, also exhibits scale models (as well as the real deal), flight suits and a

◀ HIDDEN

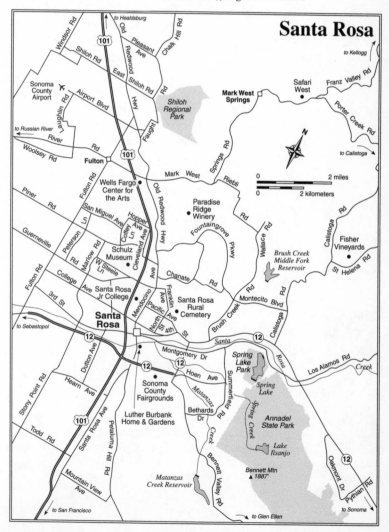

Santa Rosa

variety of aeronautical gadgetry. Closed Monday, Wednesday and Friday. ~ 2330 Becker Boulevard; 707-575-7900, fax 707-545-2813; www.pacificcoastairmuseum.org, e-mail director@pacificcoastairmuseum.org.

HIDDEN ▶

For a wild diversion, head into the hills to **Safari West**. Here, on hundreds of acres, onyx, antelope, zebras, Watusi cattle, giraffes and other endangered or threatened species roam in safety. Tours let visitors get close enough for excellent photographs at this accredited private zoo, with an open-air aviary and over 130 different bird species. By reservation only. Admission. ~ 3115 Porter Creek Road; 707-579-2551, 800-616-2695, fax 707-579-8777; www.safariwest.com, e-mail info@safariwest.com.

In the mountains outside Santa Rosa, hidden along country lanes, lies **Fisher Vineyards**. Tucked into a fold in the hills and surrounded by redwood forest, this picturesque winery is a family-style operation. The main building, a lofty board-and-batten structure in contemporary California design, was built with wood cut and milled on the site, and overlooks the surrounding vineyards. Planted primarily with cabernet sauvignon, chardonnay, and merlot vines, the winery produces a small but delicious quantity of wine each season. Visiting by appointment only. Closed weekends. ~ 6200 St. Helena Road; 707-539-7511, fax 707-539-3601; www.fishervineyards.com, e-mail info@fishervineyards.com.

LODGING

While small inns abound in the small towns in this section, there are few in the big city of Santa Rosa. You can find a couple of sizable hotels, however, as well as a smattering of motels.

AUTHOR FAVORITE

Charles Schulz, the soft-spoken cartoonist whose "Peanuts" comic strip made him famous around the world, died in 2000, just weeks after he retired from 50 years of drawing the daily cartoon. By then, the strip, in which deceptively simple and older-than-their-years characters depicted pain, loss and confusion with humor, warmth and even fuzziness, was being published in more than 26,000 newspapers. Some 20,000 "Peanuts" products were in circulation, and fans of Charlie Brown, Lucy, Linus, Snoopy and their pals had formed clubs around the globe. In 2002, his adopted home of Santa Rosa unveiled the **Charles M. Schulz Museum and Research Center**. See page 130 for more information.

Conveniently located on the border of east Santa Rosa, the **Flamingo Resort Hotel** is close to two shopping centers as well as the county fairgrounds, yet not far from the wineries of the Sonoma Valley. It has a very '50s feel to it, but the 170 rooms (half of which are on the ground floor) are well-maintained. The landscaping is attractive and links the disparate buildings. A big swimming pool and a restaurant are among the amenities; for a fee, guests also have access to the fitness center, day spa and tennis courts. ~ 2777 4th Street; 707-545-8530, 800-848-8300, fax 707-528-1404; www.flamingoresort.com, e-mail info@flamingo resort.com. MODERATE.

You can stay in the heart of Santa Rosa's fascinating Historic Railroad Square at **Hotel La Rose**, built in 1907 by the same Italian stonemasons who were responsible for the old Santa Rosa depot. It has been listed on the National Register of Historic Places and is a member of Historic Hotels of America. English country style describes the decor, with dark greens and rose-red colors. Some guest rooms sport four-poster beds. The fourth-floor attic rooms have sloping ceilings, and some are brightened by skylights. A sundeck is available to guests. ~ 308 Wilson Street; 707-579-3200, 800-527-6738, fax 707-579-3247; www.hotellarose.com, e-mail reservations@hotellarose. com. DELUXE.

A 155-room inn in the Railroad Square district, the **Hyatt Vineyard Creek Hotel & Spa** offers full convention services as well as a spa, pool and restaurant. The three-story hotel with terra-cotta tile roofs has a Mediterranean look, enhanced with interior courtyards. Throughout, the color scheme runs to yummy colors like burgundy, persimmon, aubergine and green. Large-scale furnishings and the use of stone and granite—instead of marble—add extra warmth. ~ 170 Railroad Street; 707-284-1234, fax 707-636-7130; www.vineyardcreek.hyatt.com, e-mail salessonom@hyatt. com. DELUXE TO ULTRA-DELUXE.

One of the best deals in town is the **Sandman Motel**, where 136 rooms on two floors are attractive if not spectacular. Amenities far surpass those of most motels—a heated pool, hot tub, laundry room, refrigerator in each room and a microwave in some. It's not in a pretty location, but it is close to shops and restaurants and the Sonoma County Civic Center. ~ 3421 Cleveland Avenue; 707-544-8570, fax 707-544-8710. MODERATE.

HIDDEN ▶   The **Fountaingrove Inn** on the north side of Santa Rosa is one of very few non-chain hotels in the area. Its lowrise structure of stone and redwood has 124 modest but comfortable guest rooms. Amenities include a swimming pool, a hot tub and a restaurant as well as a complimentary continental breakfast. ~ 101 Fountaingrove Parkway; 707-566-6101, 800-222-6101, fax 707-544-3126; www.fountaingroveinn.com, e-mail reservations@fountain groveinn.com. DELUXE.

    Surrounded by 92 acres of vineyards, the **Vintners Inn** has the ambience of a European estate, despite the proximity of a major highway. Its 44 spacious rooms and suites are housed in a cluster of two-story townhouses interspersed with courtyards, fountains and landscaping.

HIDDEN ▶   The 30 tent cabins at **Safari West** are a rough approximation of fine bush camps in Africa—that is, they afford a sense of wilderness while coddling guests with modern amenities. Choices include accommodations near the entrance, with views of the giraffes, and newer ones up the hill, some of which overlook a pond visited by wildlife. A combination of canvas walls and hardwood floors, the cabins are furnished minimally but tastefully, with luxurious beds and lamps fashioned from local woods. Each of the stilted cabins features a small porch for watching wildlife with a cup of coffee or a glass of wine in your hand, binoculars in the other. One real cottage is available for hedonists. Breakfast is included; lunch and dinner are available. There's a two-night weekend minimum June through August. ~ 3115 Porter Creek Road; 707-579-2551, 800-616-2695, fax 707-579-8777; www.safariwest.com, e-mail info@safariwest. com. ULTRA-DELUXE.

DINING   It's hard to think of any type of cooking that isn't available in the Santa Rosa vicinity, from burgers to Thai food to haute cuisine. Few restaurants here can match the upscale offerings in Sonoma and Napa; on the other hand, same-day reservations are usually possible. Good ethnic deals can be found in the vicinity of the Santa Rosa Junior College campus.

HIDDEN ▶   There's no way you'd find **Pamposh** without good directions; it's in a modest shopping strip that gives no hint of the exotic decor and cuisine inside. To get your taste buds hopping, start your meal with "poppers"—thin wafers of lentil flour and cumin seeds served alongside a refreshing mix of diced cucumbers, onions, mangos and peppers. Chef's specials such as chicken with apricot offer a departure from otherwise traditional Indian fare. ~ 52 Mission Circle; 707-538-3367. BUDGET TO MODERATE.

Hank's Creekside Café is a cozy spot near the corner of Farmer's Lane where many of the city's movers and shakers come for power breakfasts of crab-cake Benedict, pancakes and a wide selection of sausages including a Cajun version and a British banger. Lunch is a bit more pedestrian, with a mix of sandwiches, burgers, salads and homemade chili. At night, American homestyle food such as meatloaf grace the menu. ~ 2800 4th Street; 707-575-8839. BUDGET TO MODERATE.

Serving fresh Sonoma County cuisine in the Railroad Square district since 1990, **Mixx "Enoteca Luigi" Ristorante & Bar** makes good use of the region's agricultural bounty, including 25 wines that can be sampled by the glass. The contemporary dining room with Italianate touches and an elegant mahogany bar imported from Europe is the place to sample chicken breast stuffed with sundried tomatoes, goat cheese in pinot noir sauce, and Liberty duck with a tamarind glaze. Closed Sunday. ~ 135 4th Street; 707-573-1344, fax 707-573-0631; www.mixxrestaurant. com. MODERATE TO DELUXE.

Seafood Brasserie serves three meals a day on the Vineyard Creek Hotel property. Dinner entrées include duck, sea bass and ahi tuna as well as non-seafood items like steaks. Decor includes

AUTHOR FAVORITE

If I hadn't previously been to the location where **Latitude** opened in 2004, I would probably never have found it. This gem of a seafood restaurant, located just south of Santa Rosa in a building that formerly housed a wine-and-tourism welcome center, has indoor and outdoor seating overlooking a small manmade lake. The decor is seafaring but tasteful, with elegant, elongated Indonesian fish nets serving as chandeliers and wave patterns on the pale green carpet. Latitude lists numerous starters and salads, including a Maui-style ahi tuna *poki*, and main plates ranging from grilled seafood brochette to grilled Black Angus rib-eye. The fried calamari is the best I've ever tasted. (Their secret? They roll them in grits before frying.) ~ 5000 Roberts Lake Drive, Rohnert Park; 707-588-1800. DELUXE TO ULTRA-DELUXE.

photographs and other memorabilia from the time Grace Brothers Brewing Company operated on this site. ~ 170 Railroad Street; 707-636-7100, fax 707-636-7380. MODERATE TO ULTRA-DELUXE.

The Wine Country is not a theme park, appearances to the contrary. If you need proof, sample the exquisite Chinese cuisine at **Gary Chu's**. This excellent restaurant depends on the locals who love it. Chu's gives diners a taste of Chinese-California haute cuisine with refined fare such as walnut prawns in a sweet, creamy apple dressing, sea scallops with champagne sauce and Mongolian beef. Service is impeccable, the wine list filled with good choices, and the location central to downtown shops and theaters. Closed Monday. ~ 611 5th Street; 707-526-5840, fax 707-526-3102. BUDGET TO DELUXE.

The chefs at **Zazu** are full of clever innovations, such as pairing seared tuna with bing cherries and making the combination work. In a ramshackle building west of Santa Rosa, Zazu's weekly changing menu peddles a seasonal mix of playful American food and northern Italian fare—with a twist—split between small and big plates. Typical of the former are jingle bell peppers with house-made sausage, and poppyseed-crusted soft-shell crab; of the latter, star anise–rubbed duck and grilled rack of lamb with quinoa tabbouleh. Many housemade desserts feature fresh local fruit. Closed Tuesday. ~ 3535 Guerneville Road; 707-523-4814; www.zazu restaurant.com. ULTRA-DELUXE.

Look for the brick storefront that heralds **El Capitan**. This colorful but very modest spot turns out fresh burritos and other fast Mexican food, with daily specials that lean towards the vegetarian. ~ 544 Mendocino Avenue; 707-545-9476. BUDGET.

You cannot find fresher or tastier Thai food than what comes out of the kitchen at **Jhanthong Banbua**. Located in front of a

SKATING IN THE PEANUTS GALLERY

The Redwood Empire Ice Arena may be the only sports facility ever created by a cartoonist. It was built in 1969 by the late Charles Schulz of "Peanuts" fame for his children. Snoopy's Gallery and Gift Shop, also part of the facility, sells Snoopy memorabilia, books, clothing and life-size comic strip characters. Call ahead to confirm the arena is open to the public on the day you wish to visit. ~ 1667 West Steele Lane, Santa Rosa; 707-546-7147, fax 707-546-3764; www.snoopyshomeice.com.

motel near the Santa Rosa Junior College campus, this pretty place knocks itself out with service and a menu with something for everyone. Particularly fine are the pad thai and anything with shrimp. No lunch on Saturday. Closed Sunday. ~ 2400 Mendocino Avenue; 707-528-8048. MODERATE.

Sassafras specializes in all-American fare. Typical dishes include crab cakes and New York steak. Most classics have been tweaked: the meatloaf sandwich with ketchup and mustard, for instance, is really a bourbon-laced venison and pork terrine with plum ketchup, whole-grain mustard and toasts. No lunch on weekends. ~ 1229 North Dutton Avenue; 707-578-7600; www. sassafrasrestaurant.com. MODERATE TO DELUXE.

One of the first Wine Country restaurants to champion the region's natural resources, **John Ash & Co.** continues that mission long after its namesake departed the kitchen. Produce from nearby fields, fish from the sea and locally made cheeses and breads still star on the menu; for example, Laura Chenel and Bellwether Farm cheeses, roasted pears, Sonoma greens, fresh-picked herbs appear in many appetizers and entrées, along with locally raised beef, pork and chicken. Three large rooms, with high ceilings and plenty of windows, overlook a glass-enclosed patio that is heated in the winter and opens up when weather permits. Small plates are available in the Front Room. No lunch on Saturday. ~ 4330 Barnes Road; 707-527-7687, 800-421-2584, fax 707-527-1202; www. johnashrestaurant.com. ULTRA-DELUXE.

◄ HIDDEN

Before there were malls, there were lowrise shopping complexes like **Montgomery Village**, where locally owned stores tended to serve the upscale customer. Here you can find several mini-blocks of shops, all housed in wood structures painted dark brown. Among them are **The Competitor** (707-578-5689), which has the Wine Country's best selection of men's and women's clothing and accessories for both golf and tennis. **Copperfield's Books** (707-578-8938) is a comfortable, well-stocked store big on local authors. For fancy home accessories, the place to browse is **Ireko** (707-579-3700), which almost qualifies as an art gallery thanks to the high quality of its merchandise. ~ 2421 Magowan Drive at Farmers Lane.

SHOPPING

In and around Railroad Square, west of downtown and Route 101, you can find an assortment of offbeat stores, particularly antique shops. One of the best is **Whistle Stop Antiques,** where more than 35 dealers in antiques and collectibles are spread out over 10,000 square feet. ~ 130 4th Street; 707-542-9474.

It's Halloween all year long at **Disguise the Limit,** where you can find the paraphernalia to be a clown, a queen or an alien from outer space. Also here are toys and a few magic tricks to put up your sleeve. ~ 100 4th Street; 707-575-1477.

The **Santa Rosa Farmer's Market** is held every Wednesday and Saturday morning year-round in the parking lot at the Sonoma County Veterans Memorial Building—rain or shine. Growers from all over the region bring their produce, flowers and crafts for one of the liveliest markets in the Wine Country, located just off Route 12 east of the intersection with Route 101. ~ 1351 Maple Avenue; 707-522-8629.

Santa Rosa Wednesday Night Market is open from May through August in the downtown blocks around 4th and D streets, which are blocked to automobile traffic from about 5 to 8:30 p.m. These nights take on the flavor of a street fair on balmy summer nights, when couples and family make an evening of strolling and shopping. ~ 4th Street at Courthouse Square; 707-524-2123, fax 707-545-6914; www.srdowntownmarket.com.

NIGHTLIFE From Lily Tomlin to Diana Ross, the **Wells Fargo Center for the Arts** offers a wide variety of cultural and popular programming, some 120 performances a year. The center is host to four artistic companies, including the Santa Rosa Symphony and Healdsburg Guitar Festival. ~ 50 Mark West Springs Road; 707-546-3600; www.wellsfargocenterarts.com.

The **Santa Rosa Symphony** frequently attracts sell-out crowds to its performances at the Wells Fargo Center. The season runs from October until May on Saturday and Monday nights and

AUTHOR FAVORITE

Nothing will humble you faster than trying to learn salsa dancing, but I love to try at the **Flamingo Resort Hotel**. In addition to salsa, swing, jazz, country, rock, karaoke and live music fill the bill. Cover most nights. ~ 4th Street at Farmers Lane, Santa Rosa; 707-545-8530 ext. 727.

Sunday afternoons (with seven different concerts presented three times each). ~ 50 Santa Rosa Avenue; 707-546-8742, fax 707-546-0460; www.santarosasymphony.com.

The **Summer Repertory Theatre** is a high-energy group that stages five different major plays and musicals in the space of two months in June, July and August. The SRT sticks to the tried-and-true but has a reputation for top-notch production values. ~ 1501 Mendocino Avenue; 707-527-4343, fax 707-524-1689; www.santarosa.edu/srt.

There are some 47 parks in the Santa Rosa area, from pocket parks to places large enough to accommodate horseback riders and campgrounds.

PARKS

ANNADEL STATE PARK 🏃 🚣 Possessing a wealth of possibilities, this 5000-acre facility has 40 miles of trails through meadow and forest. A volcanic mountain flanks one end of the park and a lake provides fishing for black bass and bluegill. There's also a marsh where many of the area's 160 bird species flock. Blacktailed deer and coyotes roam the region. The park has picnic areas and pit toilets. Day-use fee, $6. ~ Off Route 12, about five miles east of Santa Rosa; 707-539-3911, fax 707-538-0769.

SPRING LAKE PARK 🏃 🚲 🏇 🚣 🛶 🚤 One of the most popular in the region, this 314-acre park is on the east side of Santa Rosa. The lagoon is open in summer only; it has lifeguards. Non-power boats can be rented and fishing is allowed; the lake contains catfish, trout, bluegill and bass. If you want to go horseback riding, you have to bring your own mount. The park has picnic areas and toilets. Parking fee, $6. ~ 5585 Newanga Avenue; 707-539-8092, fax 707-538-8038.

▲ There are 31 campsites, no electricity or water; $18 per night. ~ 707-565-2267.

YOUTH COMMUNITY PARK 🏃 🚲 A creek runs through this partially undeveloped park, situated on former vineyard and orchard grounds on the west side of Santa Rosa. Popular activities include strolling and picnicking beneath oak trees; BMX enthusiasts, armed with shovels, often create their own dirt mounds in the undeveloped portion for jumps. Although designed as a skate park, other facilities include a playground, a picnic area and restrooms. ~ 1725 Fulton Road; 707-543-3292.

◄ *HIDDEN*

▼▼▼▼▼▼▼▼▼▼▼▼▼▼▼▼▼▼▼▼▼▼▼▼
Healdsburg and Points North

North of Santa Rosa, the county of Sonoma includes the towns of Windsor, Healdsburg, Geyserville and Cloverdale, which is on the border with Mendocino County. There is more open space the farther north you travel, but every week—or so it seems—more and more grapevines are planted within sight of the main highway.

SIGHTS

It's about 25 miles via Route 101 from Santa Rosa to the city of **Healdsburg**. Once known as the "buckle in California's prune belt"—a moniker derived from the days when orchards, not vineyards, dominated the landscape—this town has evolved into a lively burg with a flourishing downtown packed with shops, restaurants and lodgings. The center of activity is **Healdsburg Plaza**, a park landscaped with palm and oak trees where people really do picnic. On summer weekends, free concerts are occasionally offered here.

At the **Healdsburg Chamber of Commerce & Visitors Bureau** you can pick up maps, brochures and other information on the region. ~ 217 Healdsburg Avenue, Healdsburg; 707-433-6935, 800-648-9922, fax 707-433-7562; www.healdsburg.org, e-mail info@healdsburg.org.

The **Healdsburg Museum** is housed in the revamped Carnegie library two blocks from the plaza. Featuring a recently expanded and redesigned permanent display, the museum focuses on regional history and offers exhibits of rare Pomo baskets as well as 19th-century artifacts such as tools and clothing; changing exhibits tend to focus on a single subject. Closed Monday. ~ 221 Matheson Street, Healdsburg; 707-431-3325, fax 707-473-4471; www.healdsburgmuseum.org, e-mail healdsburgmuseum @sbcglobal.net.

Healdsburg is centrally located for exploring several wine appellations, including the Dry Creek Valley, Russian River Valley and Alexander Valley. The roads linking the wineries provide some of the most pleasant driving anywhere in the Wine Country.

In the Russian River Valley southwest of Healdsburg, **Rodney Strong Vineyards** has a spacious and attractive visitors center with light walls and polished hardwood floors and cabinetry. The winery also offers an exhibit, a self-guided Wine Gallery Tour that explains the history of Sonoma County winemaking as well as that of the winery, which was established in 1959. Guided tours are also available daily. ~ 11455 Old Redwood Highway, Healdsburg; 707-433-6521, fax 707-433-0939; www.rodney strong.com, e-mail info@rodneystrong.com.

Dry Creek Valley, a luxurious landscape of vineyards and forest, stretches to the west of Healdsburg and is known for its plethora of family-owned wineries.

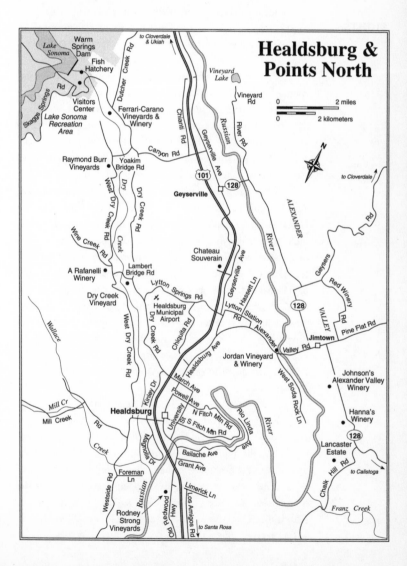

A sixth-generation member of a Swedish grape-growing family opened the **Mauritson Family Winery** in 2004. The sleek, contemporary building is easy to spot, thanks to the bright red Adirondack chairs set out on the entry terrace. Among the distinctive wines to taste here are the sauvignon blanc (lots of grapefruit aromas) and the petit syrah from the Mauritson homestead vineyard in the nearby Rockpile appellation, which is famous for producing intensely flavored red wines. Vineyard tours by appointment. ~ 2859 Dry Creek Road, Healdsburg; 707-431-0804; www.mauritsonwines.com, e-mail info@mauritson wines.com.

Dry Creek Vineyard sits in an ivy-covered building surrounded by shade trees. There's tasting every day and the winery provides picnic tables for guests. Among the excellent wines produced are chenin blancs, fumés, cabernets, chardonnays, merlots and zinfandels. ~ 3770 Lambert Bridge Road, Healdsburg; 707-433-1000, 800-864-9463, fax 707-433-5329; www.drycreek vineyard.com, e-mail dcv@drycreekvineyard.com.

Dutcher Crossing, which began producing cabernet sauvignon, chardonnay, sauvignon blanc and zinfandel from the Dry Creek and Anderson valleys in 2005, is housed in a cedar-plank building designed to resemble a century-old barn, complete with cupolas and a pitched roof. Split by an open breezeway that shelters picnic tables, the winery is surrounded by vineyards and panoramic vistas. The tasting room has hickory plank floors, a polished limestone tasting bar, a vaulted beam ceiling, and a conversational area furnished and decorated in early-American style. Private tours and tastings by appointment only. Tasting fee. ~ 8533 Dry Creek Road, Healdsburg; 707-431-2700, 866-431-2711; www.dutchercrossingwinery.com, e-mail info@dutcher crossingwinery.com.

One of the top gardens in the Wine Country can be found on the grounds of the **Ferrari-Carano Vineyards & Winery**, the last winery on Dry Creek Road before it ends at Lake Sonoma. Another highlight is the impressive underground barrel-aging cellar. Wind up a visit in the hospitality center called Villa Fiore, where fumé blanc, chardonnay, merlot and cabernet sauvignon are among the best options for tasting. Tasting fee. ~ 8761 Dry Creek Road, Healdsburg; 707-433-6700, 800-831-0381, fax 707-431-1742; www.ferrari-carano.com.

A. Rafanelli Winery, a classic family-style enterprise, now in its fourth generation, produces excellent wines in limited quantities. The winery itself consists of an old barn behind the family home. Tasting is by appointment. ~ 4685 West Dry Creek Road, Healdsburg; 707-433-1385, fax 707-433-3836; www.arafanelli winery.com.

Lambert Bridge Winery sits atop a knoll off a winding country road not far from its namesake, the only surviving single-lane, public bridge in Dry Creek Valley. Housed in a low-rise bungalow fronted with ancient wisteria vines, the winery pours its cabernet sauvignon, chardonnay, merlot, petit sirah, syrah, zinfandel and other limited-production varietals in a tasting room outfitted with a curly redwood bar and a large granite hearth. Outside, several teak picnic tables are set amid the winery's landscaped gardens. Tasting fee. ~ 4085 West Dry Creek Road, Healdsburg; 707-431-9600, 800-975-0555; www.lambertbridge.com, e-mail wines@lambertbridge.com.

Lambert Bridge Winery's landscaped gardens are where pizza-making classes are conducted in an alfresco kitchen on spring and summer weekends.

Raymond Burr Vineyards, named for the late actor made famous by his role as TV's *Perry Mason*, occupies a hillside slice of the Dry Creek Valley. Visitors can sample cabernet sauvignon, cabernet franc, chardonnay and port on the oak-shaded deck of the tiny tasting room. They can also tour the winery's orchid greenhouse by appointment on weekends. ~ 8339 West Dry Creek Road, Healdsburg; 707-433-4365, 888-900-0024, fax 707-431-1843; www.raymondburrvineyards.com, e-mail rburrwine@aol.com.

Founded in 1902 by Edoardo Seghesio, who immigrated from Italy in the late 1800s, **Seghesio Family Vineyards** exudes Old World charm. The winery produces sangiovese and other Italian varietals, but its real claim to fame is its zinfandel. Before or after tasting, visitors can play bocce ball or picnic in a redwood grove. ~ 14730 Grove Street, Healdsburg; 707-433-7764, fax 707-433-0545; www.seghesio.com, e-mail seghesio@seghesio.com.

East of Healdsburg lies the **Alexander Valley**, a region highly regarded for its distinct viticultural characteristics. Because of its warm climate, the valley is sometimes compared with the Bordeaux area of France.

Jordan Vineyard & Winery is a hilltop facility built along the lines of a Bordeaux château, and the winery is housed in a grand building that overlooks the Alexander Valley. Tours are a real treat, providing a glimpse into a winery whose elegance matches its excellence. Tours and tastings by appointment. Closed Sunday and for one week at Christmas. ~ 1474 Alexander Valley Road, Healdsburg; 707-431-5250, 800-654-1213, fax 707-431-5259; www.jordanwinery.com, e-mail info@jordanwinery.com.

A long road leads to an unpainted redwood barn housing **Johnson's Alexander Valley Winery**. There is a wealth of modern equipment around the place, which produces fine pinot noirs, zinfandels and cabernets. Family-owned, this funky little winery offers tasting anytime. ~ 8333 Route 128, Healdsburg; 707-433-2319, 800-888-5532, fax 707-433-5302; www.funvacation.net/johnsons.html, e-mail johnsons@funvacation.net.

The 1924 theater pipe organ at Johnson's Alexander Valley Winery is used for the winery's occasional concerts.

The broad veranda that wraps around **Hanna Winery**'s Mediterranean-style tasting room overlooks cabernet sauvignon and merlot vineyards as well as a chunk of the Alexander Valley. Hanna is also known for producing other award-winning wines, including the sauvignon blanc from its Russian River property. ~ 9280 Route 128, Healdsburg; 707-431-4310, 800-854-3987; www.hannawinery.com.

HIDDEN ►

Located out of sight beside a winding country road, the 53-acre **Lancaster Estate** welcomes visitors into a salon-style hospitality center for seated tastings of cabernet sauvignon, made in the Bordeaux style with small amounts of merlot, cabernet franc, malbec and petit verdot. The winery also offers tours of the vineyards in a chauffeur-driven SUV. Tours and tastings by appointment only. ~ 15001 Chalk Hill Road, Healdsburg; 707-433-8178; www.lancasterestate.com, e-mail hospitality@lancasterestate.com.

Route 101 streams north past Ukiah and several more wineries. A more interesting course lies along **Route 128**, which leads northwest from Cloverdale through piedmont country. En route, the two-lane road meanders like an old river, bending back upon itself to reveal sloping meadows and tree-tufted glades. It's a beautiful country drive through rolling ranch land. Sheep graze the hills and an occasional farmhouse stands along the roadside, its windows blinking sunlight at solitary cars.

LODGING

Numerous country inns dot the area, including some in the hearts of towns, some in rural areas and some practically across the street from vineyards. There are no large hotels in the northern part of the county, but you can find a couple of inexpensive motels.

In an area dotted with B&Bs and charming little hostelries, **Hotel Healdsburg** is a good option if you're looking for something a bit more modern. Its 55 rooms and suites come in a palette of lime greens and butter yellows, with wood floors, Tibetan rugs and sleek furnishings. Shuttered French doors lead to balconies with views of the plaza or the countryside. All accommodations have extra-large baths, high-speed internet connections, two-line portable phones, a mini-fridge and luxuries like Frette bathrobes. On site are a restaurant, a spa, a garden pool and a café/newsstand. ~ 25 Matheson Street, Healdsburg; 707-431-2800, 800-889-7188, fax 707-431-0414; www.hotelhealds burg.com, e-mail frontoffice@hotelhealdsburg.com. ULTRA-DELUXE.

The **Les Mars Hotel** was patterned on the French model: an urban inn with the charm, warmth and ambience of a chateau in the countryside. From the 17th-century Flemish tapestry and Louis IV faceted cut-glass chandelier that set the tone in the lobby to the polished, hand-carved library walls, every detail exudes refinement. The second-floor accommodations are decorated along the same lines; those on the third floor are more rustic, but all 16 rooms have custom four-poster beds and 18th- and 19th-century antiques that blend with newer pieces. ~ 27 North Street, Healdsburg; 707-433-4211, 877-431-1700; www.lesmars hotel.com, e-mail inquiries@lesmarshotel.com. ULTRA-DELUXE.

A few blocks off the Healdsburg plaza sits the **Haydon Street Inn**, a lovely bed and breakfast set in a vintage 1912 house situated near the town plaza. Each room is beautifully appointed with antique furniture and artistic wallhangings. Both the private rooms and the common areas are quite spacious. The tree-shaded lawn, comfortable living room, and wraparound front porch are a perfect expression of Main Street, America. Serving a full breakfast and afternoon refreshments, the inn has eight rooms in the main building and the separate carriage house, all with private baths and air conditioning; several rooms feature jacuzzi tubs and/or fireplaces. ~ 321 Haydon Street, Healdsburg; 707-433-5228, 800-528-3703, fax 707-433-6637; www.haydon.com, e-mail inn keeper@haydon.com. DELUXE TO ULTRA-DELUXE.

The **Healdsburg Inn on the Plaza** occupies two floors that once housed a Wells Fargo bank. There are 12 spacious rooms, each fully equipped with a fireplace, a private bath and a bay window or balcony. ~ 112 Matheson Street, Healdsburg; 707-433-6991, 800-431-8663, fax 707-433-9513; www.healdsburginn.com, e-mail healdsburginn@foursisters.com. ULTRA-DELUXE.

The ultimate Victoriana choice is the **Camellia Inn**, which retains many of its original architectural details such as 12-foot ceilings and twin fireplaces in the double parlor. Guest accommodations located in the main house are traditional with chandeliers, oriental rugs and period antiques, though newer additions tend to feature more contemporary decor. A major-league breakfast is served in the formal dining room. Camellias bloom copiously during the winter and a pool in the back is a most welcome sight after a hot day of winetasting. ~ 211 North Street, Healdsburg; 707-433-8182, 800-727-8182; www.camelliainn.com, e-mail info@camelliainn.com. DELUXE TO ULTRA-DELUXE.

> Sonoma County alone encompasses roughly 1600 square miles, far more than the entire state of Rhode Island.

Healdsburg's first B&B, the **Grape Leaf Inn** has seven guest rooms that were added to the original five in this 1900 Queen Anne Victorian. Located just a couple of blocks from the plaza, the inn's decor is Victorian in theme. Each room is named for a grape varietal; Gamay Rose, for example, has rose-colored Ralph Lauren wall coverings while Mourvedre is tucked into an octagonal turret. Every afternoon in the Speakeasy, a hidden, cellar-like room, guests are served cheese and an array of boutique wines (which are available for sale). Stay includes a full country breakfast. ~ 539 Johnson Street, Healdsburg; 707-433-8140, 866-433-8140, fax 707-433-3140; www.grapeleafinn.com, e-mail info@grapeleafinn.com. ULTRA-DELUXE.

Built in 1881 as a private summer retreat, the **Madrona Manor Country Inn** is a charming example of Gothic Victorian architecture, complete with a balconied porch, turrets and gables. The best rooms are in the main house; they are spacious (two upstairs sport a shared veranda) and furnished in serious antiques, including chaises longues and armoires. There are an additional 12 accommodations in several outbuildings on an eight-acre site as well as a carriage house. Guests enjoy the pool and a breakfast buffet. The on-site restaurant whips up eclectic California cuisine. Children under 12 are not allowed. ~ 1001 Westside Road, Healdsburg; 707-433-4231, 800-258-4003, fax 707-433-0703; www.madronamanor.com, e-mail info@madronamanor.com. ULTRA-DELUXE.

The **Hope-Merrill House** is a perennial favorite, an appealingly comfortable inn with oodles of Victorian touches. Eight guest rooms on two floors in this late-19th-century building are cozily decorated with antiques and period replica wallpaper. Unusual for a B&B, it has a pool in the garden. Across the street is the Hope-Bosworth House, with an additional four rooms. ~ 21253 Geyserville Avenue, Geyserville; 707-857-3356, 800-825-4233, fax 707-857-4673; www.hope-inns.com, e-mail moreinfo@ hope-inns.com. DELUXE TO ULTRA-DELUXE.

If you're yearning to retreat back into the '60s, check out **Isis**   ◄ HIDDEN
Oasis, a ten-acre hideaway that combines bed-and-breakfast facilities with massage, tarot readings, and past-life experiences. Set in the tiny town of Geyserville, you can wander the Egyptian-style grounds, which includes an obelisk and a labyrinth, and luxuriate in the hot tub, sauna and swimming pool. There is also a zoo with exotic animals and birds, an Egyptian meditation temple, and a "tomb room" for deep meditation. ~ 20889 Geyserville Avenue, Geyserville; 707-857-4747, 800-679-7387, fax 707-857-3544; www.isisoasis.org, e-mail isis@isisoasis.org. MODERATE.

You could dine for a week just by patronizing the restaurants on   **DINING**
and near the Healdsburg plaza. Most of the places described below are locally owned and operated and offer an eclectic choice of experiences and prices.

Dry Creek Kitchen, a sister of Charlie Palmer's Aureole restaurant in New York City, is on the lobby level of the chic Hotel Healdsburg. It is an elegant room with lots of picture windows looking out onto the patio and the town plaza. A daily changing menu exploits local products with dishes like spice-crusted duck breast, California yellowtail jack with soy-balsamic glaze and heirloom tomatoes with pickled torpedo onions. The wine list is all Sonoma. ~ 317 Healdsburg Avenue, Healdsburg; 707-431-0330; www.drycreekkitchen.com. ULTRA-DELUXE.

Healdsburg's rapid ascent into the most chic town in Sonoma County was topped in 2005 with the opening of **Cyrus**. Located next door to Les Mars Hotel, Cyrus instantly became a destination restaurant known for exciting food combinations such as hoisin-glazed squab with black-bean rice cakes and Fuyu persimmons; toasted chestnut and sherry soup with chives; and striped bass with braised cabbage and roasted butternut squash.

It is an intimate, alluring room with a vaulted dome ceiling beneath which tables are set with sterling silver and Riedel crystal. Dinner only. ~ 29 North Street, Healdsburg; 707-433-3311, fax 707-433-6633; www.cyrusrestaurant.com. ULTRA-DELUXE.

Bistro Ralph is a small but chic place that locals patronize on a regular basis. The food is interesting and adventurous, yet recognizable. You might call it California home-style, featuring fresh produce, fish and some heartier fare in a minimalist setting. The place is known for its imaginative wine offerings. Closed Sunday. ~ 109 Plaza Street, Healdsburg; 707-433-1380, fax 707-433-1974. MODERATE TO DELUXE.

You can hang out at the pretty dark-paneled bar and order your oysters or clams from a chalkboard list or be seated at your choice of booths or tables at **Willi's Seafood and Raw Bar**. Surrounded by seagoing colors like green and teal, you may have a hard time deciding among a menu with lots of small plates. Not all of them are seafood, although specialties include shrimp, ceviche and, in season, the local Dungeness crab. Willi's also serves pork riblets, skewered hanger steak and the like. ~ 403 Healdsburg Avenue, Healdsburg; 707-433-9191. MODERATE.

Tucked inside a brick facade, **Santi** is more upscale than its red-checkered tablecloths would suggest. The all-Italian menu changes seasonally but features specialties such as local braised spring lamb with soft polenta and onions; tripe Florentine; and homemade gnocchi with shrimp. Wednesday-night specials offer a main course and salad combo at a moderate price. Dinner only. ~ 21047 Geyserville Avenue, Geyserville; 707-857-1790; www.tavernasanti.com, e-mail office@tavernasanti.com. DELUXE.

HIDDEN ▶   In a cute roadside bungalow, the **Hoffman House Wine Country** is a warm and welcoming spot where soups, salads and sizable made-to-order sandwiches can be accompanied by an inexpensive

A VERY GREEN AFFAIR

From May through October, every Saturday morning and Tuesday afternoon at the North Plaza parking lot, the **Healdsburg Farmers Market** is a smorgasbord of berries, stone fruit, lettuces and artisanal cheeses and other goodies for the picnic basket. ~ North and Vine streets, Healdsburg; 707-431-1956.

glass of wine. It's one of the few places in Geyserville that's open on Monday and Tuesday. In winter, grab a table by the cozy fireplace. No dinner. ~ 21712 Geyserville Avenue, Geyserville; 707-857-3264. BUDGET.

Healdsburg's plaza is flanked with a dozen or more shops, with things for kids as well as gourmet foods and home furnishings and accessories.

SHOPPING

Susan Graf Ltd. carries a wide array of high-end designer clothing and accessories. ~ 100 Matheson Street, Healdsburg; 707-433-6495.

Three tiny wine-tasting stations can be found at **Plaza Farms**, a collective that also houses outlets for artisan food producers such as Bellwether Creamery, DaVero olive oil and Scharffen Berger chocolates. ~ 106 Matheson Street, Healdsburg; 707-433-2345.

One of the best sources for regional guides and wine-related books as well as literature is **Toyon Books**. ~ 104 Matheson Street, Healdsburg; 707-433-9270.

The posh **Saint Dizier Home** showroom specializes in Ralph Lauren furnishings but also carries deluxe accessories such as accent pillows and ice buckets. ~ 259 Center Street, Healdsburg; 707-473-0980; www.sdhdesign.com.

The Healdsburg branch of Napa's renowned **Oakville Grocery** is twice the size of the original, with an awesome assortment of condiments and wine along with fresh produce, juices and cheese. ~ 124 Matheson Street, Healdsburg; 707-433-3200.

Healdsburg Avenue boasts more antique stores than any other street in town and probably even the county. Some 20 dealers peddle their wares at **Healdsburg Classics**, which is known for its wide range of period furniture and other knickknacks. ~ 226 Healdsburg Avenue, Healdsburg; 707-433-4315.

Midnight Sun Children's Shoppe is devoted to name-brand clothing for boys and girls from infant sizes on up. ~ 107 Plaza Street, Healdsburg; 707-433-3800.

Midnight Sun Bed & Bath Shoppe carries all-natural Egyptian cotton sheets, duvets and blankets; home accents; and nightwear. ~ 355 Healdsburg Avenue, Healdsburg; 707-431-7085.

Northern Sonoma County is pretty quiet at night, but on Saturday nights there is almost always a live band (rarely is there a cover),

NIGHTLIFE

which may be blues, Latin jazz or something else playing at a local venue, like the Raven Theater. Call the **Bear Republic Brewing Company** for information and tickets. The brewpub also hosts occasional live entertainment on-site. ~ 345 Healdsburg Avenue, Healdsburg; 707-433-2337; www.bearrepublic.com.

PARKS **LAKE SONOMA** 🚶🚴🐎 🚤⛵🛥️🏄 More than 50 miles of shoreline define this lake, created by the construction of Warm Spring Dam. Add the land acreage to that of the water, and you get 17,000 pretty much unspoiled acres. The visitors center has Pomo Indian and natural history displays; it's the place to pick up hiking trail maps (there are more than 40 miles of trails) and fishing guides. The nearby fish hatchery lets visitors watch steelhead trout swim upstream. The only real beach is at the Yorty Creek Recreation Area. ~ Skaggs Springs Road, Geyserville; 707-433-9483 ext. 827, fax 707-431-0313.

⚠️ There are 97 campsites ($10 to $20 per night) and 2 group areas ($56 per night); some campsites are close enough to the lake to boat in. There's also backcountry camping; the required permits can be obtained at the visitors center. Reservations: 877-444-6777.

▼▼▼▼▼▼▼▼▼▼▼▼▼▼
Outdoor Adventures

FISHING

Lake Sonoma offers numerous secluded coves along its 53 miles of shoreline. Anglers can go for bass, channel catfish, red ear perch or Sacramento perch. A boat ramp and a full-service marina are available for those who decide to rent a boat. ~ Dry Creek Road, 11 miles north of Healdsburg; 707-433-2200.

From November through March, fishing enthusiasts can try for steelhead trout from the banks of the **Russian River** near Healdsburg.

WATER SPORTS

During the spring, summer and early fall, canoes and kayaks are a popular mode of transportation on the Russian River. **River's Edge** has them available for half- and full-day outings. ~ 13840 Healdsburg Avenue, Healdsburg; 707-433-7247, 800-345-0869, fax 707-433-7249.

BALLOON RIDES

A Balloon Over Sonoma launches from a variety of locations in the Sonoma Valley. They can accommodate up to 16 people, and following the hour-and-a-half flight, you'll be treated to a champagne breakfast (Belgian waffles? eggs benedict? steak-and-eggs?—your choice) at Kal's Kaffe Mocha Grill. ~ 109 Wikiup Meadows Drive, Santa Rosa; 707-546-3360, 707-293-7760; www.aballoonoversonoma.com.

Skaters and rollerbladers an drop in for some air at **Santa Rosa Skatepark,** equipped with three connecting bowls as well as snake runs, halfpipes and curbs. Helmets are required. ~ Youth Community Park, 725 Fulton Road, Santa Rosa; 707-543-3292. **SKATING**

Ice-skating enthusiasts strap on their blades at "Snoopy's Home Ice," the **Redwood Empire Ice Arena,** open year-round. ~ 1667 West Steele Lane, Santa Rosa; 707-546-7147, fax 707-546-3764.

Play a challenging game at the public 18-hole **Windsor Golf Club.** ~ 1340 19th Hole Drive, Windsor; 707-838-7888. **Oakmont Golf Club** features a par-72 championship course and a par-63 executive course. This tree-lined, semiprivate club rents clubs and carts. ~ 7025 Oakmont Drive, Santa Rosa; 707-539-0415, fax 707-539-045. **GOLF**

Views of Dry Creek Valley and Fitch Mountain are par for the course at **Tayman Park Golf Course,** the oldest green in the county. ~ 927 South Fitch Mountain Road, Healdsburg; 707-433-4275; www.taymanparkgolfcourse.com.

The **Joe Rodota Trail,** which is used for walking as well as pedaling, runs alongside Route 12 between Route 101 and Sebastopol before petering out. However, you can pick up the trail again north of town off Route 116 and ride into Graton. The sum of these parts is about 3 miles, virtually all of it flat; the prettiest section is between Sebastopol and Graton. **BIKING**

Bike Rentals   **Spoke Folk Cyclery** includes helmets, locks and backpacks with their rental bikes (hybrid, tandem, road). You can also buy a bike and accessories, as well as have repairs done. ~ 201 Center Street, Healdsburg; 707-433-7171. **Wine Country Bikes** rents Trek hybrids, road bikes and tandems. Guided tours are also available. ~ 61 Front Street, Healdsburg; 707-473-0610, 866-922-4537; www.winecountrybikes.com.

All distances listed for hiking trails are one way unless otherwise noted. **HIKING**

Once inhabited by Pomo and Wappo Indians, **Annadel State Park** is a mix of forest and meadow laced with 19 miles of hiking paths. The **Warren B. Richardson Trail** (2.7 miles) wanders through a forest of Douglas fir en route to Lake Ilsanjo. Spring brings redwood orchid blossoms, adding a rare experience to an already splendid hike.

Marsh Trail (3.6 miles) climbs the side of Bennett Mountain and offers grand views of Lake Ilsanjo as well as nearby mountain ranges. For a trip to an old quarry site where cobblestones were once excavated, head down the aptly named **Cobblestone Trail** (2 miles).

SIX

Russian River Area

With its headwaters in Mendocino County, the Russian River rambles south through north central California to Healdsburg. Here it turns west toward the sea, as the surrounding landscape changes from rolling ranch land to dense redwood forest. The area around Guerneville, where the river begins its headlong rush to the Pacific, has enjoyed a rebirth as a gay resort area.

Earlier a family vacation spot, the Guerneville–Forestville–Monte Rio area became a raffish home to bikers and hippies during the '50s and '60s. Then in the '70s, gay vacationers from San Francisco began frequenting the region. Today, the Russian River is San Francisco's answer to Fire Island. There are many gay resorts in and around Guerneville, and almost without exception every establishment in town welcomes gay visitors. The area is still also a popular family resort area.

This stretch of the river offers prime fishing and canoeing opportunities. As the river rumbles downslope, it provides miles of scenic runs past overhanging forests. Black bass, steelhead, bluegill and silver salmon swim these waters, and there are numerous beaches for swimming and sunbathing. From Santa Rosa, the winding, two-lane River Road follows the northern edge of the Russian River, taking you to the ocean, where it dead-ends at Goat Rock Beach.

The first people known to live in the lower Russian River were the Miwok and Pomo Indians, who established a number of villages where the bigger towns stand today. They called the river Shabaikai, or "Big Snake," after its shape. The Russian trappers and Aleuts from Alaska landed in Bodega Bay in 1809, but the area was already claimed by the Mexican government as part of Alta (upper) California. The American and European settlers arrived in the early 1850s and in short order began logging. One look at the towering redwoods was probably all it took to make them realize they had their own kind of gold mine, just as prospectors from all over the world were depleting the Sierra foothills of the real thing. (George Guerne, for whom Guerneville is named, ran a thriving saw mill on the banks of the river.) One tree in particular achieved special fame. Felled on the south side of the river in 1873, this 3000-year-old specimen stretched 275 feet—so large it was used to fashion "The Church Built from One Tree" in nearby Santa Rosa.

Eventually, the stands of redwoods were diminished to the point that other crops, including prunes, hops and tobacco, were raised in the early 1900s. Railroads anticipated the area's becoming a desirable getaway from San Francisco and began running excursions to the Russian River. Before long, hotels, resorts and summer cottages were built to house all the warm-weather visitors.

Some visitors were of a different stripe altogether. A group of San Francisco newspapermen, who had the habit of calling themselves "Bohemians," had been gathering for summer retreats in Marin County before regularly renting a 160-acre redwood grove near Monte Rio on the river in 1882. They bought the property in 1898, redubbed it Bohemian Grove, and laid the groundwork for one of the world's most famous private clubs. The all-male Bohemian Club, based in San Francisco, claims more than 2000 members. While "the Grove" encampment each summer still includes artists and scriveners, members and guests have included William Randolph Hearst, Ronald Reagan, Henry Kissinger, Richard Nixon, Bob Hope and other famous and powerful men. You can tell when each summer session is about to begin by counting the number of private jets landing at the Sonoma County Airport.

What used to be an ultra-rural hideaway is now surrounded by small towns up and down the river. And there are more visitors than ever before, eager to experience the area's climate and growing conditions, found to be well suited to a number of grape varieties. After the Europeans, especially the Italians, discovered Sonoma, it was but a matter of time before grapes were planted. (Actually, the Russians planted grapes as early as the 1830s, but very little is known about what they were or what became of them.) Families named Martini and Prati were the Russian River equivalent of the Sebastianis and the Simis elsewhere in the county and, like those colleagues, their names still grace wineries today.

Family homes, weekend cottages and just plain shacks crowd the steep banks of the river as it meanders west past a series of towns, most of them barely on the map—and some seem in danger of actually sliding off. Cazadero, just over eight miles north of Guerneville, gets more rain than anyplace else in the county (an average of about 75 inches a year, double what Guerneville gets). When winter rains swell the river—as well as the contributory creeks—some areas are routinely evacuated; many homes have been lost to water and mudslides over the past decade.

The rest of the year passes in peace, free of the damaging vagaries of Mother Nature. Although the area has become more of a year-round residential haven than it once was, the population swells noticeably in the summer, when river rafters and canoers and vacationers and daytrippers flock to the cool shade of the red-woods in this scenic region.

The entire Russian River region is an Eden of small farms, vineyards and or-chards, though the famous Gravenstein apples (introduced hereabouts by the Russians up in Fort Ross) are losing ground to grapes and other more profitable crops. As in Healdsburg and other areas, the land in this part of the Wine Country has witnessed a succession of crops, including orchards and hop fields. Today, it would

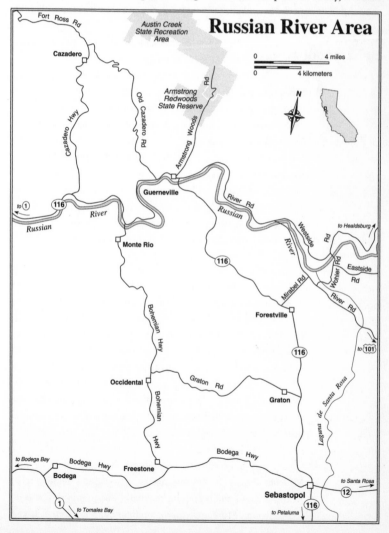

Russian River Area

seem that almost anything can grow in the fertile soil near the river. Summer and fall, the myriad two-lane roads buzz with cars filled with folks seeking to pick their own berries, hunt for pumpkins or fell their own Christmas trees. In the spring, these same roads make for dazzling drives, with the pink and white blossoms of fruit and nut trees brightening the otherwise dreary, late-winter landscape.

And of course, year-round, wine lovers poke around these same backroads, knowing that this is the Promised Land of Pinot Noir. Chardonnay is another grape known to thrive in the cool growing climate of the Russian River Valley, and the combination of the two results in some fine sparkling wine in this appellation.

Sebastopol Area

This region of the Wine Country is also an apple-growing area, although hundreds of orchards have been replanted with grapevines. Small towns such as Sebastopol and Graton are also home to numerous nurseries specializing in roses or palm trees or other growing things.

Sebastopol is Sonoma's answer to the East Bay's Berkeley, a city with a lively arts scene and a reputation for environmental activism and quirky politics. If you were thinking of importing some heavy-duty weaponry into town, think again: Sebastopol has declared itself a nuclear-free zone. It has also become something of an antique-lover's mecca, with many shops in town and south of it along Route 116, known as the Gravenstein Highway (named for a variety of apple that thrives in the region).

SIGHTS

You'll have to keep your wits about you as you traverse Sebastopol. Even before so many streets were made one-way, it wasn't exactly a piece of cake to navigate the streets in the central town. If Sebastopol is your destination, fine; park where you can and you'll be within walking distance of anything downtown. If you're headed out to the coast or north to Guerneville, heads up! The signage is good and moreover the locals are long accustomed to giving directions. There's not a lot in the way of historic sites in town, but it's a lovely place to stroll, shop, have a sandwich—or stay on for an excellent dinner—and learn a little about regional history. The town was settled in 1852 but at last count still had less than 8000 residents.

Located in a restored 1917 railroad depot, the **West County Museum** houses books, magazines, newspapers, photographs, videotapes and audiotapes on regional history in its Triggs Reference Room. More archival material illuminating west Sonoma history appear in exhibits that rotate twice a year. Closed mornings and Monday through Wednesday. ~ 261 South Main Street, Sebastopol; 707-829-6711; www.wschs-grf.pon.net/wcm.htm, e-mail grfwschs@wschs-grf.pon.net.

The **Sonoma County Farm Trails**, which sponsors the Gravenstein Apple Fair in August, publishes a map and resource guide that will lead you to farms with apples, pears, berries, cherries, peaches and vegetables you can pick yourself. ~ P.O. Box 6032, Santa Rosa, CA 95406; 707-571-8288, 800-207-9464, fax 707-571-7719; www.farmtrails.org, e-mail farmtrails@farm trails.org.

You can also pick up a Sonoma County Farm Trails map at the **Sebastopol Area Chamber of Commerce**, along with other helpful information on the area. Closed weekends. ~ 265 South Main

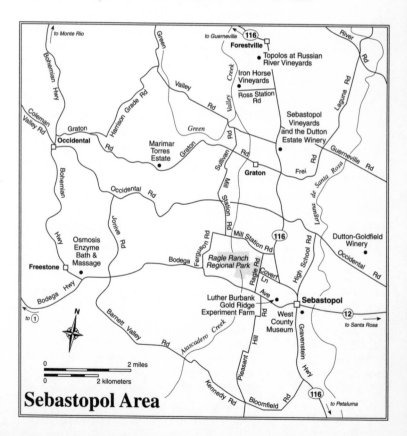

Sebastopol Area

Street, Sebastopol; 707-823-3032, 877-828-4748, fax 707-823-8439; www.sebastopol.org, e-mail info@sebastopol.org.

Perhaps less famous than Santa Rosa's Luther Burbank Home & Gardens, the **Luther Burbank Gold Ridge Experiment Farm** has its own following. Here, on 18 acres, the legendary horticulturist built a cottage, and conducted his experiments on Gravenstein apples, cherries, grapes, plums and lilies between 1885 and 1926. Most of his experiments continue to grow on the farm, including his most beloved creation, the Shasta Daisy. Access to the gardens is free, but reservations are required for guided tours of the cottage and gardens. ~ 7781 Bodega Avenue, Sebastopol; 707-829-6711, fax 707-829-7041; www.wschs-grf.pon.net.

Dan Goldfield, winemaker at **Dutton-Goldfield Winery**, takes advantage of the Russian River Valley's climatic variation by growing chardonnay and pinot noir in several vineyards known for producing grapes with distinct characteristics. Goldfield's partner, Steve Dutton, is a fifth-generation farmer whose family owns the acclaimed Dutton Ranch. The winery's tasting room is off-site, and shares the premises with Balletto Vineyards. Between them, the two wineries offer eight wines for complimentary tasting. Closed Tuesday and Wednesday. ~ 5700 Occidental Road, Santa Rosa; 707-823-3887, fax 707-829-6766; www.duttongoldfield.com, e-mail info@duttongoldfield.com.

West of Sebastopol on Route 12 in the historic town of Freestone is the five-acre **Osmosis: the Enzyme Bath Spa**. While hot-springs soaks and mud baths are possible at countless locations, Osmosis claims to be the only place in North America offering Japanese cedar enzyme baths, composed of cedar fiber, rice bran and more than 600 active enzymes. A lovely meditation garden is available for guests to use post-treatment. ~ 209 Bohemian

WHAT'S IN A NAME

The Spanish called the 58-mile Russian River "San Ygnacio" in the early 1800s. The Russians who settled in Fort Ross up the coast referred to it as "Slavianka" (Slav woman). The first record of the Spanish version of the modern name came in 1843, when it was described in a petition for a land grant as "la boca del Rio Ruso," the mouth of the Russian River.

Highway, Freestone; 707-823-8231, fax 707-874-3788; www.os mosis.com.

North of Sebastopol along Route 116 is **Graton**. Once a foundering town well off the tourist map, it has recently experienced a rebirth, thanks largely to the energetic ambitions of a local real-estate maven who undertook the restoration of many old buildings along the two-block main drag.

Without doubt, one of the prettiest vineyard settings in all California belongs to **Iron Horse Vineyards**, which is most famous ◄ HIDDEN for several types of sparkling wine. Despite a Sebastopol address, it's actually located off Route 116 in Graton. The driveway snaking into this hidden spot is bordered with flowers, olive trees, and palm trees. Hills roll away in every direction, revealing a line of distant mountains. The winery buildings, painted barn-red, follow the classic architecture of American farms. Laid out around them in graceful checkerboard patterns are fields of pinot noir and chardonnay grapes. At harvest time these will be handpicked and then barrel-aged, for the emphasis at this elegant little winery is on personal attention. The outdoor tasting area boasts a view of Green Valley and is open seven days a week by appointment. ~ 9786 Ross Station Road, Sebastopol; 707-887-1507, fax 707-887-1337; www. ironhorsevineyards.com, e-mail info@ironhorsevineyards.com.

The second generation of Duttons to grow grapes is in charge of **Sebastopol Vineyards and the Dutton Estate Winery**, which includes the oldest chardonnay vines in western Sonoma. The first generation was the first to plant grapes in Green Valley following Prohibition after they bought their premier vineyard in 1964. Today, these two labels focus mostly on chardonnay and pinot noir, but they also produce some syrah. ~ 8757 Green Valley Road, Sebastopol; 707-829-9463; www.duttonestate.com, e-mail info@ sebastopolvineyards.com.

Located a mere ten miles from the Pacific Ocean, the **Marimar Torres Estate** is ideally situated for exploiting the cool ◄ HIDDEN climate considered ideal for growing chardonnay and pinot noir grapes. Founder Marimar Torres is a native of Barcelona and a member of the family that owns Torres Wines, Spain's largest independently owned wine empire. In 2003, she converted her 60-acre Don Miguel Vineyard to all-organic farming methods. The tasting room is housed in the winery, whose stucco exterior and red-tile roof evoke Torres's Mediterranean heritage. Tours available by appointment at 11 a.m. weekdays and 10 a.m. Saturday and Sunday. ~ 11400 Graton Road, Sebastopol; 707-823-4365 ext. 101; www.marimarestate.com, e-mail info@marimarestate.com.

LODGING   For a town its size, Sebastopol is surprisingly short on lodging, including the chain variety. But you can find a couple of nifty places to lay your head, and rooms are plentiful in nearby Santa Rosa.

A large courtyard and landscaped garden make the **Sebastopol Inn** seem larger than its 31 rooms. Arranged in two two-story wings, the rooms and suites are sparkling fresh, done in country colors like blue and lemon and snappy ticking stripes; some have balconies or patios while others have jacuzzis. Other amenities include an outdoor pool and jacuzzi and an on-site coffeehouse. ~ 6751 Sebastopol Avenue, Sebastopol; 707-829-2500, 800-653-1082, fax 707-823-1535; www.thesebastopolinn.com, e-mail sebastopolinn@yahoo.com. DELUXE TO ULTRA-DELUXE.

The three-story **Holiday Inn Express Hotel & Suites** has 82 standard rooms opening onto interior corridors. It's close to Main Street, within walking distance of shops and restaurants. Continental breakfast, a pool and a whirlpool are among the complimentary amenities. ~ 1101 Route 116, Sebastopol; 707-829-6677, fax 707-829-2618; www.winecountryhi.com. MODERATE TO DELUXE.

Other lodgings lie in the towns to the west. Located on a 60-acre estate, the Mediterranean-style **Sonoma Coast Villa & Spa** offers unusual elegance for the countryside. Eighteen accommodations are arranged on a single level, opening onto a courtyard, gardens and a putting green. Most decor tends towards French and Italian country, but it's understated. All rooms are outfitted with wood-burning fireplaces as well as complimentary beverages. The villa offers spa services and, upon request, dinner to guests who may not be in the mood to travel to a nearby town. Country breakfast and afternoon wine are included. Closed Christmas week. ~ 16702 Route 1, Bodega; 707-876-9818, 888-404-2255, fax 707-876-9856; www.scvilla.com, e-mail reservations@scvilla.com. ULTRA-DELUXE.

Located ten miles east of Bodega Bay, the **Inn at Occidental** is a charming Victorian homestead encircled by a wide porch bedecked with pots of seasonal flowers and white wicker rockers. The 16 guest rooms are furnished with antique mahogany, pine beds, down comforters and fireplaces, and most come with hot tubs and decks. A two-bedroom cottage is available beside the main building. A full breakfast is included. ~ 3657 Church Street, Occidental; 707-874-1047, 800-522-6324, fax 707-874-1078; www.innatoccidental.com, e-mail innkeeper@innatoccidental. com. ULTRA-DELUXE.

DINING

Aside from fast-food joints, there are fewer dining choices in Sebastopol than one might expect for a town its size, but the situation is improving. The good news is that there seems to be at least one to fit your budget.

Housed in a renovated 1907 bank building, the 40-seat **Alice's Restaurant at 101 Main** is graced with 30-foot-high ceilings warmed up with draped fabric. This inviting arrangement sets the stage for the most acclaimed food in town. The chef has his way with local meats and produce, from lamb and wild mushrooms to desserts on the order of a crème brûlée and cheesecake. Soup and salad is included with every meal. Diners accompany these refined delights with any of more than 200 regional wines, many of which are available by the glass. Closed Tuesday and Wednesday. Breakfast available only on weekends. ~ 101 South Main Street, Sebastopol; 707-829-3212, fax 707-829-8353. MODERATE TO DELUXE.

Anyone who waxes nostalgic about food from the '50s will fall hard for **The Pine Cone**, a downtown standby that's withstood the test of time. All-American fare like tuna melts, hamburgers and

AUTHOR FAVORITE

I feel very welcome and comfortable at the **K & L Bistro**, the kind of neighborhood place that quickly attracts regulars with its atmosphere and housemade foods. The husband-and-wife team of Karen and Lucas Martin established this eatery in 2001 in downtown Sebastopol. The setting—brick walls and pictures of Paris at night—is as French as the menu, which rotates classics like bouillabaisse, mussels, duck dishes and terrine. In no time, the place became a neighborhood hangout for locals who appreciate a chef who makes everything, including veal stock *boudin blanc* and desserts from scratch. Closed Sunday. ~ 119 South Main Street, Sebastopol; 707-823-6614, fax 707-523-2067. MODERATE TO DELUXE.

honest-to-goodness creamy rich milkshakes might feel they're in a culinary time warp. By the time you've finished stuffing yourself, you may well be tempted to call the waitress "Mom." Breakfast and lunch only. ~ 162 Main Street, Sebastopol; 707-823-1375. BUDGET.

Old-timers remember Mom's Apple Pie on the Gravenstein Highway. It's still there, but it's been shoved into a corner since the lunchroom was taken over by **Stella's Café**. It's an odd set-up but good news for people looking for tasty food and reasonably priced wines. Some dishes, like skewered vegetables with curry and ginger sauce, may make you forget all about meat, but you'll find that, too. No lunch on Sunday. Closed Tuesday. ~ 4550 Route 116, Sebastopol; 707-823-6637. DELUXE.

The old-timer in nearby Graton is the **Willow Wood Market Café**, which really is a market. If you could pick just one place to soak up the ambience of life in west Sonoma, this should be it. Ultra-casual, it offers some table-and-counter seating in front, amidst the shelves stocked with canned goods and New Age merchandise, as well as four additional tables in the rear and a few more on the pretty patio. Soups and salads are healthful and fresh (in season you might order a roasted beet and tomato soup), and all-American main courses on the small menu usually include fish or roast half-chicken with mashed potatoes. No dinner on Sunday. ~ 9020 Graton Road, Graton; phone/fax 707-823-0233. MODERATE.

Several antique collectives stand on the Gravenstein Highway (Route 116) to the southeast.

SHOPPING Downtown Sebastopol is home to a number of small stores, most one-of-a-kind and locally owned.

Rosemary's Garden is chockablock with countless herbs, potpourris, ointments and soaps—everything you need to make tea, a heavenly scented bath or an appealing home. ~ 132 North Main Street, Sebastopol; 707-829-2539.

The **Antique Society** is the biggest and the best of the area's many purveyors of previously owned items. Warehouse in size, it is dust-free, with beautifully arranged collections worthy of a Macy's window. ~ 2661 Route 116, Sebastopol; 707-829-1733.

For exquisite handmade chocolates, stop by **La Dolce V.** ~ 110 North Main Street, Sebastopol; 707-829-2178.

One of the best-known places to shop for apples is **Walker Apples**, at the end of a country lane. Closed mid-November through July, the farm sells 26 varieties of apples the rest of the year. ~ Upp Road, Sebastopol; 707-823-4310.

◀ HIDDEN

Compared to nearby Guerneville, there's not much action in Sebastopol but they don't exactly roll up the sidewalks at night, either.

NIGHTLIFE

Blues or rock bands are usually on stage at **Jasper O'Farrell's**, probably the top bar in this area. In fact, there's live music, mostly blues, seven nights a week, with reggae or Cajun bands making an occasional appearance. ~ 6957 Sebastopol Avenue, Sebastopol; 707-829-2062; www.jaspers.net.

The **Sonoma County Repertory Theater** produces dramas and comedies (and once in a while, a musical) in Sebastopol. Choices range from classics to cutting-edge during the year-round season. Tickets can be bought online. ~ 104 North Main Street, Sebastopol; 707-823-0177, fax 707-824-1719; www.the-rep.com.

RAGLE RANCH REGIONAL PARK   This 156-acre parcel encompasses oak woodlands, creeks and marshes. It's very popular with nearby residents, who avail themselves of a parcourse, a soccer field, ball fields, tennis and volleyball courts, an off-leash dog park, and picnic areas outfitted with barbecue grills. Parking fee, $5. ~ 500 Ragle Ranch Road, one mile north of Bodega Highway, Sebastopol; 707-823-7262, fax 707-579-8247.

PARKS

Guerneville is famous for its gay resorts but is still a family-friendly city. It straddles the Russian River, with virtually all its commercial development on the north bank. Forestville is next in size, with a small downtown lined with services and shops. The tiny towns like Monte Rio are a cross between quaint and funky and are by and large bedroom communities.

▼▼▼▼▼▼▼▼▼▼▼▼
Guerneville Area

Several outstanding wineries can be found along heavily traveled routes such as Route 116 (Gravenstein Highway). It's on this latter boulevard that you will find **Topolos at Russian River Vineyards** (most people simply say Topolos, pronounced taupe-uh-lohs) in Forestville. This rambling complex is known for its cutting-edge techniques such as biodynamic farming, which is be-

SIGHTS

lieved to produce more vital crops by capitalizing on natural forces that tend to minimize negative impact on the land. But the real fun is in the tasting room, where a wide array of wines, including some unusual varietals, are available for sampling. Don't miss the port. ~ 5700 Route 116, Forestville; 707-887-1575, 800-867-6567, fax 707-887-1399; www.topolos.net, e-mail topolos@sonic.net.

As the biggest town on the river west of Route 101, **Guerneville** (pronounced gurn-vul) has the most restaurants, bars, shops and inns. The town was settled in 1860, once known as Stumptown and later named after a Ohio native, George E. Guerne, who built a saw- and planing-mill there in 1864.

The Russian River is the main attraction in this neck of the redwoods. Near town are a number of wineries. The **Visitors Information Center** provides maps and brochures on facilities and water sports. ~ 16209 1st Street, Guerneville; 707-869-3533, 800-253-8800, fax 707-869-9009; www.russianriver.com, e-mail news@russianriver.com. The Center also operates the **Visitors Bureau at Korbel Station.** ~ 13250 River Road, Guerneville; 707-869-4096.

As you first arrive in downtown Guerneville you will come to a traffic signal at the intersection of Armstrong Woods Road. Turning north will take you to **Armstrong Redwoods State Reserve,** where you undoubtedly will marvel at the grove of ancient redwoods dating back 1400 years and reaching heights of 300 feet. Admission. ~ 17000 Armstrong Woods Road, Guerneville; 707-869-2015, fax 707-869-5629; e-mail armvs@mcn.org.

Of course, Guerneville would never have developed into a resort destination had it not been for the waters of the Russian River. The most popular spot around Guerneville to plunge in for a swim or launch a canoe is **Johnson's Beach.** Located just two blocks from the heart of downtown, this sunny waterfront strip is also home to many summer events, including the renowned Russian River Jazz Festival. ~ South end of Church Street, Guerneville.

Founded in 1882 by three brothers, **Korbel Champagne Cellars** produces today's most popular sparkling wines. On any day of the week you may taste these award-winning bubblies. The tasting room and attached gift shop sells nine different champagnes, some of which are available nowhere else; also on the premises is a gourmet delicatessen. While guided tours are offered throughout the year, I recommend visiting during spring and summer when the winery's century-old garden, which you can tour separately, is alive

with roses, tulips and daffodils. No garden tours on Monday. ~
13250 River Road, Guerneville; 707-824-7000, fax 707-869-2981;
www.korbel.com, e-mail info@korbel.com.

Gay resorts outnumber other accommodations in Guerneville,   **LODGING**
though everyone is welcome everywhere. A couple of secluded
country inns add to the mix.

   Resting on 15 waterfront acres on the edge of downtown
Guerneville, is **Dawn Ranch Lodge**. In addition to a restaurant
and a bar, Dawn Ranch offers such facilities as a beach, a pool

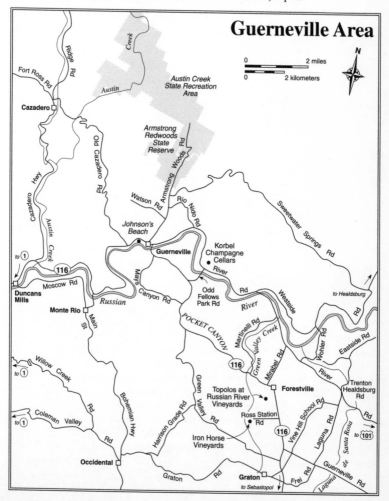

Guerneville Area

and volleyball courts. There are 55 moderate- to ultra-deluxe-priced individual cabins that were built in the early 1900s and have been renovated. Each is simply furnished with a queen-sized \bed and without TV or phones. Some two-room cabins have a woodburning stove and a sofa bed in one room. ~ 16467 River Road, Guerneville; 707-869-9500, 800-734-3371, fax 707-869-0656; www.dawnranch.com, e-mail info@dawnranch.com. MODERATE TO DELUXE.

Fondly called "Triple R," **Russian River Resort** offers 24 cheerfully decorated guest rooms situated around a hot tub area. Whereas most other resorts in the area can be described as rustic, this resort provides more modern, contemporary accommodations; each room is carpeted and has a private bath and cable TV (several have pellet stoves as well). Throughout the year, the Russian River Resort organizes 15 to 20 events celebrating major holidays and festivities such as Women's Weekend. The guests are almost exclusively gay male but lesbians and gay-friendly straights are welcome. A restaurant and several bars are located on the premises, and there's a pool. ~ 16390 4th Street, Guerneville; 707-869-0691, 800-417-3767, fax 707-869-0698; www.russianriverresort.com, e-mail info@russianriverresort.com. DELUXE.

Catering primarily to gays and lesbians, **Highlands Resort** sits on three acres. Accommodations here come in many forms. Some are individual cabins with fireplaces, private baths, and kitchenettes; others are more standard motel-style rooms. The pool suite has both a queen- and king-sized bed, a TV, a refrigerator and a

AUTHOR FAVORITE

The peace and quiet at **River Village Resort**, along with a massage, are just what I'm looking for when I get so frazzled I have to get away from it all. Some 19 cottages are arranged around a rectangular common; the gray and taupe buildings come in configurations of studios or one or two bedrooms, but the decor is roughly the same, a pale variation on gray, taupe and white. That's in keeping with the resort's dedication to getting everyone calm and relaxed. Both wet and dry spa treatments are available on site, as are barbecue grills for those who don't want to stress out by leaving the property. ~ 14880 River Road, Guerneville; 707-869-8139, 888-342-2624, fax 707-869-3096; www.rivervillageresort.com, e-mail info@rivervillageresort.com. DELUXE.

view of the pool, where sunbathing is *au naturel*. A hot tub, a continental breakfast and a guest lounge with a piano, TV, VCR and books complete the amenities. There is also space for 20 tents. ~ 14000 Woodland Drive, Guerneville; 707-869-0333, fax 707-869-0370; www.highlandsresort.com, e-mail muffins@highlandsre sort.com. MODERATE TO DELUXE.

Spread over five wooded acres along the Russian River, **The Willows** is a gay and lesbian guesthouse resort with spots for tent camping and barbecuing on the grounds. The main lodge has 11 bedrooms, most with private baths, and a spacious living room with a stone fireplace, library and grand piano. The price tag includes breakfast, tea and coffee served in the morning and afternoon. ~ 15905 River Road, Guerneville; 707-869-2824, 800-953-2828, fax 707-869-2824; www.innatthewillows.com. MODERATE TO DELUXE.

The **Fern Grove Cottages** sit at the foot of a mountain and are a five-minute walk from town. The 21 mustard-colored Craftsmen cottages were built in 1926 and are furnished with antiques. Some have jacuzzi tubs, fireplaces, wood-burning stoves, or kitchens. The grounds are full of lovely gardens and guests enjoy a buffet-style breakfast. There's a two-night minimum on peak-season weekends. ~ 16650 River Road, Guerneville; 707-869-8105, 888-243-2674, fax 707-869-1615; www.ferngrove.com, e-mail innkeepers@ferngrove.com. MODERATE TO DELUXE.

The prettiest accommodations in this neck of the redwoods belong to the **Applewood Inn**, hidden on a hillside in tiny Pocket Canyon. Belden House, the original family home built in 1922, has the older, more staid rooms, while two two-story *casas* across the courtyard offer more space and include a small balcony. With a pool, hot tub and excellent restaurant (which uses produce from its own gardens), this estate, secluded among the redwoods, is the kind of place to which you can retreat and never leave the grounds until your visit is over. ~ 13555 Route 116, Guerneville; 707-869-9093, 800-555-8509, fax 707-869-9170; www.applewoodinn.com, e-mail stay@applewoodinn.com. DELUXE TO ULTRA-DELUXE.

◀ HIDDEN

The charming **Farmhouse Inn** is a vision in yellow, with rose gardens and grapevines growing right out the front door. A stone's throw from the old farmhouse, eight attached cottages were totally overhauled in 2001 and decorated with distinction; one is done in peach-and-sage velvet, another in paisley prints, another in cream and green. All have personal saunas, fireplaces, jet tubs, and CDs and TV/VCRs. On-site amenities include a pool, restaurant and day spa. ~ 7871 River Road, Forestville; 707-887-3300, 800-464-6642, fax 707-887-3311; www.farmhouseinn. com, e-mail innkeep@farmhouseinn.com. DELUXE TO ULTRA-DELUXE.

> Russian River wines are distinctive because a 70-foot-deep stratum of gravel lies beneath the valley, forcing vine roots to reach deeper for water and adding trace minerals that give the grapes a complex flavor.

Village Inn, a refurbished woodframe complex on the river, draws a mixed clientele. This cozy country inn, set amid redwood trees, has a homey, old-time feel. All rooms come with private bath. They're trim little units: clean, carpeted and decorated with an occasional piece of art. You'll also find a good restaurant and bar with river views. ~ 20822 River Boulevard, Monte Rio; 707-865-2304, 800-303-2303, fax 707-865-2332; www.villageinn-ca.com, e-mail village@sonic.net. DELUXE.

DINING

Restaurants around Guerneville are mostly casual, the exceptions being in the nicer inns. In summer, you'll find plenty of places that welcome diners in shorts, though shirts and shoes are always a good idea.

While even remote Guerneville now offers more than a couple of places to get an espresso, none are better than the **Coffee Bazaar**. Located on Armstrong Woods Road a block off the main strip, this café's food and beverages are tasty and affordable. There is a wide range of coffee creations and a generous selection of home-baked pastries each morning. Lunch choices include soups, salads, sandwiches, quiches and calzones; many vegetarian options are available. There is plenty of seating inside, but take a sidewalk table to peoplewatch. ~ 14045 Armstrong Woods Road, Guerneville; 707-869-9706; www.coffee-bazaar.com. BUDGET.

The restaurant at **Dawn Ranch Lodge** is sophisticated and relaxing in California Modern fashion. You'll also find a sundeck for warm-weather dining. The California-cuisine menu changes seasonally. Dinner may include scampi, steak, chicken curry, and prosciutto tortellini. Dinner and weekend brunch served. ~ 16467 River Road, Guerneville; 707-869-0656, 800-734-3371; www.dawnranch.com. MODERATE TO ULTRA-DELUXE.

The walls in the dining room at the top-rated **Farmhouse Inn** are the same yellow as the exterior, making a pretty backdrop for dining. (There's also patio seating.) The seasonal menu, which changes nightly but usually includes the chef's special rabbit dish, depends on what's growing in the garden and other local sources, and on the availability of fresh wild fish. Desserts are housemade. No lunch. Closed Tuesday and Wednesday. ~ 7871 River Road, Forestville; 707-887-3300, fax 707-887-3311; www.farmhouse inn.com. DELUXE TO ULTRA-DELUXE.

Eight miles southeast of Guerneville, downtown Forestville is not exactly a gourmet ghetto. So it's nice that after Chez Marie closed, **Mosaic** moved into the building, streamlined the decor, remodeled the back room into a wine lounge, and installed a garden for alfresco dining. Chef Tai Olesky lets his creativity shine through dishes like a coriander-and-anise-rubbed pork shoulder, a coffee-encrusted filet mignon that incorporates cabernet, chocolate and bleu cheese, and a Thai-style lobster coconut curry bisque. No dinner Sunday. Closed Monday. ~ 6675 Front Street, Forestville; 707-887-7503. DELUXE TO ULTRA-DELUXE.

SHOPPING An excellent bookstore and a true community resource, the **River Reader, Inc.** has a small but strong selection of books, magazines, cards, games, music and gifts. Visitors to Guerneville will find plenty of choices for poolside reading in all categories including fiction, spirituality and regional topics. There is also a good selection of gay reading material including books and magazines. ~ 16355 Main Street, Guerneville; 707-869-2240; e-mail rreader@ sonic.net.

On the main road between Forestville and Guerneville, you'll do your sweet tooth a favor by stopping at **Kozlowski Farms**. They make and sell more than 100 different items like all-fruit preserves, chutney, spreads, dessert sauces, apple cider blends, and a variety of baked goods. Other condiments include mustards, salad dressings, salsas and teriyaki sauces, among others. The farm also has a picnic area, a deli, a bakery and an espresso bar. ~ 5566 North Gravenstein Highway (Route 116), Forestville; 707-887-1587, 800-473-2767; www.kozlowskifarms.com, e-mail koz@kozlowskifarms.com.

NIGHTLIFE **Dawn Ranch**, one of the area's first gay resorts, has a beautiful bar area that spreads through several pine-paneled rooms and extends out to a poolside deck. They offer deejays for dancing on select weekends. ~ 16467 River Road, Guerneville; 707-869-0656; www.dawnranch.com.

The **Russian River Resort** invites nonguests to enjoy the facilities and mingle with guests at the bar and around the pool. The bar isn't large but the crowd is friendly and if nothing is jumping in town, there will surely be some people hanging out at the "Triple R." ~ 16390 4th Street, Guerneville; 707-869-0691; www.russianriverresort.com.

In the middle of downtown is the **Rainbow Cattle Company**, a gay bar. Offering nothing more than a couple of pool tables, three pinball machines, bar stools, and long benches, this nightspot doesn't provide much in the way of entertainment, but it's a congenial place for socializing and drinking Monday through Friday. ~ 16220 Main Street, Guerneville; 707-869-0206; www.queersteer.com.

Home of the Rat Bastard Pale Ale, **Stumptown Brewery** is a small seven-barrel brew pub. They have a deck overlooking the river that also offers access to their two-acre beach. There's occasional live entertainment on weekend afternoons and myriad meats from the smokehouse. ~ 15045 River Road, Guerneville; 707-869-0705, fax 707-869-8169; www.stumptown.com/brews.

Blues, country, folk and rock bands alternate on Friday and Saturday at the **Forestville Club**, which has a dancefloor. Cover. ~ 6250 Front Street, Forestville; 707-887-2594.

PARKS

ARMSTRONG REDWOODS STATE RESERVE AND AUSTIN CREEK STATE RECREATION AREA 🚶 🚲 🐎 🏊 ⛵ These two parks, lying side by side, are a study in contrasts. Armstrong features a deep, cool forest of redwood trees measuring over 300 feet high and dating back 1400 years. Rare redwood orchids blossom here in spring and there is a 1200-seat amphitheater that was once used for summer concerts. Austin Creek offers sunny meadows and oak forests. Fox, bobcats, deer, wild pigs, and raccoons inhabit the region, and a nearby shallow bullfrog pond is stocked with sunfish and bass. There are almost two dozen miles of trails threading the park, including a popular trek to a few swimming holes. Facilities include picnic areas, restrooms and a visitors center. Day-use fee, $6. ~ 17000 Armstrong Woods Road, Guerneville; 707-869-2015, fax 707-869-5629; e-mail armvs@mcn.com.

▲ Austin Creek and Bullfrog Pond Campground has 24 sites and three hike-in sites, $15 per night. For restrictions and permit information, call 707-869-2015.

▼▼▼▼▼▼▼▼▼▼▼▼▼

The Russian River area is not known for fancy resort courses, but it has cool weather year-round and a couple of courses you could polish off before lunch.

Outdoor Adventures

GOLF

The **Sebastopol Golf Course** offers peaceful, countryside golfing. This public nine-hole course rents clubs. ~ 2881 Scott's Right of Way, Sebastopol; 707-823-9852.

The Alister MacKenzie–designed **Northwood Golf Club** has nine holes. Clubs and carts are available for rent. ~ 19400 Route 116, Monte Rio; 707-865-1116.

WATER SPORTS

The Russian River is *the* place to explore in a canoe or kayak. The river is a Class I from April to October, and during that time canoe and kayak rentals are plentiful. Several outfits offer everything from one-day excursions to five-day expeditions. Most folks rent for the day, canoe one way, and are picked up by the outfitter and shuttled back. The experience of floating timelessly along this magnificent river will long be remembered.

Burke's Canoe Trips offers a ten-mile day trip to Guerneville and outfit you with a canoe, lifejacket, and paddles before sending you on a self-guided ride through the redwoods. Don't despair over the thought of having to paddle back up-stream—a return shuttle is included. Reservations required. Closed mid-October through April. ~ At the north end of Mirabel Road at River Road, Forestville; 707-887-1222; www.burkescanoetrips.com.

King's Sport & Tackle rents canoes and kayaks. ~ 16258 Main Street, Guerneville; 707-869-2156; www.guernevillesport.com.

AUTHOR FAVORITE

When I think of summer, I think of floating along a river—in particular, the **Russian River**, snug in a canoe with a cold beverage and something soft on which to nap. The scenery, from rolling ranch land to dense redwood groves, is stunning. See "Water Sports" above for more information.

The Russian River is also good for a swim. Favorite spots in the area are **Johnson's Beach** in the town of Guerneville and **Monte Rio Beach** in Monte Rio.

BIKING

River Road, between Windsor and Guerneville, meanders past rolling hills and rural scenery, but carries a moderate amount of traffic.

Bike Rentals **Pee Wee Golf and Arcade** rents Trek hybrid and mountain bikes. They're open daily in summer (June to Labor Day) and weekends only in September, and March through May. Closed in winter. ~ 16155 Drake Road, Guerneville; 707-869-9321.

HIKING

In **Armstrong Redwoods State Reserve**, there are 22 miles of trails threading the park. A four-mile hike here takes you to a few swimming holes that offer relief from the sun.

SEVEN

Mendocino County

 The image of Mendocino has long been dominated by the vision of windswept cliffs, crashing surf and whirling seabirds. Yet there is another Mendocino, the inland portion that is defined by gently rolling hills, avenues of redwoods and acres of vineyards that provide the county's increasingly popular wines. If you travel along Route 101, however, you will see a lot of development, especially around Ukiah. Here, motels, shopping malls and fast-food outlets are only an exit away.

As opposed to the latter-day hippie lifestyle associated with the coastal area, the Ukiah neighborhood is all business. As the county seat, the city is home to the courthouse and lawyers' offices and most of the major services, from auto shops to appliance stores, you won't see once you get out into the country. Up in Redwood Valley and out in the larger Anderson Valley, things are more laid-back. These are the kinds of places people go to get away from it all, and there's something about this part of the world that attracts rugged individualists, even if they're wearing suits and driving minivans.

The still-rugged landscape probably has a lot to do with that attraction. Whereas Sonoma and Napa counties are well-developed and overpopulated, you can still find many places in Mendocino that must look as they did 100 years ago—thousands of acres of unspoiled wilderness (give or take a telephone line or two) and the occasional two-lane road.

You can get a glimpse into regional history at any of three museums in Mendocino County: the Grace Hudson Museum and the Held-Poage Memorial Home in Ukiah and the Anderson Valley Historical Museum in Boonville. All three look at the county from different perspectives, from the native Pomo Indians to the farmers who settled the Anderson Valley.

For the most part, however, this area's attractions fall into two categories: scenic and agricultural, including the burgeoning winery scene. Once you get off Route 101 and onto one of the smaller roads that link the interior with the coast, you'll gain an appreciation of the challenges faced by the pioneers who arrived in this rugged region.

Mendocino County's relatively late entry into the California wine business seems to have been dictated by history more than by geography or climate. The area is remote—by early-19th-century standards; the last mission was built way down in Sonoma, and the early European settlers and even gold diggers flocked to San Francisco and the Sonoma and Napa valleys, giving Mendocino not only a late start, but a slow one, in terms of development. Its remoteness from San Francisco Bay and the benefits of mass shipping didn't help, either.

However, as the merits of its grapegrowing climate became known, the region has welcomed dozens of new wineries. The price of vineyard land in Napa and Sonoma is another factor since those southern neighbors are running out of room.

The people who live in Mendocino prize the abundance of open space in their part of the world. Manmade Lake Mendocino beckons year-round, but particularly in summer when everyone around Ukiah craves relief from the fierce summer heat. Closer to the coast, hiking trails and campsites along the Navarro River serve the same purpose.

Numerous microclimates add to the mix. While it may be 95 degrees on the streets of Ukiah, you can drive ten miles north to the Redwood Valley and head up to the hills to catch one of the westerly breezes that blow in through one of several gaps. Morning fog is common in the Anderson Valley, particularly during the summer months. The so-called fog line is around Philo; east of that town, the fog burns off by mid-morning, but to the west the fog may linger all day, its tendrils adding a romantic fillip to the sight of seemingly endless redwood groves that line the roads close to the ocean.

These microclimates also greatly affect the taste of wines produced in various vineyards. Historically, white grapes such as gewürztraminer and chardonnay do well in the Anderson Valley, while zinfandel and petit sirah thrive on the warm, rocky hillsides of the interior. But so many factors, from soil to temperature to wind, come into play in winemaking that you will find all kinds of grapes planted in all sorts of places.

Other crops, particularly apples and pears, also thrive in Anderson Valley. In summer and fall, these and other fruits and vegetables are plentiful at roadside stands on or near Route 128. In many cases, these roadside produce outlets are run by the same families who started them. The Gowan family, for one, has been in the business since the 1930s. But urban escape artists as well are discovering the beauty of living off the beaten path. Some newcomers are retirees from the Bay Area who, fed up with gridlock in San Jose or the East Bay, have taken over bed-and-breakfast inns or opened guest ranches. Safe and far from the madding crowd, they may not be all that rugged, but they share the traditional streak of individuality that makes the Mendocino County experience so appealing.

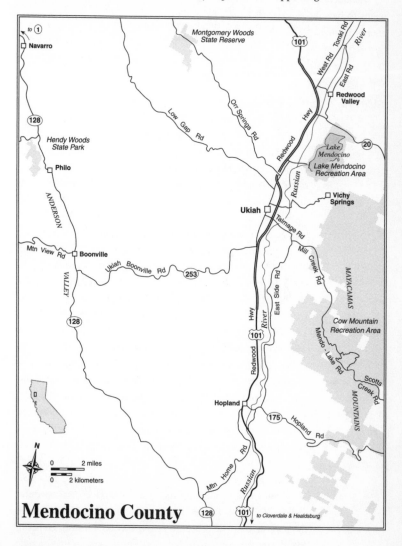

Mendocino County

Hopland–Ukiah Inland Area

There may not be a lot to see in Hopland and Ukiah, but the attractions there tend to be rather extraordinary. There's an Indian casino, a Buddhist center of learning, a museum dedicated to art and Pomo Indian basketry, and a plaque honoring ladies of the night. Beyond these quirky points of interest are at least 20 wineries, most of which have tasting rooms open daily to the public. With a grand total of about 50 wineries, Mendocino will never catch up to Napa's 300-plus wineries or Sonoma's 200-plus, but the wines are gaining in popularity and recognition with every passing year. Most of the inland producers are located close to Route 101.

SIGHTS

It's not hard to guess how the town of **Hopland** got its name. While there are brewpubs in both Hopland and Ukiah, the hops have long been supplanted by grapes. The town was founded in 1859 when three local men opened a saloon. In those days it was known as Sanel (Hopland is still in Sanel Valley); it was renamed in the early 1890s. Surrounded by hills and intersected by Route 101, it's still a quiet town.

Housed in a rare old hop kiln, **Milano Family Winery** oozes historic Mendocino County with its second-floor redwood tasting room and oodles of stained glass. It was already a winery when Ted and Deanna Starr bought the place in 2001. Visitors are welcome to buy a bottle of wine—perhaps cabernet sauvignon, chardonnay, port, syrah or zinfandel—and picnic at shaded tables with views of the vineyards and orchards. ~ 14594 South Route 101, Hopland, 707-744-1396, fax 707-744-1138; www.milano winery.com, e-mail wines@milanowinery.com.

HIDDEN ►

The Indians are getting even with the White Man, quarter by quarter, at the **Hopland Shokawah Casino** complex, located just over three miles east of Hopland via Route 175. Hundreds of slot and video machines are kept busy, even on weekday mornings, in the cool, dark recesses of the large game room here. There are also table games. ~ 13101 Nokomis Road, Hopland; 707-744-1395, fax 707-744-1698; www.shokawah.com, e-mail shokawah@pacific.net.

When you return to Hopland, you will be facing an impressive facility just across Route 101. Turn left and then right to reach the parking lot. The Brutocao family has been raising grapes in Mendocino for more than half a century, and you may sample

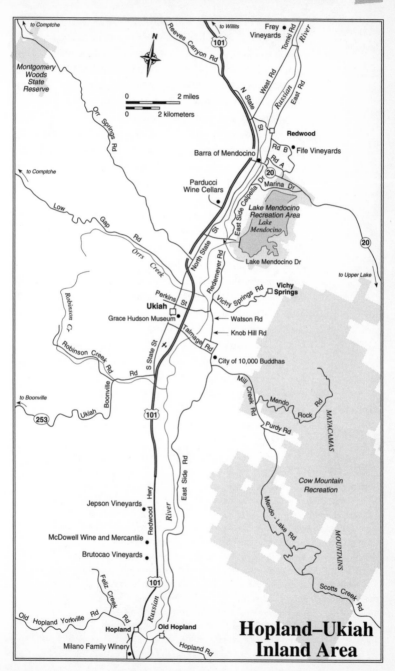

to Comptche

Montgomery
Woods
State
Reserve

to Willits

to Comptche

Orr Springs Rd

Reeves Canyon Rd

101

N

Frey
Vineyards

N State St

West Rd

Russian River

Tomki Rd

East Rd

0   2 miles
0   2 kilometers

Redwood

Rd B
Rd A

• Fife Vineyards

Barra of Mendocino •

20

Low   Gap   Rd

Marina Dr

**Parducci
Wine Cellars**

Orrs Creek

East Side Calpella Dr

North State St

*Lake Mendocino
Recreation Area*
*Lake
Mendocino*

20

Lake Mendocino Dr

to Upper Lake

Robinson C.

Redemeyer Rd

Perkins St

Vichy Springs Rd

□ **Vichy
Springs**

Ukiah

Grace Hudson Museum •

S State St

Talmage Rd

← Watson Rd

← Knob Hill Rd

Robinson Creek Rd

Rd

• City of 10,000 Buddhas

to Boonville

253

Ukiah

Boonville

Russian River

East Side Rd

Mill Creek Rd

Mendo
Rock
Rd

Purdy Rd

*Cow Mountain
Recreation*

MAYACAMAS

101

Redwood Hwy

Jepson Vineyards •

McDowell Wine and Mercantile •

Brutocao Vineyards •

Mendo - Lake Rd

MOUNTAINS

Feliz Creek

Old Hopland Yorkville Rd

101

Russian River

Hopland   **Old Hopland**

Hopland Rd

Scotts Creek Rd

Milano Family Winery •

Hopland–Ukiah
Inland Area

the fruits of their labor at the **Brutocao Vineyards**. Their wine-making facilities also harbor a tasting room in addition to a gift shop, a bar and a restaurant. A smaller tasting room is also located on Route 128 north of Philo. ~ 13500 South Route 101, Hopland; 707-744-1066, 800-433-3689, fax 707-744-1046; www.brutocao cellars.com, e-mail info@brutocaocellars.com.

McDowell Wine and Mercantile gives McDowell Valley Vine-yards excellent exposure right on the highway in an 1897 building rigged to resemble a country store. The tasting room showcases McDowell's viognier, syrah and other Rhone varietals. ~ 13380 South Route 101, Hopland; 707-744-8911, fax 707-744-1826; www.mcdowellsyrah.com.

Between Hopland and Ukiah are several wineries, one of the most interesting of which is **Jepson Vineyards**. Its product line includes sauvignon blanc, chardonnay, viognier, merlot, syrah and brandy. The brandy comes from colombard grapes, which thrive in this part of the Sanel Valley. You can sample the brandy in the tasting room for a small fee; you will need to make an appointment to see the exotic machinery and intricate techniques used to create it. ~ 10400 Route 101, Ukiah; 707-468-8936, fax 707-468-0362; www.jepsonwine.com, e-mail mboeckx@jepsonwine.com.

Approaching Ukiah from the south, you can take the Talmage Road exit and follow it east to where it ends at the most unusual attraction in Mendocino County. A magnificent gilded gateway

HIDDEN ▶ announces the entrance to the **City of 10,000 Buddhas**. Here, amid some 437 acres, the buildings of what used to be a mental hospital

sights

are being put to use as classrooms and temples. Arranged along the walls of the temple are some 10,000 small statues of the Buddha, as well as impressive larger statues displayed outdoors. As unusual as this place is, it's not a curiosity and should be visited only by people interested in praying, studying or learning about Buddhism. That said, there is a vegetarian restaurant on the premises (see "Dining," below) well worth a detour. There is a bookstore with half its titles in English and a large assortment of Buddhist items ranging from restitution beads to Buddha icons. Sign in and ask for directions at the guest services desk. ~ 2001 Talmage Road, Ukiah; 707-462-0939, fax 707-462-0949; www. drba.org.

Ukiah, the county seat, is a real working town with activity centered downtown near the civic buildings. Some old Victorians can be found if you drive along the pretty back streets.

If you're eager to pick up maps and brochures, you can head straight to the **Greater Ukiah Chamber of Commerce** by taking the Perkins Street exit off Route 101 and heading west to School Street. There's an information desk and a wall full of information to the left as you approach the desk. Closed Saturday and Sunday. ~ 200 South School Street, Ukiah; 707-462-4705, fax 707-462-2088; www.ukiahchamber.com, e-mail info@ukiahchamber.com.

Otherwise, continue north on Route 101 and exit at East Gobbi Street; turn west and then north onto Main Street, which leads to the heart of Ukiah. The best things about the **Grace Hudson Museum** and **Sun House** are the baskets made by the indigenous Pomo Indians; the next best things are the paintings and photographs of these native Americans that adorn the museum walls. Grace Hudson and her husband (a scholar of basketry) lived in Sun House; she is the artist behind the paintings of Pomo life. The museum, which also hosts history and anthropology exhibits on a rotating basis, is open to the public; Sun House is open for half-hour guided tours. Closed Monday and Tuesday. ~ 431 South Main Street, Ukiah; 707-467-2836, fax 707-467-2835; www.grace hudsonmuseum.org, e-mail gracehudson@pacific.net.

The only other place in town to learn about regional history is the nearby **Held-Poage Memorial Home and Research Library**, where archival materials including photographs and maps are available to the public; the library alone has some 5000 volumes. The house is a Queen Anne Victorian that was the home of Mendocino County Superior Court Judge William D. L. Held and Ethel Poage Held. The library has limited hours but the Mendocino County Historical Society will make an effort to open by appointment. Closed mornings and Saturday and Sunday. ~ 603 West Perkins Street, Ukiah; 707-462-6969; www.pacificsites.net/~mchs, e-mail mchs@pacific.net.

Despite no evidence of the world's oldest occupation on the streets of Ukiah nowadays, you can find a memorial honoring it. Just south of Hayes Music (200 South State Street at West Church Street) on the righthand side of the street, look for a granite boulder in front of an office building. A **bronze plaque** reads: "To the ladies of the night who plied their trade upon this site." The plaque marks the location of what was a ladies' "boarding house" in the 1930s.

After meandering around downtown Ukiah, it's time to go winetasting. Scoot right up Route 101 to **Parducci Wine Cellars**, the first and largest in the area. Founded in 1932 by Adolph Parducci, it was run by family members until the late 1990s. You can taste and tour (by appointment only) here, though the winery itself is up on a hill and the tasting room is in a white stucco California Mission–style building. Parducci's moderately priced sauvignon blanc and chardonnay, in particular, have been well-received. ~ 501 Parducci Road, Ukiah; 800-362-9463, fax 707-462-7260; www.parducci.com, e-mail tastingroom@parducci.com.

HIDDEN ▶   Up the road in the Redwood Valley, **Fife Vineyards** makes so many excellent wines that the tasting room can't offer them all, every day. If you're lucky they'll be pouring estate-grown zinfandel. You can see these vines as well as petit sirah growing on the hillside in front of the winery. For all its quality, the winery is quite modest, except for the knock-out view of Lake Mendocino, way below to the south. Tours by appointment only. ~ 3621 Ricetti Lane, Redwood Valley; 707-485-0323, fax 707-485-0832; www.fifevineyards.com.

HIDDEN ▶   The owner of **Barra of Mendocino** has been in the grape-growing business his entire life and knows more about winemaking in Mendocino County than just about anybody. Charlie Barra and his wife Martha are becoming less involved in tasting-room activities, but you could still be lucky enough to run into them. Tours of the winery are offered by appointment, but winetasting occurs at Redwood Valley Cellars, which is in the shape of an inverted wine glass (which means the tasting room is circular). Be sure to sample the pinot blanc and the petite sirah. There are shaded picnic facilities. ~ 7051 North State Street, Redwood Valley; 707-485-0322 (Redwood Valley Cellars), 707-485-8771 (Barra of Mendocino), fax 707-485-6784; www.barraofmendo cino.com, e-mail rvv@barraofmendocino.com.

Frey Vineyards (pronounced "fry") makes gewürztraminer, chardonnay, sauvignon blanc, cabernet sauvignon, syrah, petit sirah and other reds and whites, all of which are certified as organically farmed and processed. If you plan to visit this winery (the nation's first organic winery) set on a 700-acre ranch, you need to call ahead. Tastings by appointment only. ~ 14000 Tomki Road, Redwood Valley; 707-485-5177, 800-760-3739, fax 707-485-7875; www.freywine.com, e-mail info@freywine.com.

Motels outnumber hotels and inns in eastern Mendocino County, though there are some interesting choices—one in Hopland and another on the outskirts of Ukiah. Straddling the highway, the bigger city makes a convenient overnight stop for travelers heading elsewhere. The old Palace Hotel downtown was renovated in the 1970s but lack of patronage caused it to close soon thereafter. Now the old hotel sits empty while ivy vines climb all over its brick facade.

LODGING

The Hopland Inn opened in the late 19th century as a rest stop for stage and train travelers between San Francisco and Oregon.

The accommodations at **Lawson's Station** are surprisingly upscale for such a tiny town, and a welcome replacement for the two other Hopland hotels that have closed. Seven 500-square-foot spa suites are handsomely decorated à la Hilton and feature balconies, fireplaces, spa tubs and other amenities in a two-story adobe-style building. In-room massage available by reservation. ~ 13441 South Route 101, Hopland; 707-744-1977, 866-744-1977; www.lawsonsstation.com, e-mail info@lawsonsstation.com. DELUXE TO ULTRA-DELUXE.

In downtown Hopland, the **Hopland Inn** is an eye-catching 1890 Victorian. All 21 rooms are decorated in a mix of original and reproduction antiques. If you stay here, you won't have far to go if you sample the two local brandies or any of a long list of single-malt scotches in the bar. Continental breakfast is included. ~ 13401 South Route 101, Hopland; 707-744-1890, 800-266-1891, fax 707-744-1219; www.hoplandinn.com, e-mail innkeeper@hop landinn.com. DELUXE.

The only bed and breakfast in Ukiah is the **Sanford House**, one of the prettiest homes in an older neighborhood where everyone seems to have a green thumb. Topped with a turret in one corner, the Queen Anne–style Victorian has five upstairs rooms adorned with family antiques, dark carpeting and pastel wallpaper in various designs. The house was built in 1904 by longtime state legislator John Bunyon Sanford, and is greatly enhanced by reading chairs on the front porch and a garden with a koi pond in the back. Full organic breakfast is included. ~ 306 South Pine Street, Ukiah; 707-462-1653, fax 707-462-8987; www.sanford house.com. DELUXE.

The **Voll Motel** is a 21-room roadside rest stop. A couple of accommodations are on an upper floor, but most are right on the parking lot and, while clean, truly borderline. At these prices, however, you can't expect a beauty queen. ~ 628 North State Street, Ukiah; 707-463-1610. BUDGET.

HIDDEN ▶ Located three miles east of Ukiah, the **Vichy Springs Resort** dates to 1854 and has long attracted visitors with its special springs, which are not only warm but as bubbly as a glass of good champagne. Mark Twain, Robert Louis Stevenson and Jack London all paid visits here. As a state landmark, it's home to California's oldest warm-springs retreats. The prettiest accommodations at this 700-acre property are in the cottages arranged in a horseshoe pattern on a slight rise, but there are also comfortable guest rooms in the inn. The resort is open to day visitors as well, who, like guests, can avail themselves of the waters and various spa treatments at this peaceful hideaway. ~ 2605 Vichy Springs Road, Ukiah; 707-462-9515, fax 707-462-9516; www.vichysprings.com, e-mail vichy@ vichysprings.com. DELUXE TO ULTRA-DELUXE.

DINING The concept of five-star dining has not arrived in Hopland or Ukiah, but there are some nice places to dine. In addition to loads of fast-food places, you can find good, inexpensive meals at a number of spots.

The main reason to recommend **Hopland Shokawah Casino** as a restaurant is that it is open 24/7. No matter what time you arrive, you will be able to stop your stomach's cries. The menu includes burgers and cheap prime rib as well as a breakfast that doesn't cost much more than a dollar or two. ~ 13101 Nokomis

Road, Hopland; 707-744-1395, 877-546-7526, fax 707-744-1698; www.shokawah.com. BUDGET TO MODERATE.

Seafood pasta, vegetable tempura and leg of lamb with creamy polenta, ratatouille and rosemary demiglace typify the menu at **Shotgun**, the restaurant on the ground floor of Lawson's Station. In addition to tables in the elegant, club-like dining room, there is patio seating. ~ 13441 South Route 101, Hopland; 707-744-1977. MODERATE TO DELUXE.

For an early breakfast or ultra-casual lunch, drop into the **Bluebird Café**. All the locals do. Grab a counter stool or find an available table and someone will bring you a menu and, most likely, a friendly smile. The milkshakes and burgers are fabulous, but you can also find less expected fare such as vegetarian and seafood dishes, as well as homemade breads and desserts. Housed in an 1870s building, the café features many original fixtures, including the sign, a large clock outside, and the lighting above the counter. No dinner. ~ 13340 South Route 101, Hopland; 707-744-1633. BUDGET TO MODERATE.

Inside the Brutocao Schoolhouse Plaza in downtown Hopland, **The Crushed Grape Grille** offers a full palate of Italian-style fare with a California flair. Wood-fired pizzas and fresh pasta dominate the menu, while a lovely outdoor patio and bocce ball courts fill out the scenery. The lounge hosts live music during the summer. Brunch served on Sunday. No dinner Sunday. Closed Monday. ~ 13500 Route 101, Hopland; 707-744-2000, fax 707-

AUTHOR FAVORITE

I like to think I'm indulging my system first and stomach second when I order from the certified all-organic menu at the **Ukiah Brewing Co. & Restaurant**. In a turreted building on a downtown corner, this eatery has a big bar, bare floors and soaring ceilings. Everything is organic here, from the food to the beer (all house labels) to even the local wine. The menu varies but typical are pesto fettuccine primavera, seared polenta, coconut curry tofu and grilled ribeye steak, in addition to burgers, pizza and lots of side orders. ~ 102 South State Street, Ukiah; 707-468-5898, fax 707-467-9088; www.ukiahbrewingco.com. BUDGET TO MODERATE.

Text continued on page 188.

A Touch of New England

Mendocino, which sits on a headland above the sea, is New England incarnate. Settled in 1852, the town was built largely by Yankees who decorated their village with wooden towers, Victorian homes, and a Gothic Revival Presbyterian church. The town, originally a vital lumber port, has become an artists' colony. With a shoreline honeycombed by beaches and a villagescape capped with a white church steeple, Mendocino is a mighty pretty corner of the continent.

The best way to experience this antique town is by stopping at the **Kelley House Museum**. Set in a vintage home dating from 1861, the museum serves as a historical research center (open Tuesday through Friday) and unofficial chamber of commerce. The museum is open from June through August, and Friday through Monday from October through May. Closed Wednesday. Admission. ~ 45007 Albion Street; 707-937-5791, fax 707-937-2156; www.mendocinohistory.org, e-mail kelleyhs@mcn.org.

Among Mendocino's intriguing locales are the **Chinese Temple**, a 19th-century religious shrine located on Albion Street; the **Presbyterian Church**, a National Historic Landmark on Main Street; and the **MacCallum House**, a Gingerbread Victorian on Albion Street, which has been reborn as an inn and restaurant. Another building of note is the **Masonic Hall**, an 1865 structure adorned with a hand-carved redwood statue on the roof. ~ Ukiah Street.

Then after meandering the side streets, stop at the **Mendocino Art Center**. Here exhibits by painters, potters, photographers, textile workers and others will give an idea of the tremendous talent contained in tiny Mendocino. It's also a great place to shop. In addition, the complex houses a local theater company. ~ 45200 Little Lake Street; 707-937-5818, 800-653-3328, fax 707-937-1764; www.mendocinoartcenter.org, e-mail mendoart@mcn.org.

Mendocino Headlands State Park, located atop a sea cliff, offers unmatched views of the town's tumultuous shoreline. From the bluffs you can gaze down at placid tidepools and wave-carved grottoes.

Adjacent to the park is the historic **Ford House**, an 1854 home with a small museum, which also serves as a visitors center for the park. ~ 735 Main Street; 707-937-5397, fax 707-937-3845; e-mail fhvc@mcn.org.

WHERE TO STAY   Set in a falsefront building which dates to 1878, the 51-room **Mendocino Hotel** is a wonderful place, larger than other nearby country inns, with a wood-paneled lobby, full dining room, and living quarters adorned with antiques. There are rooms in the hotel with both private and shared baths as well as quarters in the garden cottages out back. ~ 45080 Main Street; 707-937-0511, 800-548-0513, fax 707-937-0513; www.mendo cinohotel.com, e-mail reservations@mendocinohotel.com. MODERATE TO ULTRA-DELUXE.

The queen of Mendocino is the **MacCallum House Inn**, a Gingerbread Victorian built in 1882 by William Kelley and given to his daughter, Daisy, as a wedding gift. The place is filled with charm and antiques from a bygone era, and includes the MacCallum Suites, a luxury mansion on Mendocino's highest hill. Gourmet breakfast and wine hour included. ~ 45020 Albion Street; 707-937-0289, 800-609-0492, fax 707-937-2243; www.maccallumhouse.com, e-mail info@maccallumhouse.com. DELUXE TO ULTRA-DELUXE.

FINE DINING   Mendocino's best-known dining room is well deserving of its renown. **Café Beaujolais**, situated in a small Victorian house on the edge of town, serves designer dishes. Dinner, served seven nights a week, is ever changing. Perhaps they'll be serving scallops with roasted corn sauce and local heirloom tomatoes, or mixed greens with entrées like duck breast with fresh cherry sauce, pan-seared salmon with sherry shallot *beurre blanc*, or peppered lamb loin with ratatouille. Excellent cuisine. Closed from the day after Thanksgiving until January 31. ~ 961 Ukiah Street; 707-937-5614, fax 707-937-3656; www.cafebeaujolais.com, e-mail cafebeau@mcn.org. DELUXE TO ULTRA-DELUXE.

BREAKFAST   A morning ritual for locals and visitors alike is to climb the rough-hewn stairs to the loft-like **Bay View Café** for coffee, French toast, or fluffy omelettes. On sunny afternoons, the deck overlooking Main Street and the coastal headlands makes an ideal lunch spot, especially for fish and chips or a jalapeño chile burger. Seasonal dinner hours. ~ 45040 Main Street; 707-937-4197, fax 707-937-5300. BUDGET TO MODERATE.

SHOPPING   Housed in the town's old Victorians and Cape Cod cottages is a plethora of shops. Most are located along woodframe Main Street, but also search out the side streets and passageways. One particularly note- worthy gallery is the **William Zimmer Gallery**, which houses an eclectic collection of contemporary and traditional arts and crafts. ~ Lansing and Ukiah streets; 707-937-5121; www.williamzimmergallery.com, e-mail info@ williamzimmergallery.com. Be sure to also check out **Highlight Gallery**, featuring displays of handmade furniture, contemporary art, jewelry and woodwork. ~ 45052 Main Street; 707-937-3132. The **Mendocino Art Center** houses numerous crafts studios as well as four art galleries; they also offer workshops. ~ 45200 Little Lake Street; 707-937-5818, 800-653-3328; www.mendocinoartcenter.org, e-mail mendoart@mcn.org.

744-2020; www.brutocaoschoolhouseplaza.com, e-mail info@ brutocaoschoolhouseplaza.com. MODERATE TO DELUXE.

HIDDEN ▶   Deep inside the City of 10,000 Buddhas, the **Jun Kang Vegetarian Restaurant** is comfortable, despite fluorescent lighting and bare floors; framed pictures and other wallhangings warm the place up. Before you order you can look at 20 pages of pictures of the dishes, which incorporate lots of fresh vegetables and a goodly amount of tofu. Everything is available for take-out, and locals in the know make a habit of dropping in. Lunch only. Closed Tuesday. ~ 2001 Talmage Road, Ukiah; 707-462-0939. BUDGET TO MODERATE.

One of Hopland's most popular eateries has established an
HIDDEN ▶   outpost up the road. The **Bluebird Cafe & Catering Company** is located across the street from the airport due south of downtown and is open daily for breakfast and lunch, and dinner on the weekend. ~ 1390 South State Street, Ukiah; 707-462-6640; www. mendofood.com. BUDGET TO MODERATE.

There's one near every courthouse: a lunch spot where, sooner or later, you'll probably encounter every lawyer and judge in town. In Ukiah, that spot is **Schat's Courthouse Bakery and Café**. Sandwiches have delightful names like Subpoena, Legal Eagle, Melvin Belli, and Not Guilty (the vegetarian option) and are available with roast beef, turkey, ham, Louisiana hot sausage, roast chicken or turkey. Or all of the above. Salads, quiches, pizzas, soups, burritos and build-your-own-baked-potato also appear on the docket. And remember, if you are up early, you can get espresso and baked things here as early as 6 a.m. Breakfast, lunch and dinner are served. Closed Sunday. ~ 113 West Perkins Street, Ukiah; 707-462-1670, fax 707-462-6434; www.schats.com, e-mail zach@schats. com. BUDGET TO MODERATE.

Longtime Mendocino County chefs Bridget Harrington and husband Craig Strattman thrilled the cuisine-challenged local
HIDDEN ▶   populace when they opened **Patrona Restaurant** in 2004. A showcase for the foods, wine and eco-friendliness of the county, this downtown hit changes its menu with the seasons, but typical dishes include tempura-battered quail and penne in a creamy tomato sauce. The 140-bottle wine list features mostly local choices. ~ 130 West Stanley Street, Ukiah; 707-462-9181; www. patronarestaurant.com. MODERATE TO DELUXE.

In a cute bungalow on the north side of town, **Ruen Tong** serves excellent Thai food, using fresh ingredients and a light hand. Somehow it suits the little bungalow it occupies, where the open floor plan adds a sense of space; there's also patio seating. Thai silks and crafts and ubiquitous photographs of the royal family make the restaurant festive. Daily specials are recommended here; Ruen Tong comes up with some winners featuring unexpected ingredients such as pumpkin. Outside seating available. ~ 801 North State Street, Ukiah; 707-462-0238. BUDGET TO MODERATE.

Offbeat merchandise is the name of the game when it comes to retail choices in inland Mendocino. Don't expect the kinds of boutiques that proliferate in the cute coastal towns. At the other end of the spectrum are the "big-box" stores next to the highway in Ukiah just east of the airport.

SHOPPING

The gift shop in the **Brutocao Vineyards Tasting Room,** which faces Route 101, is a cut above the usual, featuring an excellent array of food- and wine-related books as well as the usual bottle tags and tableware. ~ 13500 South Route 101, Hopland; 707-744-1664; www.brutocao.com.

The best stores in Ukiah are strung along Church Street between Perkins and Clay streets, where the parking is generally free and plentiful. The **Mendocino Book Company** is a spacious and gracious store with a helpful staff and a wide selection of regional guidebooks along with fiction, nonfiction and children's books. Closed Sunday. ~ 102 South School Street, Ukiah; 707-468-5940.

Candles, home accessories, potpourri and the like are beautifully displayed at the aptly named **Habitat.** Closed Sunday. ~ 110 South School Street, Ukiah; 707-462-3920.

NATURAL GOODS

Just inside the Hopland city limits, **Real Goods Solar Living Center** showcases products utilizing renewable energy sources as well as items manufactured from natural fibers and alternative materials. Merchandise includes natural bed and bath products, cotton clothing, and gourmet kitchenware. More than just a retail store, the center also presents water-conservation demonstrations and offers guided tours of the facilities. ~ 13771 South Route 101, Hopland; 707-744-2100, fax 707-744-1342; www.realgoods.com.

Mendocino Bounty, accessible from the lobby of the Mendocino Conference Center, has a quirky collection of food-related gifts and other knickknacks (not to mention one of the few espresso machines in the neighborhood). Closed Sunday. ~ 200 South School Street, Ukiah; 707-463-6711.

Tierra-Art, Garden, Wine opened in 2006, specializing in local products such as organic wines from small wineries, paintings, sculpture and native plants. Closed Sunday through Tuesday. ~ 312 North School Street, Ukiah; 707-468-7936.

NIGHTLIFE **Hopland Shokawah Casino** is open 24/7 for gaming, including slot machines, video poker, table games and a full bar. ~ 13101 Nokomis Road, Hopland; 707-744-1395; www.shokawah.com.

The **Mendocino Ballet** presents the *Nutcracker* each holiday season and other ballets, featuring local dancers and professional guest artists, throughout the year at various locations in Ukiah and around the county. ~ 205 South State Street, Ukiah; 707-463-2290; www.mendocinoballet.org, e-mail ballet@pacific.net.

The **Ukiah Civic Light Opera** was founded in 1989 and showcases a wide variety of productions from mid-summer through spring. The group produces a major musical in the spring and other performances throughout the rest of the year. In November and January, they do dinner theater productions. The best way to learn what's going on is to call their offices. ~ 707-462-9155, fax 707-468-7975; www.uclo.org.

The **Ukiah Brewing Co. and Restaurant** has live music, from jazz and fusion to rock and reggae, four nights a week. ~ 102 South State Street, Ukiah; 707-668-5898; www.ukiahbrewingco.com.

Just across the border in Lake County via Routes 175 or 20, **Konocti Harbor Resort** features the only big-name entertainment in the area. Major rock, soul, blues and country bands appear regularly. Cover. ~ 8727 Soda Bay Road, Kelseyville; 707-279-4281, 800-660-5253; www.konoctiharbor.com.

PARKS **LAKE MENDOCINO RECREATION AREA** A quick drive from downtown Ukiah, this manmade lake was created in 1958 by the Army Corps of Engineers, which dammed the Russian River at Coyote Valley. Now 1720 acre-feet of water provide recreational opportunities and much-needed relief on hot summer days. Fishing, swimming, boating, waterskiing and windsurfing are major sports. The lake is flanked by foothills that encompass nearly 700 acres of protected wildlife habitat. The **Visitors Center**, which is .7 mile south of Route 20 at the Marina Drive entrance, has exhibits on natural history and American Indian culture. ~ Entrances are at Marina Drive (east of East Side Calpella Road) and at Lake Mendocino Drive (east of North State Street). Park headquarters are at 1160 Lake Mendocino Drive; 707-462-7581, fax 707-462-3372; www.spn.usace.army.mil/mendocino.

▲ There are 300 tent/RV sites; $10 to $22 per night. Limited availability October to mid-April. Reservations accepted: 877-444-6777; www.reserveusa.com.

MONTGOMERY WOODS STATE RESERVE 🏃 Located 15 miles west of Ukiah via Comptche–Orr Springs–Ukiah Road, this reserve has expanded from the original nine acres donated by Robert Orr in 1945 to its present size of 1323 acres. A two-mile hiking trail leads along Montgomery Creek, connects five of the reserve's memorial redwood groves and leads to a stand of Douglas fir. Walking this route is the only way to get a close look at the salamander and newt habitats that provide sustenance for snakes, frogs and large toads. ~ Off Orr Springs Road, about 15 miles northwest of Ukiah; 707-937-5804.

The Anderson Valley is relatively small, but it has its own invisible dividing line, the so-called fog line. The closer you get to the ocean, the greater the likelihood that a day that starts foggy will stay socked in all day. As

▼▼▼▼▼▼▼▼▼▼▼▼
Anderson Valley

"BOONTLING"

As Route 128 rolls down into Anderson Valley, it passes **Boonville**, a farming community of about 2000 folks. Back in the 1880s, this town invented a kind of local pig Latin, "boontling," known only to residents. With a vocabulary of over 1000 words, it neatly reflected Anderson Valley life. A photo became a "Charlie Walker" after the Mendocino fellow who took portraits. Because of his handlebar whiskers, "Tom Bacon" lent his name to the moustache. Rail fences were "relfs," heavy storms became "trashmovers," and pastors (those heavenly skypilots) were "skipes." Vestiges of the old lingo remain—restaurants, for instance, still boast of their "bahl gorms," or good food. They also produce good wine in these parts, and several award-winning wineries dot the Anderson Valley.

a result, the cooler, western end of the valley is well suited to growing pinot noir, chardonnay and gewürztraminer. Planted up above the fog, zinfandel can also do quite well closer to the ocean. Chardonnay also grows well in the sunnier and warmer interior surrounding Boonville, as does some sauvignon blanc.

For visitors northbound from San Francisco or Sonoma, the standard route through the Anderson Valley is via Route 128, which cuts northwest from Route 101 around Cloverdale in northern Sonoma and links the inland part of the county with the coast. The road is a corkscrew for the first few miles, featuring a few hairpin turns that make drivers glad that they are driving in hills, not mountains. Eventually, those kinks are loosened as the road reaches the halfway point between Yorkville and Boonville. By the time the road straightens out, drivers are likely to feel they've been delivered into a secret valley, tucked away from the hustle and bustle of civilization and protected by all those twists and turns.

And in a way, they have been delivered. Delivered, at least, from fast-food joints and shopping malls, interstates and traffic lights. It is peaceful out on Route 128, even more so along the handful of alternative roads that snake through the surrounding hills in a maze of remote connections that only locals ever fully comprehend.

SIGHTS   With a handful of intriguing exceptions, the attractions in this scenic Mendocino valley are all wineries. It's a dream of an itinerary, a gorgeous drive that's rarely crowded, leading along a necklace of wineries that seem perfectly spaced for slow-paced exploring. If you're driving out to the valley from Ukiah, you'll get there faster if you take **Route 253**, the scenic two-lane road through the hills, to the intersection with Route 128.

Steve Ledson, owner of the Ledson Winery and the Ledson Hotel in the Sonoma Valley, is a member of the Cunningham family, which has been growing grapes in the Anderson Valley since 1865. In the summer of 2006, he remodeled a historic building in "downtown" Boonville and installed the **Zina Hyde Cunningham** tasting room. The winery makes carignagne, chardonnay, pinot noir, sauvignon blanc, petite sirah, zinfandel and a Bordeaux-style blend, using grapes from Mendocino, Lake and Sonoma counties. A bocce ball court and picnic tables can be found behind the building. Tasting fee. ~ 14077 Route 128, Boonville; 707-895-9462, fax 707-895-9460; www.zinawinery.com.

Just west of downtown Boonville, the **Anderson Valley Historical Museum** is headquartered in a little red schoolhouse, with auxiliary space in a glorified shed at the end of a grassy field. Exhibits tell the story of Anderson Valley pioneer life in photographs and household and farm tools, and there is a small display of Pomo basketry. Out back are old pieces of equipment from the valley's logging and early agriculture days. Closed Monday

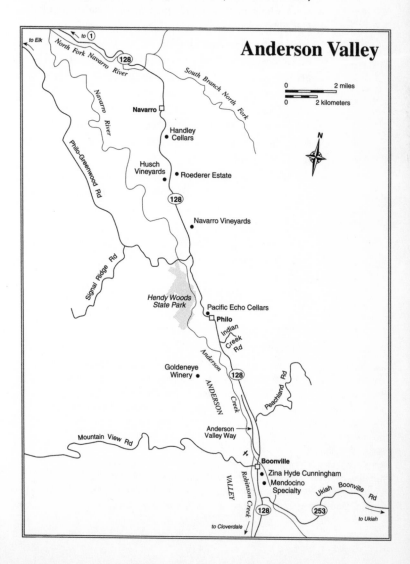

through Thursday. ~ Located one mile north of Boonville at Anderson Valley Way off Route 128; 707-895-3207.

The cool weather in the Philo area is considered excellent for raising grapes like pinot noir and chardonnay, premium champagne varietals. One of the best producers of California sparkling wines, **Scharffenberger Cellars** has a tasting room in a 1916 Craftsman bungalow just off the highway (the main winery is behind it). Tours by appointment only. ~ 8501 Route 128, Philo; 707-895-2957.

Navarro Vineyards, best known for gewürtztraminer, also makes other premium whites as well as pinot noir. This is a relaxed place, even by Anderson Valley standards, and the lovely landscape of rolling hills cries out for a picnic under an arbor of grapevines. Tours are by appointment only, though wine tasting is available daily. ~ 5601 Route 128, Philo; 707-895-3686, 800-537-9463, fax 707-895-3647; www.navarrowine.com, e-mail sales@navarrowine.com.

Husch Vineyards, on everyone's list of favorite family wineries, uses only grapes grown on the family-owned vineyards. The winery makes more than a dozen wines; don't miss the chardonnay, sauvignon blanc or pinot noir. ~ 4400 Route 128, Philo; 707-895-3216, 800-554-8724, fax 707-895-2068; www.huschvineyards.com, e-mail tastingroom@huschvineyards.com.

Topping a terraced vineyard with views of the wooded hills to the west, the 580-acre **Roederer Estate** is French right down to the 18th-century floor tiles in the tasting room. Antique wood prints

- -

HIGHLAND ENDEAVORS

Like its neighbors in the tiny appellation of Yorkville Highlands, located south of the Anderson Valley, **Maple Creek Winery** is a small, family-run concern in one of the most bucolic settings in the Wine Country. Tom Rodrigues, an artist who designed the labels for Far Niente's wines and whose works are displayed in the rustic tasting room, and his wife Linda Stutz, a former interior designer, bought the hilly property in 2001. They named the 180-acre parcel after the creek that runs through it, and began producing limited amounts of chardonnay, merlot, pinot noir and zinfandel as well as a late-harvest symphony and a proprietary blend called Cowboy Red. Tasting fee (applicable to purchase). ~ 20799 Route 128, Yorkville; 707-895-3001; www.maplecreekwine.com, e-mail linda@maplecreekwine.com.

of winery life in early-20th-century France decorate the wall opposite a long tasting bar. Visitors can sample the bubbly—all made in the classic *methode champenoise*—at the bar or at tables in the bistro-like setting. Roederer also makes a still pinot noir and chardonnay. Tasting fee. ~ 4501 Route 128, Philo; 707-895-2288; www.roedererestate.com, e- mail info@roedererestate.com.

The tasting room at **Handley Cellars** would make a nice stop whether you sample wine or not. The views are delightful and the space doubles as a gallery for African, Indonesian, Asian, Indian and Latin American art. But you should try the wines, especially the chardonnay estate, Anderson Valley. ~ 3151 Route 128, Philo; 800-733-3151, fax 707-895-2603; www.handleycellars.com, e-mail info@handleycellars.com.

LODGING

The Anderson Valley is not the kind of place where you'll find a traditional motel, much less any chain lodging. The handful of accommodations in this bucolic valley are all highly individual, and all but a couple are located far enough off the highway to guarantee a quiet night's sleep.

The two-story, red-frame **Boonville Hotel** provides the most sophisticated lodgings in the valley. Not that they're fancy—in fact, they're pared-down. Furnishings have been handcrafted by regional artisans to give each of the six rooms and two suites a crisp, distinctive look. All the accommodations on the second floor open onto a central hallway. Two units behind the hotel have separate entrances and allow children and pets. ~ Route 128 at Lambert Lane, Boonville; 707-895-2210, fax 707-895-2243; www.boonvillehotel.com. MODERATE TO ULTRA-DELUXE.

On a hill overlooking Boonville, three deluxe cottages on 550 acres are available for short-term rentals of two or more nights. All are contemporary in style and have kitchens, TV/VCR, CD players, and fireplaces or woodstoves. Two cottages sleep two; the third has two bedrooms. Up to two dogs are welcome with no additional fee. Best of all, the ranch property—known as **The Other Place**—has a pond where your canine companions can go swimming (plus a fenced area where they can safely play). Rates are lowest during midweek and highest on weekends and holidays. There is a three-night minimum in April, May and October. No credit cards. ~ P.O. Box 49, Yorkville, CA 95494; 707-894-5322; www.sheepdung.com. ULTRA-DELUXE.

◄ HIDDEN

HIDDEN ▶   **Anderson Creek Inn,** located at the end of a lane off a road that runs parallel to Route 128 on the south side, is a contemporary bed and breakfast. Three of its five spacious rooms have fireplaces and all have king-size beds and private baths. The ranch-style house is surrounded by rolling hills dotted with old oaks and redwoods and has an on-site pool. Full breakfast is included. ~ 12050 Anderson Valley Way, Boonville; 707-895-3091, 800-552-6202; www.andersoncreekinn.com, e-mail innkeeper@anderson creekinn.com. DELUXE TO ULTRA-DELUXE.

The **Apple Farm** has been a fixture for quite some time. The farm sells apples and related products and offers occasional cooking classes. In part to accommodate those weekend chefs, the owners constructed three cottages, right in the middle of the orchards. Each has its own decor but all are done in the same style, with a large bedroom and bath (one has an outdoor shower) and countrified colors like apple red, butter yellow and sky blue. The gardens alone are worth a visit; some 2000 trees include more than 60 varieties of apples. The Farm prints a brochure with dates of their Farm Weekend Classes; if you plan to visit at any of those times you will have to make reservations far in advance for the classes, the rooms or both. ~ 18501 Greenwood Road, Philo; 707-895-2461; www.philoapplefarm.com. ULTRA-DELUXE.

AUTHOR FAVORITE

Off the road linking Philo and the coast and just a stone's throw from the entrance to Hendy Woods State Park is a private road leading up—way up—to the wonderful **Highland Ranch.** The setting is glorious, a highlands vale surrounded by forests intersected with hiking and horseback riding trails for the lucky guests of this hideaway. The ranch has eight cottages sparingly but attractively furnished, each with a fireplace and a small front porch. At breakfast and dinner everyone gathers in the century-old farmhouse; lunch and afternoon tea are also served. Amenities include horseback riding, swimming, boating, fishing in a big (stocked) pond, hiking, clay pigeon shooting, mountain biking, massage, yoga and wall-to-wall peace and quiet. Everything's included at this casual but extremely well-run retreat. ~ On a private road off Philo-Greenwood Road just west of Hendy Woods State Park, Philo; 707-895-3600, fax 707-895-3702; www.high landranch.com, e-mail stay@highlandranch.com. ULTRA-DELUXE.

The cheapest—in fact, the only inexpensive—lodging in the Anderson Valley can be found in **Hendy Woods State Park**. Four extremely basic cabins, with little more than bunk beds and no indoor plumbing, are available for a song. It's cheaper to camp, but on cold nights the security of these primitive accommodations may seem mighty appealing. ~ Philo-Greenwood Road, Philo; 707-895-3141, district office 707-937-5804. BUDGET.

Out on the coast, south of Route 128, you'll find the **Elk Cove Inn**. A message in a guest room diary here reads: "A view, with a room." The view is of knobby coast and simmering surf of ice blue and shaggy dunes falling away. The room is perfect for watching it all: a comfortable cottage with dramatic beamed ceiling, gas fireplace at the foot of your featherbed, carafe of port and chocolate truffles waiting on the nightstand. In the morning, there's an elaborate buffet in the main 1883 Craftsman-style house, a short walk from the four bluff-top cottages. There are seven guest rooms in the main house, some with dormer windows overlooking the ocean, others with doors opening onto riotous gardens. Four oceanfront cottages, four suites and a European day spa complete the picture. A restaurant serves up organically grown comfort food for dinner. ~ 6300 South Route 1, Elk; 707-877-3321, 800-275-2967, fax 707-877-1808; www.elkcoveinn.com, e-mail innkeeper@elkcoveinn.com. DELUXE TO ULTRA-DELUXE.

DINING

The restaurant scene here is sparse but eclectic, from a relentlessly authentic coffeehouse to a Mexican café to a hotel dining room where most of the food could be classified as gourmet. You can also find a hamburger joint as well as take-out food in delis and small markets and, in season, a couple of top-notch roadside stands. All are friendly and none is really expensive. Call ahead, especially in off-season, if you plan to dine out mid-week, as most places rely heavily on tourists for their clientele.

Particularly recommended for dinner is the **Boonville Hotel**, an outstanding California cuisine restaurant with a gourmet menu. Entrées run along the lines of mussels steamed with red Thai curry, crusted Alaskan halibut, and grilled rib-eye steak. Dinner only. Closed Tuesday and Wednesday. ~ Route 128, Boonville; 707-895-2210, fax 707-895-2243; www.boonvillehotel.com. DELUXE.

Libby's is owned by a former cook at the Boonville Hotel, a plain diner enlivened by colorful Mexican tablecloths. Ambience is irrelevant here, though, because the food is so wonderfully fresh and beautifully prepared. A simple cheese quesadilla, for example, with a requested addition of shrimp, arrives as a plump and flaky meal in itself, adorned with a lively salsa and sour cream to balance things out. Specialties include enchiladas and several dishes incorporating flavorful *mole* sauce. Closed Monday. ~ 8651 Route 128, Philo; 707-895-2646, fax 707-895-9510. BUDGET TO MODERATE.

The Mendocino coast (see "A Touch of New England"), less than 18 miles from Philo, is worth a drive for travelers looking for more upscale fare than is available in the Anderson Valley. In Albion and up and down the coast highway are half a dozen fine dining establishments within ten miles of one another.

SHOPPING   Besides the obvious wine purchases to be considered, chances to shop in this rural area are few and far between. From late spring into fall, however, you may find roadside stands open. Travelers bound for the coast will find boutiques galore in the nearby town of Mendocino.

For the freshest of seasonal fruit, look under **Gowan's Oak Tree**, which has been providing homegrown produce here since the 1930s. With a swing for the kids, shaded picnic groves and a public restroom, this white clapboard roadside stand is an ideal pit stop. The bounty is best in mid- to late-summer. ~ 6600 Route 128, Philo; 707-895-3353.

Apples and all manner of apple and other fruit products such as chutney are available at **The Apple Farm,** where purchases are made on the honor system. ~ 18501 Greenwood Road, Philo; 707-895-2461.

NIGHTLIFE   Out here in farming country, people get up with the sun—or the fog—and so visitors can't expect much action after dark. But Ukiah or Mendocino is less than an hour away.

PARKS   **HENDY WOODS STATE PARK** 🚶 🚴 ⛵ One of the most beautiful parcels in the Anderson Valley is that occupied by this 850-acre state park, an enclave of pristine old- and second-growth redwood forest on and near the banks of the Navarro River. The site was originally purchased in the 19th century by Joshua Hendy, a San Francisco foundry owner who exhibited little if any interest in logging or otherwise developing the property. After World

War II, title was transferred to the Masonite Corporation, which set aside the best part of the old-growth forest to be preserved as the Joshua Hendy Grove. (Now two pieces survive: the 80-acre Big Hendy Grove and the 20-acre Little Hendy Grove.) In the late 1950s the site was deeded to the state by the Save-the-Redwoods League; the state park was developed and dedicated in 1963. Most of the campsites are deep in shade; the ones set in sunlight are indicated on the map available from rangers at the park's entrance, which is located half a mile off Route 128 three miles west of Philo. Restrooms, visitors center, showers, telephones and accessible sites are among the amenities at this popular but low-key park; leashed dogs are welcome, though not allowed on trails. Day-use fee, $6. ~ Philo-Greenwood Road, Philo; 707-895-3141; district office 707-937-5804, fax 707-895-2012.

▲ There are 90 campsites (no water or electricity), $20 to $25 per night; and four cabins, $50 per night (for up to six people; $4 surcharge for second vehicle). ~ 800-444-7275.

Outdoor Adventures

While the Mendocino coast is famous for fishing and boating, the interior Wine Country is more geared to hiking and swimming.

GOLF

This is not the golfing paradise that Napa and Sonoma counties are, but there is one place to play in Ukiah.

The major links are at the **Ukiah Municipal Golf Course**, an 18-hole par-70, 5859-yard course that won't discourage novices. Carts are available. ~ 599 Park Boulevard, Ukiah; 707-467-2832; www.ukiahgolf.com.

SWIMMING

Summers get really toasty in inland Mendocino, and the only way to cool off—aside from driving all the way out to the coast—is to find the nearest swimming hole.

Protected beaches make **Lake Mendocino** a wonderful place to cool off during hot summer days. ~ 1160 Lake Mendocino Drive; 707-462-7581.

The **Ukiah Municipal Swimming Pool** is the largest public facility for water lovers in town. ~ 511 Park Boulevard, Ukiah; 707-467-2831.

The **Navarro River** starts drying up in midsummer, but spring and early summer are good times to take a dip. There are several access points, including Hendy Woods State Park; the best swim-ming is near the town of Navarro.

FISHING Out on the coast, you can fish for salmon and other deep swim-mers, but all the fish are not in the sea. No fishing is allowed within Hendy Woods State Park because it fronts the part of the Navarro River upstream from the Philo-Greenwood bridge pro-tected as spawning habitat.

In **Lake Mendocino**, anglers go for large- and smallmouth bass, striper, crappie, blue gill and catfish. Bring your own fish-ing supplies. ~ 1160 Lake Mendocino Drive, Ukiah; 707-462-7581; www.spn.usace.army.mil/mendocino.

HIKING You'll find some easy and moderate trails in Mendocino County. Spring is the best time to hike, when the trails lead past bloom-ing wildflowers and the weather, which can be blistering hot in the summer, is mild. All distances listed for hiking trails are one way unless otherwise noted.

Low Gap Park Loop (1.5 miles roundtrip) can be easily hiked in one or two hours. To reach the trailhead, take the North Ukiah/North State Street exit from Route 101 and go .6 mile south to Low Gap Road, then west for a mile to the park entrance, which will be on your left. The trail parallels a creek through oak, bay laurel and California buckeye trees. Like many hikes, this mod-erate one is highly recommended for a spring morning, when wildflowers are abundant. The area gets quite hot in summer, and poison oak is always a threat in decent hiking weather.

There is a two-mile nature trail in **Montgomery Woods State Reserve** north of Ukiah. It takes you through tall trees, with steps carved into fallen redwoods. Watch out for poison oak, which is plentiful here. Pick up a printed guide at the trailhead.

A series of trails loop through the forests at **Hendy Woods State Park**. Most are level or have an easy grade. The **Gentle Giants trail** in the 80-acre Big Hendy Grove is a short handicapped-accessible route. **Eagle Trail** (3 miles), the longest, runs from the visitors center to the day-use area, about half of it tracing the Navarro River. On the far side of the park, **Azalea Creek Trail** (.5 mile) meanders along with various loops like **Hermit Hut** (.6 mile) and **Water Tank Loop** (.6 mile) offering alternatives. The hillier outer perimeter trails at Big Hendy provide another 1.6 miles of hiking.

Index

Lodging Index

LODGING SERVICES

Dining Index

HIDDEN GUIDES

Adventure travel or a relaxing vacation?—"Hidden" guidebooks are the only travel books in the business to provide detailed information on both. Aimed at environmentally aware travelers, our motto is "Where Vacations Meet Adventures." These books combine details on unique hotels, restaurants and sightseeing with information on camping, sports and hiking for the outdoor enthusiast.

PARADISE FAMILY GUIDES

Ideal for families traveling with kids of any age—toddlers to teenagers—Paradise Family Guides offer a blend of travel information unlike any other guides to the Hawaiian islands. With vacation ideas and tropical adventures that are sure to satisfy both action-hungry youngsters and relaxation-seeking parents, these guides meet the specific needs of each and every family member.

Ulysses Press books are available at bookstores everywhere. If any of the following titles are unavailable at your local bookstore, ask the bookseller to order them.

You can also order books directly from Ulysses Press
P.O. Box 3440, Berkeley, CA 94703
800-377-2542 or 510-601-8301
fax: 510-601-8307
www.ulyssespress.com
e-mail: ulysses@ulyssespress.com

HIDDEN GUIDEBOOKS

____ Hidden Arizona, $16.95
____ Hidden Baja, $14.95
____ Hidden Belize, $15.95
____ Hidden Big Island of Hawaii, $13.95
____ Hidden Boston & Cape Cod, $14.95
____ Hidden British Columbia, $18.95
____ Hidden Cancún & the Yucatán, $16.95
____ Hidden Carolinas, $17.95
____ Hidden Coast of California, $18.95
____ Hidden Colorado, $15.95
____ Hidden Disneyland, $13.95
____ Hidden Florida, $19.95
____ Hidden Florida Keys & Everglades, $13.95
____ Hidden Georgia, $16.95
____ Hidden Hawaii, $19.95
____ Hidden Idaho, $14.95
____ Hidden Kauai, $13.95
____ Hidden Los Angeles, $14.95
____ Hidden Maine, $15.95
____ Hidden Maui, $14.95
____ Hidden Miami, $14.95

____ Hidden Montana, $15.95
____ Hidden New England, $18.95
____ Hidden New Mexico, $15.95
____ Hidden Oahu, $14.95
____ Hidden Oregon, $15.95
____ Hidden Pacific Northwest, $18.95
____ Hidden Philadelphia, $14.95
____ Hidden Puerto Vallarta, $14.95
____ Hidden Salt Lake City, $14.95
____ Hidden San Diego, $14.95
____ Hidden San Francisco & Northern California, $19.95
____ Hidden Seattle, $14.95
____ Hidden Southern California, $19.95
____ Hidden Southwest, $19.95
____ Hidden Tahiti, $18.95
____ Hidden Tennessee, $16.95
____ Hidden Utah, $16.95
____ Hidden Walt Disney World, $13.95
____ Hidden Washington, $15.95
____ Hidden Wine Country, $13.95
____ Hidden Wyoming, $15.95

PARADISE FAMILY GUIDES

____ Paradise Family Guides: Kaua'i, $17.95
____ Paradise Family Guides: Maui, $17.95
____ Paradise Family Guides: Big Island of Hawai'i, $17.95

Mark the book(s) you're ordering and enter the total cost here ⟹ [   ]

California residents add 8.75% sales tax here ⟹ [   ]

Shipping, check box for your preferred method and enter cost here ⟹ [   ]

☐ BOOK RATE   FREE! FREE! FREE!

☐ PRIORITY MAIL/UPS GROUND   cost of postage

☐ UPS OVERNIGHT OR 2-DAY AIR   cost of postage   [   ]

Billing, enter total amount due here and check method of payment ⟹

☐ CHECK   ☐ MONEY ORDER

☐ VISA/MASTERCARD _____ EXP. DATE _____

NAME _____ PHONE _____

ADDRESS _____

CITY _____ STATE _____ ZIP _____

MONEY-BACK GUARANTEE ON DIRECT ORDERS PLACED THROUGH ULYSSES PRESS.

ABOUT THE AUTHORS

MARTY OLMSTEAD is a freelance writer based in Sonoma, California. She is author of Ulysses' *Hidden Tennessee* and *Hidden Georgia* and of *The California Directory of Fine Wineries* (Wine House Press), as well as co-author of *San Francisco & the Bay Area* (Windsor Publications, Inc.). Her articles have appeared in numerous national and regional publications, including *Travel & Leisure*, *Wine Country Living*, the *Los Angeles Times*, *TWA Ambassador*, *America West*, *Odyssey* and the *San Francisco Chronicle*. She writes a weekly newspaper column on the Wine Country for the *Marin Independent Journal*.

RAY RIEGERT is the author of seven travel books, including *Hidden San Francisco and Northern California*. His most popular work, *Hidden Hawaii*, won the coveted Lowell Thomas Travel Journalism Award for Best Guidebook. In addition to his role as publisher of Ulysses Press, he has written for the *Chicago Tribune*, *San Francisco Chronicle*, and *Travel & Leisure*. A member of the Society of American Travel Writers, he lives in the San Francisco Bay area with his wife, co-publisher Leslie Henriques, and their son Keith and daughter Alice.

ABOUT THE ILLUSTRATOR

DOUG McCARTHY, a native New Yorker, lives in the San Francisco Bay area with his family. His illustrations appear in a number of Ulysses Press guides, including *Hidden Tennessee*, *Hidden Kauai* and *Hidden Baja*.